EDUCATION AND THE STRUGGLE

FOR DEMOCRACY

EDUCATION AND THE STRUGGLE

FOR DEMOCRACY

The politics of
educational ideas

Wilfred Carr and
Anthony Hartnett

Open University Press
Buckingham • Philadelphia

Open University Press
Celtic Court
22 Ballmoor
Buckingham
MK18 1XW

and

1900 Frost Road, Suite 101
Bristol, PA 19007, USA

First Published 1996

A catalogue record of this book is available from the British Library

ISBN 0 335 19520 2 (pb)   0 335 19521 0 (hb)

Library of Congress Cataloging-in-Publication Data
Carr, Wilfred,
   Education and the struggle for democracy : the politics of educational ideas / Wilfred Carr and Anthony Hartnett.
      p.   cm.
   Includes bibliographical references and index.
   ISBN 0–335–19521–0   ISBN 0–335–19520–2 (pbk.)
   1. Politics and education—Great Britain.   2. Education—Great Britain—Philosophy.   3. Democracy—Great Britain.   I. Hartnett, Anthony.   II.   Title.
LC93.G7C37   1996
379.41—dc20   95–24923
                                                                CIP

Typeset by Graphicraft Typesetters Ltd, Hong Kong
Printed in Great Britain by Biddles Ltd, Guildford and Kings Lynn

In memory of
Mary Ellen Oates
(1894–1980)

And

For

Elizabeth Stephen JWH
and in memory of MH

CONTENTS

PREFACE AND

ACKNOWLEDGEMENTS

This book is the outcome of its authors' changing aims and aspirations. It began life in October 1989 as a short study of the National Curriculum which had been introduced as part of the Educational Reform Act of 1988. This apparently simple task was soon to be complicated by the fact that this curriculum seemed to be in a state of permanent revision and change. During the next few years, numerous educational changes were introduced, so creating the impression that the entire educational system was in an almost perennial state of revolutionary flux. This state of affairs caused us to reflect upon how, in a democratic society, it had been possible for a government to introduce so many radical educational policies with such little regard for evidence, argument or serious public debate. Such reflections inevitably led us to consider more fundamental questions about the relationship between education and society, about the political role of education and about the distinctive versions of 'liberal education' and 'liberal democracy' that had been constructed in the political, cultural and economic environment of nineteenth-century England. As we began to explore these questions, it became obvious that any study of the educational changes of the 1980s and 1990s which omitted all reference to the English political and educational traditions would be unsatisfactory. And as we began to consider the historical origins of these traditions, it became increasingly necessary to shift the focus of our study from a limited discussion of the National Curriculum to a wider-ranging discussion of the role that education should play in sustaining the core values and aspirations of a liberal democracy. It was, we concluded, only by locating our assessment of the educational changes of the 1980s and 1990s in the context of this more fundamental issue that we could be confident that our analysis would be adequate to the task we had initially set for ourselves.

In this transition from short book to long book, from clearly delineated work to wide-ranging study, from focused objectives to divergent aspirations, we have had to deal with a range of topics and issues that are not usually to be found within the covers of a single volume. We have also found it necessary to ignore the conventional academic demarcation lines which divide the study of education from the study of politics and which separate the 'theoretical' questions dealt with by the philosophy, sociology and history 'of education' from the more pressing questions confronted in what is conventionally called 'policy research'. Our dissatisfaction with these academic demarcations and divisions emerges throughout the book. Suffice to say that the book is intended to revive and exemplify a method of analysing educational change which is more comprehensive and critical than prevailing academic orthodoxies normally permit.

It is indicative of the times in which we now live that, in order to write this book, we have had to circumvent numerous obstacles and impediments, often emanating from the most unlikely and least expected sources. It is therefore particularly important that we should fully acknowledge the help and support we have received from a large number of individuals. Stephen Kemmis and Michael Naish spent many hours discussing the book with us when it was in its embryonic stages and they have both continued to provide a constant source of stimulation, guidance and advice. Michael Golby, Gary McCulloch and Waltraud Boxall read earlier drafts of the book and made invaluable comments and suggestions. Fred Inglis gave us the benefit of his detailed understanding of the cultural and political aspects of post-industrial societies. Robin Betts provided shrewd advice about the political and historical aspects of the book. We are also grateful to Michael Apple, Dallas Cliff, Ruth Jonathan, Jon Nixon, John Quicke and Brian Wilcox for their helpful – if sometimes critical – comments on many of the ideas and arguments expressed in the book. Thanks are also due to Paul Booth for providing reading lists on various aspects of economic and political history and to Wendy Spalton and her staff in the Education Library at the University of Liverpool for making the task of locating books and journals as trouble-free as possible. The efforts of Helen Cross and Gill Cranny in helping with bibliographical enquiries are also much appreciated.

We have been extremely fortunate in having Ann Whorton and Angela Macaulay to type and retype the numerous draft versions of the book. By combining endless tolerance with technical competence, they have made it possible for us to enjoy all the advantages of modern information technology without having to suffer any of the *Angst*, 'viruses' or other computer-related anxiety diseases that tend to infect those who lack their sophisticated expertise. On a sadder note, we would like to record an enormous debt to Kath Moore who typed many of the early drafts of the book but who died in May 1994. During her illness Kath expressed the hope that she would be able to see the book through to its completion and it is a matter of deep regret that this was not to be the case.

We are indebted to successive generations of MA and MEd students at the Universities of Liverpool and Sheffield for enduring, in a good natured way, our earlier attempts to grapple with some of the ideas and arguments expressed in the book. Finally we would like to thank John Skelton, Shona Mullen and Pat Lee of the Open University Press for transforming our manuscript into a book.

No one could write a book covering the range of issues, topics and themes that this one does without having to omit, select, compress and compromise. We are also aware that many of our interpretations and arguments will be disputed and that our treatment of particular individuals, historical periods and contemporary events may, on closer inspection, be found to contain discrepancies, simplifications, inaccuracies and faults. But despite its lacunas and limitations, we hope that the book will still be of interest to those who feel that the educational changes of the 1980s and 1990s have made the need to develop a more democratic system of education an urgent political and academic task. We have tried to make some modest contribution to the accomplishment of this task. No one is more aware than we of the limitations of our contribution or of how much more remains to be done.

Wilfred Carr, Division of Education, University of Sheffield
Anthony Hartnett, Department of Education, University of Liverpool

INTRODUCTION: THE POLITICS OF

EDUCATIONAL IDEAS

> I wish that you would fear neither truth nor falsehood but that you
> would give ear least of all to those who never believe themselves free
> unless they prevent the freedom of others, who work never more
> diligently or vehemently than when shackling, not only the bodies, but
> also the minds of their brethren. May you be on the side of all those
> who believe all the citizens alike have an equal right to freedom.
> (John Milton, *In Defence of the People of England*)

The deintellectualization of educational policy

In education, as in so much else, we are living through difficult times. Over
the past two decades there has been an unprecedented level of argument
about the basic purposes of education, about how schools and their curriculum ought to be organized and controlled and about how teachers ought to
be educated and trained. Teachers have been criticized for their incompetence, teacher educators lambasted for their obsession with progressive educational theories, and schools blamed for a variety of social ills ranging from
a deterioration in moral standards to national economic decline. Furthermore, the tasks for which teachers and schools are being held responsible
have accumulated at such a rate as to destroy any hope that they can all be
achieved. In these circumstances it is unsurprising to find that there is now
a growing confusion in the minds of teachers about the limits of their
professional responsibilities and the nature of their educational role. Nor is
it surprising that schools and other educational institutions are beginning to

voice serious misgivings about the adverse educational consequences of many of the new demands that are now being made on them. More tragic, however, is the way in which these confusions and demands have thoroughly demoralized the education professions and created a culture of anxiety that operates at a level and to a degree that was previously unknown.

Although this constellation of criticism, anxiety and frustration obviously reflects a deep-seated sense of unease about the present state of contemporary schooling, it is not so obvious how this unease ought to be understood or expressed. One obvious source of the current malaise is the enormous number of educational 'reforms' that were introduced in England during the 1980s and 1990s, many of which were given solid statutory status in the Educational Reform Act of 1988. These include: the imposition on all state schools of a subject-based National Curriculum; the introduction of an elaborate and compulsory national system of assessment; an increase in support for independent schools; a reduction in the powers of teachers and local education authorities; the introduction of local management of schools; an increase in parental choice concerning their children's schools; and the establishment of procedures for controlling the content and organization of teacher education. Many other changes – ranging from those made to the funding and organization of universities to those made to the system of post-16 education and training – could be cited. But it is hardly necessary. Nobody doubts that much of the current turmoil in education is in large part due to the sheer volume of radical educational policies introduced by successive Conservative governments during the 1980s and 1990s – policies which have been formulated and implemented with little or no reference to the educational professions and which have put control of the educational system firmly in the hands of politicians and unelected quangos.

Things were not always so. Prior to the 1980s educational policy in Britain was largely determined through the collective deliberations of teachers, politicians, local education authorities, employers, and others with a legitimate interest in education. At their best, these deliberations were based on a combination of practical experience, rational argument, theoretical insight and accumulated wisdom, and allowed the conflicting interests of different groups to be acknowledged and their legitimate disagreements to be resolved. Today all this has changed. With the educational reforms of the 1980s and 1990s now largely implemented, and with the mechanisms and procedures that allow the state to control virtually all aspects of the education system now firmly established, it has become increasingly difficult to sustain the belief that educational policy should be formed through public dialogue and collective debate. Indeed, one of the sure signs of the 1990s is the way in which any informed or enlightened educational thinking is derided as 'mere theorizing' and dismissed as utopian pie in the sky that flies in the face of ordinary common sense. In many ways we seem to be witnessing the successful attempt to deintellectualize educational discussion and debate and abandon any pretence that educational policy has to be grounded in social and political ideals.

The effects of this attempt to deintellectualize educational thinking are obvious enough. One has been to erode the self-confidence of those who have sought to establish a theoretical rationale for a set of educational and political principles which could provide a guiding strategy for education and direct its future development. Another has been – quite literally – to demoralize educational policy by treating attempts to examine the moral basis of educational policy as an 'ideological' approach that is no longer appropriate. Yet another has been to reinforce the belief that educational policy can be determined, explained and defended by a pragmatic appeal to 'ordinary common sense' and 'what everybody knows'. The attractions of basing educational policy on a comforting faith in common sense are readily apparent. Unlike 'theory', common sense is an essentially unproblematic way of thinking: an uncritical mode of thought based on beliefs, ideas and assumptions which are regarded as self-evidently true. What is commonsensical is *ipso facto* unquestionable and not in need of critical examination or justification. But what is also distinctive of common sense is that it is an inherited way of thinking that is the product of precedent, ideology and tradition and, as such, inevitably impregnated with the myths, superstitions and prejudices of the past.[1]

From the perspective of common sense, 'theory' is seen as 'irrelevant jargon' and inevitably treated with suspicion and mistrust. 'Theory', as Terry Eagleton puts it, 'is not the kind of thing one might expect to hear on the top of a bus' and differs from common sense precisely 'because it involves rejecting what seems natural and refusing to be fobbed off with shifty answers from well meaning elders'.[2] Educational theory, in so far as it seeks systematically to assess the validity of the central postulates of conventional educational thinking, is simply a way of thinking about education that strives to be more coherent and more adequate than ordinary common-sense thought can allow. But this does not entail abandoning common sense in favour of some purely 'theoretical' view of education. What is being abandoned is an unquestioning acceptance of established educational dogmas and creeds so that a more critical, reflective and informed attitude can be adopted towards what common sense uncritically accepts. Properly understood, educational theory does not replace common sense so much as transform it, by subjecting its beliefs and justifications to systematic criticism. In this sense, educational theorizing is always a subversive activity, self-consciously aimed at challenging the irrationality of conventional thinking in order to make educational ideas and beliefs less dependent on the myths, prejudices and ideological distortions that common sense fossilizes and preserves.

There is little reason to think that all common-sense educational beliefs are true and ample reason to suspect that many of them are false. Once it is conceded that common sense does not have any particular claim to be correct and that educational theorizing is no more than an attempt critically to reassess the validity of common-sense educational assumptions, then the basis on which the attacks on educational theory have been erected begins to crumble. For it then becomes apparent that the attempt to defend educational policy by appealing to some nebulous 'common sense' is not a way of dispelling 'theory'. On the contrary, it is simply a strategy for insulating

the inadequacies of politically dominant 'educational theories' from systematic exposure and for rejecting as 'ideological' any alternative educational
ideas.

This kind of blanket refusal to envisage any alternative understanding of
education to that which common sense embodies is one of the most persist-
ent features of the current educational reforms. But the hostility towards
alternative educational views is never based on a detailed examination of the
arguments through which they are advanced. Nor is any attempt made to
answer the claim that the view of education which recent policies sustain is
itself an ideological view based on an impoverished and outdated 'theory'
about the role of education in society. Instead, by dismissing all progressive
ideas as 'fashionable theory' and by opening up the blind alley of 'common
sense', the current anti-intellectual rhetoric is simply an ideological device
for closing down serious educational debate by portraying opponents to
current educational reforms as dangerous 'theorists' who need to be
marginalized rather than given a convincing answer. It is thus a strategy that
discourages any fundamental rethinking of conventional educational ideas.
It also discourages all serious attempts to develop an educational strategy for
the future which takes account of intellectual advances, new economic circumstances and changing cultural conditions. It is thus unsurprising to find
that progressive educational innovations – whether in curriculum, pedagogy
or assessment – which seek to take account of these kinds of social change
are now being treated with derision and that the validity of traditional
educational practices is being ritually reasserted. Nor should it come as a surprise if one of the practical consequences of implementing recent policies
will be to create an educational system that only avoids the dangers and
insecurities of political, economic and cultural change by preserving the
dogmas and certitudes of the past. Still less should it come as a surprise to
find that the dominant discourse of education has become thoroughly in-
fected by a rampant anti-intellectualism which makes it respectable to
believe that educational theory no longer has any significant part to play in
the formation of educational policy. But to the extent to which nationally
prescribed policy has been detached from rationally justified theory, education has become less a *rational* enterprise fed by the resources of argument, evidence and debate and more a *rationalized* enterprise which compels
teachers and schools to conform to educational ideas and 'theories' which
are never officially formulated or defended and to which few would willingly
subscribe.

This book speaks to all those who are concerned by this contemporary
deintellectualization and demoralization of educational policy. For a central
argument of the book is that the difficulties now confronting education will
not be resolved simply by introducing still more policies for improving the
technical expertise of teachers, raising standards or increasing the effectiveness of schools. They will only be adequately resolved when fundamental
moral and political questions about the role of education in promoting a
desirable form of social life are openly acknowledged and more consciously
addressed.

A central claim of this book is that the current uncertainties and confusions surrounding education can only be understood by placing recent educational reforms within a perspective which will allow these reforms to be brought into more open confrontation with critical questions about the kind of society that they help to sustain. To this end, it seeks to assess the extent to which these reforms are compatible with a vision of the role of education in promoting the core values of a democratic society in the closing years of the twentieth century. Only by articulating a vision of education grounded in democratic values will it be possible to ensure that non-technical, non-utilitarian questions about the moral and social purposes being served by recent educational changes are neither neglected or ignored. And only by doing this will it be possible to articulate a morally principled response to these changes and determine how educational policy might be redirected so that it can better serve democratic aspirations and ideals. By offering arguments for this kind of educational change and by making practical suggestions about what it entails, this book not only aims to challenge many of the common-sense assumptions now governing educational policy. It also seeks to contribute to the intellectual resources which will help the educational professions to resist contemporary political pressures to perpetuate schooling in its present form and devise reasonable and practical ways of bringing contemporary schooling into closer harmony with democratic values and ideals.

The fragmentation of educational theory and the depoliticization of educational debate

The current lack of any adequate theoretical resources for discussing the significance of recent educational reforms for the future development of democracy, is not only a measure of the success of those who have sought to discredit educational theory while simultaneously promoting their own theoretical conceptions and ideological beliefs. It also reveals a basic contradiction within modern democratic society – a contradiction between the obvious need for members of a democracy publicly to debate the social and political principles underlying its educational policies and the obvious failure of these policies to address questions about the kind of education which genuine participation in such a public debate requires. It is only in a democracy which does not take seriously the need to equip its future members with the intellectual understandings, civic virtues or social attitudes necessary for participating in public debate, that democratic discussion of recent educational reforms can be treated as irrelevant and largely ignored.

One of the inevitable results of this lack of concern with the democratic purpose of education has been to deprive educational theory of any clear understanding of its own cultural or political role. Indeed, in many ways educational theory appears, like education itself, to be fragmented, confused and quite incapable of providing any coherent view of what its purpose should be. Educational theorists often behave as if they constituted a unified intellectual community, but this simply conceals the fundamental disagreements between them about how educational theorizing ought to be conducted and understood. Sometimes it seems that there are now so many different 'educational disciplines' and so many different 'paradigms' within each of these disciplines, that whatever identity educational theory can claim to possess stems more from its institutional embodiment in conferences and journals than from any internal intellectual unity. Beleaguered from without and fragmented from within, educational theory now displays all the characteristics of an endangered species on the verge of extinction.

But things were not always so. At one time 'educational theory' was simply the label attached to wide-ranging intellectual enquiries which aimed to provide comprehensive accounts of the nature and purpose of education by integrating a general theory of society with a theoretical understanding of the role of knowledge, ethics and politics in social life. Because 'education', 'ethics', 'knowledge', 'politics' and 'society' were treated as elements of a unified object of enquiry, this kind of theorizing was informed by an understanding of education as a socially embedded and historically located political project that always incorporates a coherent vision of the kind of future a society is trying to build. And because of this, it always embodied an acute awareness of the fact that the purposes education serves, the kinds of knowledge it legitimizes and the kinds of social relationship it sustains can only be adequately assessed by considering the extent to which they facilitate or impede progress towards the realization of a more desirable form of social life.

Any full-length account of the demise of this tradition of educational theorizing would have to give serious attention to the late nineteenth-century movement to establish a 'science of education' which could replicate the aims, methods and achievements of the natural sciences.[3] It would also need to show how, during the 1950s, the legitimacy of traditional educational theorizing was severely eroded by two related claims which, at that time, received widespread support. One was the 'end of ideology' thesis as propounded by Daniel Bell: the claim that, in modern liberal democracies, ideologically inspired proposals aimed at creating the good society were no longer tenable.[4] The other was the dominant positivist view that 'normative' or 'prescriptive' social, political or educational philosophies should be regarded as old-fashioned failures to keep up with modern scientific times. When combined, these two claims were sufficient to persuade educational theorists more or less to abandon the traditional approach to educational theorizing – with its unsatisfactory mixture of value judgements, ideological commitment and empirical assertions – and to redefine educational theory in a non-ideological and more academically respectable way.[5]

It was against this background that, during the 1960s, the traditional approach to educational theory was subjected to a barrage of heavy-handed attacks and denounced as an outmoded form of 'grand theorizing'. The revelation of these horrors led to educational theory being purged of its unacceptable features and replaced by a somewhat arbitrary collection of academic disciplines. Before the end of the 1960s these disciplines – the philosophy, psychology, sociology and history 'of education' – had managed to carve up their newly conquered domain among themselves. Education departments were reorganized, courses were restructured, professional identities were changed, new journals and academic societies were established all displaying total allegiance to the image of educational theory as a form of interdisciplinary enquiry in which the 'findings' of the foundation disciplines could be integrated into principles for formulating educational policy and guiding educational practice.[6]

With hindsight, what is now so noticeable about the numerous enquiries undertaken in the name of this kind of educational theory is not what they have achieved, but what they have failed to achieve. What they have failed to achieve is any notable success in producing the kind of interdisciplinary answers to the educational questions that this kind of educational theory was supposed to provide. Numerous answers to these questions were constantly being produced from within the confines of the single educational disciplines. But wherever and whenever attempts were made to 'integrate' these answers the results were always unsatisfactory and the points of disagreement between the disciplines remained exactly where they were. But, given that the way in which psychologists understand these questions is very different from the way in which they are understood by either historians or sociologists, and given that philosophers can never agree among themselves – let alone with the other educational disciplines – about how these questions are to be understood, it is difficult to know why anybody seriously expected this kind of 'interdisciplinary' educational theory ever to get off the ground.

The failure of educational theory to provide answers to the questions it was supposed to resolve has been compounded by a failure to reach any agreement about what these questions should be. To the more positivistically minded educational theorists, educational questions are predominantly empirical questions about, for example, how curriculum knowledge can best be organized and taught, learning outcomes can be maximized, school effectiveness can be improved, teaching quality can be enhanced or educational standards can be raised. But because non-empirical questions about why certain kinds of knowledge are included in the curriculum, or about the justification for the evaluative criteria governing the ways in which the concepts of 'effectiveness', 'quality' or 'standards' are being used, are ignored, this form of educational theorizing often serves simply to legitimize the institutional norms and political interests that determine what is to count as 'official' curriculum knowledge and that shape the criteria governing the way in which evaluative educational concepts are being understood and applied. It is thus no accident that this kind of theorizing is always conducted from a posture of 'value neutrality' that allows educational theorists to legitimate their indifference to major political, social and moral concerns. Nor is it surprising that this kind of educational theory is so frequently used by politicians and policy-makers to confer academic legitimacy on policies and practices which fit in with the political status quo.

A similar indifference to the larger political debate can be detected in the contribution to educational theory made by the philosophy of education. Much of the philosophy of education since the 1960s has defined its primary task as one of clarifying the meanings of basic educational concepts by analysing the terms used to express them in 'ordinary language'. The twin dangers incurred by confining the philosophy of education to this kind of 'conceptual analysis' are obvious. The first is that, by examining the meaning of educational concepts without any reference to the particular form of social life in which they are embedded, the philosophy of education runs the risk of offering a logical guarantee to that particular interpretation of educational concepts which happens to be dominant in the 'ordinary language' of a given social and cultural milieu. The second is that, by failing adequately to appreciate the ways in which the meanings of educational concepts have been challenged and revised over time, the philosophy of education has obscured the historical process of ideological contestation and political struggle through which the meanings now attached to educational concepts have evolved. It is because it so often appears to be treating the meanings of educational concepts as determinate and logically fixed – rather than as indeterminate and socially constructed – that this kind of philosophy of education is so frequently accused of serving to underpin, rather than to expose, ideology.

Although the history of education has readily accepted the historical nature of educational concepts and practices, its separation from the philosophy of education and from the sociology of education has meant that it has all too often treated its subject matter in an unsatisfactory way. For example, the separation of the 'philosophy of education' from the 'history of educational ideas' has tended to conceal the extent to which the philosophical ideas of the past are embedded in the educational institutions and practices of the present. Similarly, the separation of the 'history of education' from the 'sociology of education' has meant that the educational events of the past have tended to be abstracted from the larger social, economic and cultural totalities in which they were embedded. The collective effect of these academic divisions has been to create a body of educational theory in which the history of educational ideas is disconnected from the history of philosophical ideas and the history of educational institutions is detached from the larger intellectual, political and economic structures of which they were an integral part.

One type of educational theory that sought to avoid this effect was an approach to the sociology of education which aimed to expose the interconnections between forms of curriculum, pedagogy, assessment and school organization and the larger ideology of the society in which they operate and apply. This emerged in the 1970s under the general name of 'reproduction theory': a form of educational theorizing which focused on the crucial role that education plays in the process whereby a society reproduces in its new members the forms of consciousness and social relationships characteristic of contemporary social life.[7]

Although reproduction theory has undoubtedly made an important contribution to our understanding of how education operates to maintain the ideologies and social structures of society, it has nevertheless suffered from two related limitations. First, by portraying the reproductive process as an autonomous process over which individuals have little power or control, it has tended to obscure the extent to which this process is always contested by those holding different views about the future direction that society should take and the role that education should play in its realization.[8] Second, although reproductive theory offers the basis from which to erect a negative critique of contemporary schooling, it can only acquire this critical role by first presuming a widespread intuitive commitment to the educational values intrinsic to the liberal democratic vision of society. But to the extent that the critical force of reproduction theory relies 'upon certain key judgements and critical intentions that constitute part of the liberal frame of mind in contemporary society',[9] it always presupposes an acceptance of the normative political philosophy within which the liberal democratic vision of society is vindicated. While the sociology of education remains separate from this kind of political philosophy, its contribution to current educational debate will remain partial and incomplete. And without a form of educational theory which interweaves 'empirical' and 'explanatory' sociology of education with 'conceptual' and 'prescriptive' political philosophy, it will remain incapable of explicating people's intuitive anxieties about current educational reforms.

The lessons to be drawn from the foregoing analysis are fourfold. The first is that in the course of its late twentieth-century transformation into a series of academic disciplines, educational theory has become fragmented into a collection of isolated and often contradictory 'findings' which, because they cannot find a place in any unified or integrated whole, are incapable of producing a coherent response to fundamental political questions about what the social purpose of education should be. Thus, the depoliticization of educational debate that resulted from the disappearance of these questions from the educational agenda and the fragmentation of educational theory were not two unrelated events. Rather, the disappearance of these questions was itself one of the consequences of replacing a version of educational theory in which fundamental political and moral questions about the purpose of education were accorded formal recognition, with a version of educational theory in which they could no longer be regarded as questions of significant theoretical concern.

Thus, the second lesson is that the changes to the overall academic division of labour, resulting from the internal restructuring of educational theory in the 1960s, should not be treated as an isolated event that emerged out of abstract arguments about 'what educational theory is' but as one aspect of a complex process through which a previous way of understanding the role of education in society was gradually transformed. The transition from a form of educational theory in which 'education', 'politics' and 'society' were understood as indivisible aspects of a unified object of enquiry, to a form of educational theory which sharply distinguishes the study of education from the study of politics, and even more sharply from the study of society and its history, not only signified a transition to a new way of understanding educational theory. It also signified a transition to a new way of understanding the relationship between education and society.

The third lesson to be learned is that any discussion of recent educational reforms cannot be conducted from within the confines of 'philosophy', 'sociology', 'history' or any of the other so-called 'educational disciplines' and that the only way adequately to address the issues to which these reforms give rise is to revive that tradition of educational enquiry which treats educational issues as aspects of the larger problems of culture and society. What, in other words, has to be revived is a late twentieth-century version of that earlier tradition of educational theorizing of which Huxley, Arnold, Tawney, Williams and others were major exponents. Within this tradition Plato's *Republic*, Rousseau's *Émile* and Dewey's *Democracy and Education* have the status of canonical texts precisely because they provide the intellectual resources for nourishing a rational debate about what the future role of education in society should be. What the restoration of this tradition thus requires is an approach to educational theorizing that conducts its arguments not only with the architects of current educational policies but also as part of that historically extended argument in which the voices of Plato, Rousseau, Dewey and others have played a decisive role.

The fourth lesson to be learned is not that the 'philosophy', 'history' and 'sociology of education' are irrelevant but that they have to be integrated into a unified theoretical perspective which relates contemporary educational reforms to the philosophical arguments and political ideas in which they are embedded and connects these arguments and ideas to the broader historical, social and ideological contexts in which they were initially formulated and expressed. What is required therefore is a theoretical perspective which is simultaneously 'philosophical', 'sociological' and 'historical'. It is 'philosophical' in the sense that it recognizes how the philosophical analysis of political ideas such as 'democracy', 'freedom', 'equality' and 'autonomy' has played a central role in creating modern educational structures, institutions and practices. It is 'sociological' in the sense that it recognizes how the interpretations given to these political ideas by philosophers of the past are deeply entrenched in, and continue to be reproduced through, the educational institutions of the present. And it is 'historical', in the sense that it makes explicit how the structures and practices of contemporary schooling are not 'natural' or timeless entities, but historically constructed and ideologically reproduced artefacts which have their roots in a period which has long since passed and whose contemporary significance can only be fully understood by understanding the political, economic and cultural circumstances in which they were initially invented.

The theoretical framework required for this book is, then, one which recognizes how any analysis of current educational reforms which is restricted to examining the particular arguments on which they have been erected will seriously underestimate the extent to which these arguments are themselves nothing other than the latest episode in the complex process of ideological contestation and political struggle through which education and society have evolved and changed. Only by means of a theoretical framework that treats the process of educational change and the process of social change as mutually constitutive and dialectically related processes can the full significance of what is now happening in, and to, education be adequately grasped and the possibilities of more desirable forms of educational change be realistically envisaged.[10]

Education and democracy: a theoretical framework

The educational reforms introduced in Britain since the beginning of the 1980s did not, of course, appear out of a political vacuum. They were a central part of the 'Thatcher revolution': a systematic attempt to reverse the historical trend towards a more democratic and egalitarian society and to foster the progressive development of the kind of liberal society in which individual freedom and *laissez-faire* economics would play a decisive part. In particular, they were part of a political strategy designed to create the kind of non-interventionist state which would be deeply sceptical about any attempt to use education as a political instrument for extending democracy. In the kind of liberal society being promoted, 'democracy' would be primarily valued as a political mechanism for protecting individual freedom and the future of education would be determined by the only mechanism which can safeguard and preserve individual liberty: the market.

One of the successes of this political strategy has been to create a political climate in which previously accepted educational policies and structures could be called into question. What, in particular, has been undermined is the legitimacy of those post-war educational reforms – particularly the 1944 Education Act and the comprehensive reorganization of secondary education – which were designed to promote equality of educational opportunity and so help the eradication of those social and economic inequalities that were preventing the majority of people from exercising their democratic freedoms. It has thus stimulated a renewed debate about the historical tensions within the liberal democratic tradition between the 'liberal' commitment to individual freedom and the 'democratic' commitment to a more equitable distribution of power.

Since any serious discussion of contemporary educational reforms cannot escape this tension, fundamental questions inevitably arise about the extent to which these reforms are consistent with the aspirations and ideals of a democratic society. What part will they play in the development of a more democratic society? What view of the relationship between democracy and education do they imply? Because these questions cannot be answered in a neutral way, any assessment of recent reforms cannot avoid entering into a general political debate about how the democratic role of education is to be interpreted and understood. It is only by clarifying what democracy should mean for schooling, pedagogy and curriculum in the closing years of the twentieth century that it will be possible to engage critically with questions about whether recent educational changes legitimately express and uphold democratic values and ideals.

Assessing the democratic legitimacy of recent educational change is not helped by the fact that, historically, the English educational system has never adapted to the growth of democracy.[11] Democratic rights in England were conceded slowly and various undemocratic institutions still remain: an unelected House of Lords, a peculiar electoral system, and a hereditary monarchy with considerable symbolic power. Moreover, education, like democracy, has evolved in such a way that old aristocratic educational institutions – such as the ancient universities and the élite public schools – have not only survived but continue to provide the criteria of success for the new state educational institutions that have been created. Thus modern universities largely imitate the structure and culture of the old universities; polytechnics define their own success by becoming 'universities'. This tradition of 'instant oldness' is now being continued by the city technology colleges and 'opted-out' grant-maintained schools which Mrs Thatcher called 'independent state schools'.

What this has meant is that although the educational system has expanded to meet the needs of a democratic society (by bringing schooling to more of the population for longer periods), the power of pre-democratic educational traditions and practices has continued to be felt. Clearly, if new educational institutions are always to be judged by criteria devised by and for old institutions, they are bound to fail. For example, if certain sorts of assessment, such as traditional GCE O-level and A-level examinations, were the specialism of certain institutions (for example, grammar schools) and suited certain kinds of children (those middle-class children with 'academic' interests and abilities) then it would be difficult for new institutions (for example, comprehensive schools) which aspired to educate children from all social classes and cater for all interests and abilities, to compare favourably unless the assessment system was radically changed. Such a change would require a fundamental rethinking of questions concerning access to higher education and the need to develop curriculum and teaching methods that would make education appropriate to the interests of previously excluded social groups. More generally, it would require a wide-ranging political debate about how the educational system could be transformed so that it no longer served the pre-democratic purpose of excluding certain social groups, but the democratic aim of offering genuine educational opportunities to all.

While it remains the case that new educational institutions and practices are judged by the criteria established by old institutions and practices, the power of pre-democratic educational traditions to distort and constrain any rational debate about the democratic role of education will remain entrenched. New educational institutions, innovative curriculum development, progressive pedagogies and new forms of assessment will constantly be opposed by a rhetoric of traditional standards, quality and academic excellence derived from the educational traditions of the past. Over the past 20 years, as this rhetoric has increasingly become the official discourse of education, educational arguments and debates have had to be conducted in a language which embodies educational assumptions and vocabularies which speak to pre-democratic traditions and prevents fundamental concerns about the democratic role of education from being adequately expressed. The only way to widen the educational debate, therefore, is to develop a language which refuses to be restricted to the official discourse of education and allows complex issues about the role of education in the future development of a democratic society to be articulated and discussed.

Such a debate is particularly important at the present time. As recently as 20 years ago, there was still a widespread commitment to educational reforms that were underpinned by a compelling vision of the importance of education in fostering a more democratic society. Moreover, most educational policy-makers and educational theorists confidently assumed that the democratic advances and achievements that had helped to galvanize this vision in the past would remain unchallenged and unchanged into the twenty-first century. Today, this confidence has been severely undermined, the process of democratization has lost its momentum and there is a widespread feeling that the time has come openly to concede that the relationship between education and democracy needs to be radically rethought.

A useful starting point for doing this is an explicit recognition of how the current educational changes are simply the latest episode in a long and still incomplete historical process of social transformation that began in the second half of the eighteenth century – a process that Raymond Williams has called 'the long revolution':

> We are living through a long revolution . . . It is a genuine revolution transforming men and institutions; continually extended and deepened by the actions of millions, continually and variously opposed by explicit reaction and by the pressure of habitual form and ideas.[12]

This 'long revolution' was instigated by what is commonly called 'the Enlightenment' – that eighteenth-century intellectual and political project aimed at exposing the injustices and inequalities of the existing aristocratic societies of western Europe. Williams argues that because we are still living through the 'long revolution' ushered in by the Enlightenment, it continuously transforms our experience of political, economic and cultural life. Politically, it takes the form of a 'democratic revolution' reflected in 'the rising determination, almost everywhere, that people should govern themselves'. Economic life is being transformed by an 'industrial revolution' which, despite its already massive impact, is still 'at a comparatively early stage'. The transformation of cultural life reflects the aspiration for universal education – the aspiration 'to extend the active process of learning . . . to all people rather than limited groups'.[13]

About this 'long revolution' Williams made three related points. First, despite the progress that has already been made, it is still at a very early stage. In democracy, industry and education 'what we have done seems little compared with what we are certain to try and do'.[14] Second, the desire for greater democracy, for the expansion of education and for new kinds of industrial organization continues to be contested, frustrated and resisted, not only passively by the dead weight of custom and tradition, but also actively and openly by those whose interests such progress threatens. Finally, Williams warns that we will always misunderstand the processes of democratic, industrial and cultural change if we treat them as independent processes rather than an interdependent part of the larger and more complex 'long revolution' through which our present forms of social life have evolved. Thus he writes:

> We cannot understand the process of change in which we are involved if we limit ourselves to thinking of the democratic, industrial and cultural revolutions as separate processes. Our whole way of life, from the shape of our communities to the organisation and content of education . . . is being profoundly affected by the progress and interaction of democracy and industry . . . This deeper . . . revolution is a large part of our most significant living experience . . . We must keep trying to grasp the process as a whole, to see it . . . as a long revolution, if we are to understand . . . the reality of our immediate condition and the terms of change.[15]

Once it is accepted that 'the process of change in which we are involved' can only be understood by grasping 'the process as a whole' then some of the main organizing principles for any discussion of recent educational changes become clear. The first, and most obvious, is that 'educational change' and 'democratic change' should not be understood as separate processes. Still less should the current educational reforms be regarded as the culminative achievement of democratic progress and educational reform. Rather, they should be seen as the latest stage in the still incomplete 'long revolution' – a revolution in which 'democratic progress' and 'educational reform' are two indivisible and intrinsically related parts. What this means is that any attempt to treat 'the history of education' and 'the history of democracy' as two separate histories must be firmly resisted. To do otherwise would be to remain blind to the possibility that the understanding of 'education' now dominant in modern democratic societies would not have taken its contemporary form unless the dominant understanding of 'democracy' had not already been radically revised and transformed. The 'history of education' and the 'history of democracy' must thus be regarded as two elements of the single historical process through which our contemporary system of education *and* our contemporary system of democracy have simultaneously evolved. Only this kind of history can ensure that an analysis of current educational change is neither confined to that particular definition of 'education' to which contemporary democracy subscribes, nor constrained by that particular view of 'democracy' that contemporary definitions of education serve to legitimate and sustain.

This first organizing principle entails another. Since the system of education in a democratic society always reflects and refracts the definition of 'democracy' which that society accepts as legitimate and true, the educational changes occurring in a democracy at any time will reveal how that democratic society has interpreted itself in the past and how it intends to interpret itself in the future. This means that any analysis of recent educational reforms will inevitably be about the past, the present and the future: about the terms in which we make sense of the past, the ways in which these affect our understanding of the present and how our understanding of the present affects the way we try to deal with the future. It will have to explore the way in which the relationship between education and democracy is now understood, examine the philosophical ideas and political theories on which this understanding is based and expose the ideological framework within which this understanding continues to be sustained. It will also have to offer a historical interpretation of the sequence of events that led to the present situation and, on this basis, suggest how in the future our understanding of the democratic role of education may be revised. Only by doing this can the analysis offered in this book ensure that questions about the extent to which the educational reforms of the 1980s and 1990s are consistent with democratic values and ideals are adequately formulated and addressed.

The organization of the book

These two organizing principles largely determine the structure and content of the book. The purpose of Chapter 1 is to demonstrate how education is irrevocably linked to politics, how there are contested and different political viewpoints about the nature of the 'good society', and why the contestable nature of what constitutes the good society is especially important in education. The chapter identifies different conceptions of education and shows how these are related to different conceptions of the good society. These general insights into how political and educational issues are linked are illustrated by examining the educational and political theories of Plato and Rousseau.

The purpose of Chapter 2 is to reveal, both conceptually and historically, the complex nature of 'democracy' and the implications of this for any understanding of the role of education in a democratic society. In order to do this it outlines two different conceptions of democracy and the very different views of education they entail. The chapter also explores how, in the nineteenth century, two distinct political traditions – liberalism and democracy – combined to form the liberal democratic tradition within which the English system of education has evolved. The chapter concludes with an analysis of John Dewey's attempt to resolve the historical tensions between liberalism and democracy and to show how this required the progressive reconstruction of educational institutions and practices.

The purpose of Chapters 3 and 4 is to show how the dominant ideas and assumptions that now condition and inform the English educational system reflect the peculiarities of the English educational tradition within which it was constructed. The purpose of Chapter 3 is to examine the intellectual, cultural, political, economic and ideological contexts and milieu within which state schooling in England developed in the nineteenth century and which established the parameters within which the debate about education took place. It argues that the nineteenth-century solutions to the problems raised by industrialization helped to establish an educational tradition which was structured by the core values of the old aristocratic order and was more relevant to pre-industrial society than to an emerging democratic culture. Chapter 4 examines the main educational reforms and policy changes of the twentieth century and considers how successful they were in creating a more democratic form of education. It concludes by identifying several characteristics of the English educational tradition which, by speaking largely to an old aristocratic social order, has prevented the development of an educational system appropriate to a modern democratic society.

Chapters 5 and 6 critically assess the educational reforms of the 1980s and 1990s first by relating them to 'New Right' political ideas and, second, by relating these political ideas to their nineteenth-century origins. Chapter 5 shows how the English democratic and educational traditions were exploited by the New Right both to revive nineteenth-century liberalism and to undermine the post-war social democratic consensus. It also considers the political, cultural and economic problems facing English society in the 1970s and why the New Right 'solutions' to these problems were so politically attractive. Chapter 6 is concerned with the rise of the New Right coalition and the implications of this for democratic education. It considers how and why the New Right was able to emerge as a major political force, the ways in which its ideas were translated into educational policies, the extent to which these policies are consistent with the aims and values of a democratic society and the ways in which they confirm the characteristics of the English educational tradition.

In the light to this assessment of New Right educational reforms, the Conclusion outlines an alternative educational strategy which is more consistent with the self-avowed aspirations of a liberal democratic society as it enters the twenty-first century. It argues that such a strategy must be informed by a democratic theory of education which regards the political values of freedom and equality as interdependent rather than antithetical and gives full recognition to the crucial role of education in rebuilding democratically organized public life. On this basis, it outlines a democratic vision for the future of education and makes some positive suggestions about how it may be advanced. In doing this, the Conclusion also reiterates a central argument of the book: that the democratic vision of education has always been resisted and opposed and will only effectively be advanced by re-engaging in the historical struggle to promote a form of democratic life in which the freedom and dignity of all can be secured.

1 EDUCATION, POLITICS

AND SOCIETY

Education is a process of shaping society a generation hence. Whether the shape is well chosen is a question in public moral philosophy, whose other name is political theory.

(Martin Hollis)[1]

Introduction: the language of educational debate

Although many people still take the view that 'education should be kept out of politics', questions about the social, economic and cultural purposes of education have always been the subject of contentious political debate. During the nineteenth century this debate was stimulated by the social upheavals set in motion by the Industrial and French revolutions and it often took the form of a conflict between those who wanted education to reflect the new economic realities of industrialized society and those who wished to continue with that form of liberal education which had been developed in the pre-industrial age. A century later, in the social climate created by the Second World War, political debate revolved around questions concerning the adverse social effects of selection and the desirability of the comprehensive ideal of equality of educational opportunity. In the economic crisis of the 1970s, however, these egalitarian issues began to be superseded by issues concerning the need for schools to become more responsive to the economic needs of society in general, and the labour requirements of industry in particular. This gave rise to a political debate that echoed many historical concerns: the dissatisfaction of employers with the educational standards of their recruits; criticism of the ways in which schools foster an aversion to careers in industry; and the failure of the education system to be more directly responsive to national economic needs. Throughout the 1980s and 1990s the nineteenth-century conflict between 'liberal' and 'vocational' education has resurfaced and given rise to a concerted political effort to redefine the role of schools in a modern industrial society.

Central to this political effort has been the reintroduction of a particular form of educational discourse: a language which serves to define educational problems in a particular way and to support an implicit political stance towards their resolution. The central issues to which this new discourse draws attention are those associated with economic failure and decline – problems for which the education system is, at least in part, to be held responsible. Nowhere is this discourse more clearly represented than in the remarks of Parry Rogers, the chairman of the Institute of Directors, who, in 1986, insisted that: 'We have gone astray . . . in what we expect of our educational system . . . it must be redirected to be an integral part of our economic system; its job is to supply to the world of employment the human skills that are – and will be – needed.'[2]

The main reason for introducing this educational discourse was to shift the educational debate of the 1960s – a debate captured by the language of 'child-centred education', 'equality of opportunity', 'progressive pedagogy' and 'mixed-ability teaching' – to the more utilitarian issues defined by a rhetoric of 'standards', 'parental choice', 'consumers', 'accountability', 'school effectiveness' and 'value for money'. But the language of educational debate is not neutral: educational notions such as 'standards', 'school effectiveness' and 'teacher accountability' are not merely neutral terms through which educational ideas can be expressed. Rather they always have a politically loaded meaning which favours the educational interests of some and neglects those of others. Examining and critically challenging the prevailing educational discourse is not a prelude to entering the contemporary debate: it is an indispensable dimension of the debate itself.

One indication of how the dominant educational discourse actually sets the terms within which the educational debate is conducted, is the way in which the attempts to legitimize the educational changes of the 1980s have involved revising the conventional distinction between the concepts of 'education' and 'training'. One example is the assertion in the DES (1985) document *Better Schools* that 'education and training cannot always be distinguished . . . they are complementary'.[3] Another is the announcement in 1986 by Lord Young, as Secretary of State for Employment, that the distinction had officially been obliterated: 'the difference between education and training is very slight . . . Training is merely the practical application of education'.[4] Of course, these attempts to impose a particular understanding of what education means are not uncommon and often provide the focus for argument and debate between individuals and social groups with different political interests and beliefs. This is most evident in those cases where champions of progressive teaching methods dismiss traditional teaching as 'anti-educational', or where advocates of 'traditional' teaching methods dismiss progressive methods in a similar way. But it is important to recognize that such disagreements are not so much verbal disagreements about what is correctly to be called 'education' as political disagreements about the evaluative criteria for determining what 'education' should mean. The evaluative criteria judged as central by those favouring progressive methods (for example, developing the interests and understandings of each individual child) may be judged to be insignificant or even irrelevant by those favouring traditional methods. Moreover, the fact that the parties to this dispute are both using the concept of education in different ways does not mean that their dispute is purely terminological or that they are not talking about the same thing. It simply means that the disputants share the same basic *concept* of education but have different *conceptions* of education and hence different views about how this concept is to be understood.

What this indicates is that the concept of education is an example of what W.B. Gallie has called 'essentially contested concepts' – concepts whose meanings are 'contested' in the sense that the criteria governing their proper use are constantly challenged and disputed.[5] Such disputes are 'essential' in the sense that arguments about these criteria turn on fundamental political values and beliefs. It is for this reason that questions about whether some person is actually 'educated' or whether some particular kinds of school offer 'real' education are always a matter of political dispute. It is for the same reason that the problems to which the educational debate is addressed are always *enduring* problems that present and re-present themselves over time in different forms but which have no general routine, or 'once and for all' solutions.

Since education is an 'essentially contested concept' it is always possible to evaluate any educational proposal by evaluating the particular conception of education it advocates and the particular political interests and values it incorporates. Such a proposal may advocate replacing a widely institutionalized conception of education (such as the 'liberal' conception of education) because it no longer enables the society adequately to meet some new social predicament (such as economic decline). Alternatively, it may propose the means for revitalizing an existing conception of education. For example, a conception of education as 'vocational' will constantly need to be 'modernized' to take account of changes in the nature of work (such as the rise of new technologies and the decline of traditional manufacturing industry).

The contestability of the meaning of education also explains why its meaning is so frequently the focus of political conflict not only between political parties but also between various interest groups who have more or less power to influence the political processes through which the educational system is controlled. These groups compete with each other to control decisions not only about the aims and content of education but also about the conception of education that is to be officially recognized. In this situation, rival groups try to ensure that their own conception of education becomes part of the politically dominant educational discourse and institutionalized in the organization and practices of the schooling system. Since the Educational Reform Act of 1988 was clearly the outcome of a process of contestation about what education should mean, it would be productive to ask 'what' and 'whose' conception of education it embodies, and what rival conception of education it displaced and why.

The actual strategies used to displace or revitalize an existing conception of education may, of course, be either well or ill considered. A historical example of an ill-considered strategy is provided by the curriculum prescribed for England's state secondary schools in the 1904 Regulations. Aldrich argues that this was ill considered because it was based 'upon the public school model' and 'not upon the scientific and technical work of the institutions and higher grade schools'.[6] The National Curriculum introduced in 1988 may be understood as part of a strategy designed to revitalize a 'liberal' conception of education so that it would more effectively address the predicaments created by the economic and cultural decline of the 1960s and 1970s. The fact that the list of liberal arts subjects in the National Curriculum is virtually identical to that laid down in the 1904 Regulations raises the possibility that it, too, will be judged by history to represent, no less than those Regulations, an ill-considered attempt to revitalize an existing conception of education in response to the contemporary needs of society.

Education and political ideology

The numerous educational changes introduced by successive Conservative governments throughout the 1980s were invariably presented and justified in a way which emphasized their non-ideological character: as 'commonsense' reforms designed to make the educational system more effective and efficient. However, this should not be allowed to conceal the extent to which the shift in the dominant discourse of education that accompanied these reforms created and nurtured a climate of debate in which the particular conception of education intrinsic to the political ideology of the Conservative Party could be presented as unproblematic and self-evidently desirable. It thus marked a shift away from the more humanistic and egalitarian social democratic political ideology that had dominated most of the 1960s and 1970s to the more utilitarian political ideology of Thatcherism: an ideology which signalled a return to market forces, individual responsibility and economic freedom.

Because of this shift in political ideologies, what was to count as a 'political issue' changed and the agenda of significant 'educational problems' was radically revised. The topics of educational debate that were dominant in the 1960s – the status of the public schools, comprehensive reorganization, compensatory education and multicultural curriculum – reflected the extent to which inequalities of class, race and gender were officially recognized to be issues of major political concern. In the 1980s, with the emergence of a political ideology which defined the major political problems in terms of a concern with economic and moral decline, egalitarianism could be portrayed as the 'cause' of rather than the 'solution' to these problems and the issue of equality could be more or less eliminated from the agenda of serious political debate. In this new situation, educational policies that had been introduced in the 1960s to promote egalitarian principles could be legitimately attacked and policies which emphasized 'moral standards' and the economic utility of education could be persuasively advanced. Indeed, once this new political ideology had been established, it became a matter of 'common sense' to replace educational policies that had been introduced to compensate students for their social, cultural and economic disadvantages, with policies designed to vocationalize education and raise moral standards: policies that, two decades earlier, would have been regarded as politically unacceptable and educationally naive.

Nowhere is the way in which a change in the dominant political ideology can transform the language of educational debate more clearly evident than in the history of the *Black Papers* (1969–75).[7] When the first of these appeared in 1969 their vehement attack on the 'egalitarian threat' to educational standards caused by comprehensive reorganization emanated from a political perspective that lay outside the parameters of the official political ideology of the time. As a result, the authors of the *Black Papers* were derided as eccentric traditionalists advancing reactionary arguments which were irrelevant to the contemporary educational debate. By the 1980s, however, the views of the *Black Papers* were much more compatible with the dominant political ideology, and the Conservative Research Department could convincingly portray their authors as early protagonists of educational ideas whose time had come:

> Ten years ago those Conservatives and other deeply concerned groups who wished to reverse the socialist tide in education found it difficult to gain a hearing: their campaign for proper standards, high quality teaching and clear tests of ability was frequently derided as a grossly unfair attempt to undermine a broadly successful system. Today the case for fundamental reform is widely accepted.[8]

The transformation to the dominant discourse of education that occurred in the 1980s was, then, an indispensable part of the process whereby a political ideology that had legitimized a conception of education which emphasized the development of the 'whole person' was replaced by a political ideology that sustained a conception of education which emphasized its economic role in training an efficient workforce, creating a culture of entrepreneurship and enterprise, and fostering a positive view of industry and wealth creation. In much of the contemporary debate, the political ideology underlying this conception of education has remained largely unarticulated and undisclosed and hence has served to foreclose any more fundamental debate about the particular view of the relationship between education and society that it tacitly sustains. One way of making it more visible and explicit – and hence of widening the educational debate – is to give some serious consideration to the central thesis of Walter Feinberg's book *Understanding Education*.[9] In this, Feinberg argues that 'education is best understood by recognising that one of the functions of education . . . is that of social reproduction'.[10]

To speak of education as social reproduction ... is to recognise its primary role in maintaining intergenerational continuity and in maintaining the identity of a society across generations ... At the most basic
level, the study of education involves an analysis of the processes whereby
a society reproduces itself over time such that it can be said of one
generation that it belongs to the same society as did generations long
past and generations not yet born.[11]

In serving as an instrument of social reproduction, education performs two
specific functions. First, there is 'the reproduction of skills that meet socially
defined needs. These skills include not only those related to specific economic functions but also those habits and behaviour patterns that maintain
social interaction in a certain structured way.'[12] Second, there is 'the reproduction of consciousness or of the shared understanding ... that provides
the basis for social life'.[13]

Once it is acknowledged that 'reproduction is the focal point of educational understanding',[14] then it becomes clear that understanding the form,
content and control of education is always a matter of understanding 'the
specific habits and skills needed for an economic system to function'[15] and
the ideological mechanisms for producing the form of consciousness that
social continuity requires. To recognize this is to admit that current educational changes cannot be understood in isolation from the economic and
ideological structures within which the process of social reproduction is
played out. It is also to admit that future possibilities for significant educational change are always constrained by structures and processes of reproduction that have been inherited from the past.

To recognize the reproductive role of education is also to recognize that
the different conceptions of education that now exist have their historical
origins in 'the perceived needs ... of existing societies and can always be
traced to the ability of some to capitalise on this need by persuading or
coercing others to address it in a certain way'.[16] Any evaluation of the contemporary relevance of existing conceptions of education will therefore have
to be informed by an understanding of the specific social functions they
were initially designed to perform in the reproduction of social life. In order
to develop such an understanding, Feinberg distinguishes 'two major social
functions of education, two paradigms that can begin to provide an understanding of the possibilities that exist for progressive change'.[17] In the first
of these paradigms the social functions of education are primarily economic
and vocational. This is the paradigm of education that involves

those areas that provide deliberate instruction in a code of knowledge,
a set of principles and techniques designed to further the participation
of an individual in the market through the mediation of skills that
possess an exchange value ... It would include not only all those performances that involve simple rote procedures in which one has been
instructed, but also those performances that involve the ability to deal
with contingencies through the application of well-grounded scientific understanding. Hence, this category would include not only the

simplest kind of vocational training, but education into a craft or profession as well, and it is primarily concerned with the transmission of
technically exploitable knowledge.[18]

The social functions of Feinberg's second paradigm are primarily political and
cultural. Its purpose is to provide:

> those forms of instruction primarily intended to further social participa-
> tion as a member of the public through the development of interpretive
> understanding and normative skills. This form of instruction is often
> called general education. It is that component of education that prepares
> students for a common life regardless of the nature of their vocation and
> is often thought that because general education projects a life in common
> . . . it requires a common curriculum . . . General education, as education
> for participation in a public, ideally implies a community of equals,
> active partners engaged in a process of self-formation.[19]

As Feinberg implies, these two paradigms of education sustain different
modes of educational discourse and legitimize particular views of society. For
example, within the discourse of general education the primary reproductive
function of education is political: to prepare pupils for a form of social life
in which free and equal individuals can collectively participate in formulating the common good of their society. Its view of society is thus democratic
and egalitarian and it clearly exercised a decisive influence on the Education
Act of 1944 and on the policy of comprehensive reorganization of education
that dominated the 1960s.

In this paradigm, education is intimately related to the need of a democratic society for an educated public and it is invariably invoked in support
of a conception of education which recognizes the role of education in
promoting the active development of the kinds of general understanding,
social intelligence and cultural awareness that active democratic participation requires. It thus supports a system of education which gives curriculum
space to such subjects as social studies, economics and civic education and
in which the primary task of the teacher is to organize the conditions under
which pupils can formulate and resolve social, moral and political problems
on the basis of collaborative enquiry and a shared concern for the common
good. It eschews those authoritarian teaching methods (such as direct instruction and the inculcation of facts) which breed anti-social attitudes (such
as narrow self-interest) in favour of teaching methods (such as enquiry-based
learning) which foster the qualities of mind and social attitudes which participation in public life both presupposes and requires.

The primary social function of the paradigm of vocational education is
economic: to contribute to the regeneration and modernization of industry
and so advance the economic development and growth of modern society.
It sustains a conception of education appropriate to a meritocratic society
in which all individuals have equal opportunity to compete for economic
rewards on the basis of their talent, skills, efforts and achievements. It is
sharply critical of traditional distinctions between education and training,

'high-status' academic knowledge and 'low-status' technical knowledge and proposes forms of education which provide the knowledge, attitudes and skills useful to future workers, producers and consumers in a market economy. Curriculum knowledge is thus evaluated on the basis of its instrumental utility and particular emphasis is given to the practical application of knowledge and the acquisition of marketable skills. For this reason, vocationally relevant subjects are given pride of place and other subjects – such as literature, art and history – are organized and taught in ways which maximize their market value. Subjects which may promote the critical evaluation of contemporary society – such as social studies – tend to be marginalized and pupils are taught about 'the world of work' in ways which ensure that critical questions about the norms and values infecting this 'world' are not seriously addressed. Teaching is itself based on that body of technical knowledge and practical skills which can most effectively and economically 'deliver' predetermined learning outcomes.

The essential features of these two paradigms can be presented as shown in Table 1. It is important to make three points about this table. First, the fact that the paradigms have been described in an ahistorical way should not obscure the fact that each is the product of a particular historical period and emerged in response to new social circumstances. Second, although the paradigms have been portrayed as mutually exclusive, this should not be allowed to obscure the extent to which, in practice, they merge and overlap. Third, the educational changes of the 1980s cannot simply be interpreted as the result of the paradigm of general education being replaced by the paradigm of vocational education. Rather, as with any major educational reforms, they were the negotiated outcome of a process of conflict, disagreement and compromise between individuals and groups about the primary social functions that education should serve; the actual outcome reflecting the degree of political power that one or more of these groups had managed to attain. Similarly, although many of the educational policies of the 1980s and 1990s were clearly intended to advance the conception of education intrinsic to the vocational paradigm, these policies have often been reinterpreted and modified as they have been mediated through the very different conception of education held by most teachers and implemented within the paradigm of 'general education' characterizing the culture of most schools. It is for this reason that the practical manifestations of either 'general' education or 'vocational' education at any one time always reflect how the tensions and contractions between them have been reconciled and resolved as their conflicting educational principles are absorbed and integrated into the existing discourse, organization and practice of schools.

Once the recent educational changes are understood in this way certain conclusions about the contemporary educational debate begin to emerge. The most obvious is that the contemporary educational debate is part of that much wider debate about which existing patterns of political, economic and cultural life ought to be reproduced and which ought to be modified or transformed. Of course, this does not mean that the educational debate is simply a reaction to external political pressures or a response to society's

Table 1 Two paradigms of education

	Vocational education	*General education*
Political orientation	Technocratic	Democratic
Main reproductive function of education	Economic regeneration	Public participation
Political and social values	Meritocratic	Egalitarian
Guiding educational metaphors	Relevance, enterprise	Participation, collaboration
Policy exemplars	Technical and Vocational Educational Initiative (TVEI)	1944 Education Act
Type of school	Technical colleges	Comprehensive community schools
School organization	Managerial	Democratic
Curriculum organization	Differentiation of subjects. Grouping on basis of vocational needs. Weak division between classroom and world of work.	Differentiation of subject matter around common activities. Weak division between classroom and community.
Curriculum knowledge	Technical knowledge and practical skills	Critical knowledge, cultural awareness and social understanding
Teacher's role	Managerial, maximizing learning outcomes	Co-ordinator organizing learning around common tasks
Teaching methods	Practical instruction	Projects, group work, collaborative enquiry

demands. What it means is that debates about education always reveal the ideological tensions occuring in a society as it struggles to come to terms with changing cultural circumstances and new economic conditions. It is for this reason that participating in the contemporary debate is never simply a matter of arguing for or against particular educational policies; it is also a matter of arguing for or against the political assumptions implicit in the educational discourse through which these policies are mediated. For example, to employ the discourse relevant to the paradigm of general education is not only to argue that subjects such as the humanities, literature and the liberal arts should be directed towards the development of the qualities of mind that participation in social life requires. It is also to argue that vocational subjects should always incorporate some opportunities for reflectively understanding and critically examining the norms and values of the world of work. Conversely, to employ the discourse of vocational education is to assume that the subject matter of general education should be taught and learned in ways which emphasize its market value and that vocational subjects should be restricted to providing the knowledge and skills required for successful market participation.

Thus, another conclusion to emerge is that to participate in the contemporary educational debate is also and always to take a particular view about the society of which education is a product and which education itself helps to produce and sustain. It is precisely because the contemporary educational debate can be read in terms of contested interpretations of society that it should not be regarded primarily as a debate about the extent to which education should prepare individuals *either* for public life *or* for the world of work. Rather it is a debate about whether education should respond to political demands to reproduce the particular 'world of work' which contemporary society has created by implicitly accepting the political ideology on which recent educational changes have been erected.

If the contemporary educational debate were to be conducted in these terms, certain questions would have to be addressed. Is general education able to perform its social function in a society in which public participation is increasingly reduced to market participation?[20] How can the contradictions between the demand for an educated public and the educational demands of a market economy be resolved? Has the dominant educational discourse produced a distorted understanding of the purpose of general education by concealing its social and political function? To insist that questions like these be explicitly confronted not only helps to dispel the illusion that there can be a neutral discourse through which educational issues can be debated in a non-political way. It also helps to explain why educational questions are always a particular expression of political questions about which existing patterns of social life ought to be reproduced and, conversely, why political questions about how society ought to be changed always give rise to educational questions about the conception of education that a more desirable form of social life presupposes and requires.

Education and the good society

Since education plays a major role in the process of social reproduction, any debate about contemporary educational policy cannot avoid some discussion about the kind of society that education should foster and promote. To discuss what the future shape of society should be is to raise issues about the nature of the 'good society': issues about the kind of social, educational and political arrangements that will best enable members of society to live satisfying and worthwhile lives. It follows from this that the defence or critique of particular educational policies can always be read as a defence of particular vision of the good society. Just as different educational policies are related to rival conceptions of education, so rival conceptions of education are related to rival conceptions of the good society.

The efforts of political philosophers to describe and justify a morally compelling vision of the good society have a long and illustrious history. But in the current political and intellectual climate, attempts to construct a vision of the good society are invariably denounced as dangerous utopianism that, in practice, always lead to fanaticism and despotism. One of the first to express this aversion to any notion of the good society was the conservative political theorist Edmund Burke (1729–97) who, in his *Reflections on the Revolution in France*, argued that implementing radical political ideals will always lead to 'madness, discord, vice, confusion and unavailing sorrow'.[21] More recently, Karl Popper, in his influential *The Open Society and its Enemies*, dismissed the idea of the good society as a a utopian illusion that has, throughout history, had appalling social and political consequences.[22]

But, as Arblaster and Lukes point out, the distinction between those political philosophers (such as Burke and Popper) who are 'realists ... with a concrete sense of the actual and concerned with reforming it in the light of the possible' and those (such as Plato and Rousseau) who are 'utopians ... the myth makers and ideologists ... dedicated to the construction and imposition of abstract models or blueprints of the good society'[23] is both tendentious and misleading. It is tendentious because it advances the cause of the realist, implying that any political ideals which realists themselves regard as 'impractical' or otherwise 'unrealistic' can simply be dismissed as 'utopian'. It is misleading because it conveys the impression that whereas 'utopians' wish to implement some vision of the good society, realists do not. But the opposition of realists to 'utopianism' is never simply based on an opposition to the notion of the good society *per se*. Rather it is always based on the realization that the implementation of any radical vision of the good society, would, by reconstructing existing political and social arrangements, destroy the vision of the good society that the realist wishes to promote and preserve. As Arblaster and Lukes put it:

> in criticizing what are held to be utopian plans and projects, a different view of what general principles should determine the life and structure of society is implied and this is bound to be so since criticisms of utopianism are essentially moral and evaluative, implying not an unattainable moral neutrality but simply a different moral standpoint or vision.[24]

The difference between realists and utopians is, then, a difference in their particular visions of the good society, and attacks on utopianism are best understood as attempts to legitimize a relative satisfaction with the social and political status quo. This can easily be illustrated by the ways in which realists and utopians characteristically interpret the core social principles of freedom, equality and justice.

For most modern realists, individual freedom is invariably regarded as the key feature of the good society. Moreover, individual freedom is usually interpreted as the freedom of individuals to pursue their own private interests with minimal interference from the state. On this view, the good society is one which embraces what Sir Isiah Berlin has called 'negative' liberty – and which he defines as 'the extent to which someone is or should be left to do or be what he is able to do or be without interference from other persons'.[25]

This negative conception of freedom implies that a good society is a society in which all individuals are free to pursue their own private goals. In such a society 'equality' simply means that all individuals have the same formal rights and individuals are not seen as unfairly disadvantaged by virtue of their social origins, wealth, race or gender. The educational system of such a society is consistent with this view of equality in so far as it is organized to ensure that individual students formally have an equal opportunity to succeed.

Since most realist versions of the good society – particularly those of classical liberals – incorporate a commitment to the principle of negative liberty, they invariably regard society as no more than an association of private individuals and view the state as a necessary evil which will always use its power to infringe the liberty of its members. But for many radicals, the realist commitment to the 'minimal state' ignores the fact that, in such a society, most individuals are unable effectively to exercise their freedom because of widespread social and economic inequalities. It is for this reason that radicals often wish to change society so that it no longer restricts individual freedom to a privileged few or confines the role of the state to protecting the freedoms of a minority of its members. It is for the same reason that they advocate a vision of the good society in which freedom is interpreted not as a negative freedom, from external constraints, but as the 'positive' freedom of all individuals to determine those matters which affect their own lives. As Berlin puts it:

> The positive sense of the word 'liberty' derives from the wish on the part of the individual to be his own master. I wish my life and decisions to depend on myself, not on external forces ... I wish, above all to be conscious of myself as a thinking, willing, active being, bearing responsibility for my choices and able to explain them by references to my own ideas and purposes. I feel free to the degree that I believe this to be true, and enslaved to the degree that I am made to realise that it is not.[26]

In a society which embraces this ideal of 'positive' liberty, the principle of equality means that all individuals are equally able to exercise and enjoy their freedom. The good society, on this view, is one which provides the political, social and economic conditions for all its members to exercise their freedom on equal terms.

In most modern societies, because individuals and social groups have different views about how the political ideals of freedom and equality should be interpreted, they also have different ways of interpreting the key political concept of justice. For example, those holding a realist view of the good society will tend to interpret justice as 'retributive': that is, as a means of punishing those who illegitimately infringe the rights and freedoms of others. However, those who support a more radical or utopian conception of the good society will favour a view of justice as 'social' or 'redistributive'; that is as a just and fair way of distributing benefits and burdens (primarily through taxation and welfare provisions) so as to ensure that the unbridled activities of free individuals are constrained by the state in ways which prevent unacceptable inequalities and promote the positive liberty of all.

Since questions about what form the good society should take (questions, for example, about the relative importance of 'retributive' and 'redistributive' justice) are always political questions about the kind of society which can serve the needs of its members and, since education plays a central role in reproducing society, it is always possible, and frequently desirable, to evaluate any conception of education by evaluating the assumptions it makes about what constitutes a good society. As different conceptions of freedom, equality and social justice have their natural home in different conceptions of the 'good' society, so, too, do different conceptions of education. And just as different conceptions of freedom, equality and social justice yield different principles for the distribution of benefit and burdens, so they also yield different principles by which educational aims, curriculum content and teaching styles can be determined. For example, a conception of education tied to a view of the good society in which a 'negative' conception of liberty and a 'retributive' conception of justice are dominant will yield different educational aims and curricula than one tied to a view of the good society in which 'positive liberty' and redistributive justice are dominant.

Because different conceptions of education are inextricably linked to different conceptions of the good society they are also linked to different conceptions of the 'good life' for the individual. This is because, central to any conception of the good society is the claim to be able to define the political and social arrangements that will best enable each individual to live a life which is morally desirable and personally fulfilling. However, this distinction between the good society and the good life does not mean that these represent two separate ways of understanding education. What they represent are two different routes to the same destination. We can either start by asking what is the 'good life' for each individual and then create a society in which education prepares each individual to live such a life, or we can start by asking what makes a good society and then create an education system which prepares individuals to become suitable members by living the good life appropriate to such a society. This becomes evident by considering those recent educational changes explicitly designed to foster a more entrepreneurial society on the grounds that it is only in a free-market society that individuals can live the good life. According to this view:

> It is only in the free competitive market that men and women can realise themselves and their aspirations without interference from others . . .
> In the real market, the economic market, they are themselves, acting for themselves, and responsible for their own actions in a sense which is not and cannot be true of the political market.[27]

On this particular view, the 'good life' is regarded as something to be lived and pursued predominantly through the occupation of economic roles (producers, consumers, workers) and the good society is seen as one in which a free competitive market is allowed to flourish. The particular conception of education it sustains is therefore one that involves the transmission of the knowledge and skills that will fit individuals for life in a market society. The 'good life' does not consist of being the occupant of a political role, such as a citizen. Nor is political activity – such as participation in public discussion or decision-making – seen as an essential part of the good life or an important requirement of the good society. Indeed, on this view excessive political activity is often regarded as undermining the individual's access to the good life and hence detrimental to the maintenance of the good society.

Education and political philosophy

Because questions about the future direction that education should take are inseparable from questions about the nature of the good society, the conventional demarcation lines separating political philosophy from educational policy should always be treated with suspicion. Educational policies, though they may be presented and discussed in isolation from any particular conception of the good society, always incorporate a commitment to some normative political philosophy and hence to the view of the good society that this commitment unavoidably entails. It follows from this that political philosophy cannot be expunged from education and that it plays a much more central role in educational decision-making than most politicians and policy-makers are usually prepared to admit. Historically, the close connection between political philosophy and educational policy has always been taken for granted, and it is for this reason that periods of fundamental social change have invariably been accompanied by the emergence of political philosophies advocating conceptions of the good society and the conceptions of education they imply. The most influential of these have undoubtedly been the political and educational philosophies of Plato and Rousseau.

Plato (c.428–c.348 BC) was born into a distinguished Athenian family. Although his social position made politics his natural career, two important events led him to decide otherwise. The first of these was the Peloponnesian War which overshadowed his youth, and ended in defeat for Athens, the demise of democracy and the emergence of tyranny. In his analysis of the causes and consequences of the war, Plato concluded that since democracy is a form of society 'which treats all men as equal whether they are equal or not'[28] and leaves 'every individual free to do as he likes'[29] it creates an insatiable desire for freedom that inevitably leads to anarchy. Since anarchy removes any limitations or constraints on individual actions, it always creates a desire for the restoration of law and order and so produces the conditions for the emergence of tyranny. For Plato, the tyranny which followed the Peloponnesian War was an entirely predictable and inevitable outcome of the inherent failings of democracy. For Plato, a democratic society always contains the seeds of its own destruction.

Plato's indictment of democracy was also based on a second crucial event in his early life: the trial and execution in 399 BC of his teacher Socrates. Plato was convinced that Socrates' trial was a gross abuse of power by elected politicians who lacked the intellectual capacity to understand or exercise political authority. This not only confirmed Plato's hostility to democracy but also convinced him that political authority required virtue (*arete*) and should be confined to that small minority – the aristocracy – who possessed true knowledge of the good society. Democratization inevitably meant that the right of the aristocracy to rule was either disregarded or undermined.

Given these convictions it is hardly surprising that when Plato set up his famous Academy – the first European university – his main objective was to outline his idealized vision of the good society and the kind of education required for its creation and preservation. About eight years after establishing the Academy, Plato set out his vision in *The Republic* which, like all Plato's works, is written as a dialogue with Socrates as the main speaker representing Plato's views.

The opening sections of *The Republic* pose the basic questions of the book: what is justice, and what is the just society? In his answer, Socrates suggests that any society must fulfil three basic needs: the *economic* need to produce the goods and wealth on which the material survival of its members depend; the *military* need for a society to protect itself against external enemies; and the *administrative* need to be effectively governed. The good society is one which is able to satisfy those needs for production, defence and administration in a harmonious and balanced way. Socrates then claims that, by virtue of the differences in their innate natural ability and aptitudes, human beings belong to one of three categories. First, there are those individuals who are governed by basic bodily desires and whose primary concern is the pursuit of pleasure. Second, there are those who by nature are competitive, courageous and brave and predisposed to the pursuit of honour and glory. Third, there are those who are driven by the search for knowledge, wisdom and understanding and who have been blessed with the intellectual ability to pursue these ends.

Socrates then argues that these natural divisions between individuals indicate the kind of social role they should perform. Those predisposed to pursue pleasure are best suited to meeting the productive needs of society by becoming workers; those who are naturally strong, brave and courageous are destined to become soldiers; and those naturally endowed with a capacity for rational thought are best suited to become rulers. From this, Socrates concludes that since the good life for the individual is a life doing what, by nature, s/he is predestined to do, and since the good society is one that can satisfy its economic, military and administrative needs, the ideal society is one in which there is a harmonious correspondence between the nature of the individual and his/her social role. Thus, both the good of society and the good life for the individual require a rigid division of labour so that individuals can live according to their nature and social groups can live in harmony with each other. The ideal society, concludes Socrates, is one in which 'the worker, the warrior and the ruler each do their own business; this is justice and will make the city just'.[30]

Given this view of the relationship between the individual and society, the whole system of education outlined in *The Republic* is geared to identifying individuals in terms of their dominant aptitudes and abilities and educating

them for their appropriate social role. To this end, the educational programme outlined in *The Republic* is made up of five key stages. The first
involves acquiring basic reading and writing skills together with an inculcation of moral and political beliefs. The second stage is a period of military
training, and the third involves a study of theoretical subjects such as maths
and science. The fourth stage is, in effect, a systematic study of philosophy.
Only those who have successfully completed this stage can go on to the fifth
stage which offers preparation for political leadership. Individuals are only
allowed to follow this programme as far as their natural ability permits and
at the end of each stage they are subjected to rigorous testing designed to
identify those who should be allowed to continue. For those destined for the
labouring class, education ends at the first key stage and is replaced by
vocational training, while those destined to become soldiers terminate their
employment at the third stage. Only those with the intellectual ability to
become political leaders are allowed to complete all five stages, and become
members of a small intellectual élite: an aristocracy who will become the
future rulers of society.

Generally, then, the educational system outlined in *The Republic* was designed to adjust individuals to their unchangeable nature and to allocate
them to their proper place in society. As such, it had a crucial role in producing and sustaining a conception of the good society in which individuals
are not only able to achieve the good life for themselves but also contribute
to the harmonious functioning of society. But, at the same time, it was also
an education system geared to the overriding need to produce political leaders who, by virtue of their intellectual and moral superiority, could define
the well-being of all inferior individuals and guarantee the maintenance and
preservation of the good society.

Plato's justification for this view of education was based on his view that
true knowledge of 'virtue' – knowledge of what the good society is, and
hence of what its proper regulation and control requires – could only be
taught to and learned by an intellectually gifted minority undergoing a
certain kind of theoretical education and philosophical training. Thus, for
Plato, there is a close affinity between education and the legitimation of
political authority. For Plato, those with a certain kind of education should
have the power to decide what is in the best interests of others. Only in a
society whose rulers had a philosophical knowledge and understanding of
the good life and the good society could truth and justice prevail. In a well-
known passage in *The Republic*, Socrates asserts that:

> Unless philosophers are kings ... or things of this world have the spirit
> and power of philosophy, and political greatness and wisdom meet in
> one, and those of a common nature who pursue either to the exclusion
> of the other are compelled to stand aside, neither cities nor the human
> race will ever have rest from their evils ... and only then will this our
> ideal state behold the light of day.[31]

Although Plato's *Republic* is a brilliant exposition of how any conception
of education must be grounded in a political vision of the good society, a

more critical reading inevitably leads to the conclusion that Plato's answers to the questions he correctly formulated are unacceptable in the modern world. What vitiates Plato's answers is his impoverished and limited view of the intellectual abilities and political capabilities of ordinary human beings and his belief that there is some kind of absolute knowledge of what constitutes the good life and the good society that can be acquired only by an aristocratic élite. But perhaps the major weakness of Plato's conception of education is that it was deliberately designed to prevent the re-emergence of a democratic society by ensuring that the majority of people would be denied the educational opportunity to develop their knowledge and understanding in ways which would allow them to participate in the political life of their community.

The political and educational philosophy expounded in Plato's *Republic* has exercised enormous influence on the evolution of education in the western world. However, although Plato clearly intended *The Republic* to be a blueprint for the creation of a good society, it served to legitimize the perpetuation of an aristocratic society in which it was assumed that individuals are 'by nature' unequal and everybody has a pre-ordained position in the social order. Indeed, prior to the eighteenth century, most European societies were based on a Platonic system of social relationships in which the relationship between an educated 'higher class' and the 'uneducated lower orders' required that the lives of the lower orders 'should be regulated for them, not by them. They should not be required or encouraged to think for themselves . . . it is the duty of the higher classes to think for them and to take responsibility for their lot.'[32]

In the political and cultural conditions of the eighteenth century, the Platonic ideas sustaining aristocratic societies were seriously and successfully challenged by the philosophies of the Enlightenment – philosophies which were to contribute considerably to the intellectual climate that not only led to the displacement of the traditional aristocratic forms of society but also stimulated the need for a philosophical account of the good society in which political power was more equally distributed and education was a universal provision available to all. The Enlightenment philosopher who most clearly articulated these demands for political equality and public education was Jean-Jacques Rousseau (1712–78).

Although Rousseau's political philosophy is radically different from that of Plato, the social context in which it was developed and the political problems to which it was addressed were similar. Rousseau, like Plato, was deeply opposed to the existing political and social order and, like Plato, he was convinced that this situation could only be adequately resolved by re-examining the basic question of political authority: who should rule. For Rousseau, the orthodox Platonic response obscured the extent to which a 'society' was an artificially constructed entity which had destroyed the freedom and dignity of individuals who, in pre-social times, had lived according to 'nature'. Prior to the founding of society, individuals had lived according to their natural inclinations but, as societies were formed, individual bonds of servitude and inequality were inevitably and necessarily created. For Rousseau, to be a member of society was always to some extent to be enslaved and unfree – a situation which he dramatically described in the paradox which opens his seminal work, *The Social Contract*: 'Man is born free and everywhere he is in chains.'[33]

The 'chains' constraining human freedom derive from the ways in which social and political institutions that had initially been introduced to provide impartial justice had become the instruments used by the politically powerful to oppress, exploit and enslave the politically weak. Like Plato, Rousseau argued that the reform of existing social and political institutions was a precondition for the emergence of individuals who think and act, not as self-interested individuals, but as free citizens of an integrated political community who have a shared regard for the common good. In *The Social Contract* Rousseau posed the same question that Plato had sought to answer in *The Republic*: who should have political authority?

Rousseau argued that to answer this question by identifying an intellectually gifted aristocracy who have true knowledge of the good society led to the creation of the kind of tyrannical society that Plato had been so keen to avoid. For Rousseau the only way to avoid tyranny was to make the consent of all members of society the sole source of legitimate political authority. For Rousseau the good society is one in which all individuals consent to the laws by which their lives are regulated and their natural freedoms curtailed. To this end, Rousseau proposed a form of society based on the 'Social Contract': an agreement between all members of society to surrender their 'natural' freedom in return for the 'civic' freedom appropriate to life in society. By entering into this 'Social Contract' individuals recognize that for their freedom to be preserved they must be prepared to establish a co-operative law-making body which enables them to participate actively in the collective formulation of the common good encaptured in the 'General Will'. Thus, for Rousseau, the good society is one whose members accept the legitimacy of its laws because they have been involved in their creation and have agreed to impose them on themselves.

For Rousseau, the 'General Will' is not an aggregation of individuals' private preferences but a collective judgement expressing the common good. But he recognized that because, in society as it existed at that time, people acted primarily as private individuals rather than as public members of a community, it is necessary to consider the social and cultural conditions under which the 'General Will' of a society could be formulated and expressed. One such condition was that the 'negative' freedom of individuals to pursue their own interests must be extended to include the 'positive' freedom to determine their own shared social life. But Rousseau also recognized that under the corrupting influence of the institutions of existing society, people were no longer willing to subordinate their private interests to the public good. How, then, could the good society – a society based on the Social Contract and directed by the 'General Will' – be created? Rousseau's answer was that people would only agree to participate in the creation and development of such a society if they were suitably educated. For Rousseau, as for Plato, the task of transforming an existing corrupt form of society into a good society was a task for education. Six months after the publication of *The Social Contract*, Rousseau published his classical treatise on education, *Émile*.[34]

The Social Contract and *Émile* were regarded by Rousseau as inseparable parts of a single whole rather than as two independent works. If the aim of *The Social Contract* is to define the good society, the aim of *Émile* is to describe the kind of education that would serve to bring this society into existence. It is for this reason that, though Rousseau says that Émile's education is to be restricted 'to the education of the house',[35] it is nevertheless intended as a scheme of universal public education. It is for the same reason that Émile has to be taken out of existing society and educated privately. Only by being withdrawn from the corrupting influence of modern society at an early age can he learn to 'see with his own eyes and feel with his own heart'.[36] And only by first recapturing his 'natural innocence' will Émile learn to accept the General Will and seek the common good. Thus for Rousseau, as for Plato, the purpose of education was to recognize and develop the natural capacities of individuals so that they may come to create a society in which these natural capacities can be adequately exercised and enjoyed. But for Rousseau, the aim of education is not to transcend natural inclinations and desires but to follow them. 'That man is truly free who desires what he is able to perform and does what he desires. This is my fundamental maxim. Apply it to childhood and all the rules of education spring from it.'[37]

The purpose of the first stage of Émile's education is to make Émile 'Nature's pupil' by ensuring that all his learning is derived from first-hand experience. As Rousseau famously put it: 'Nature not man is the schoolmaster and he learns all the quicker because he is not aware that he has any lessons to learn.'[38] At the second stage of his education – which begins at the age of 12 – Émile is subjected to a new form of instruction geared to learning practically useful knowledge about the world in which he lives through solving problems in a natural setting. The general rule of education governing this stage is 'learning by doing'. As Rousseau puts it: 'Teach by doing whenever you can, and only fall back upon words when doing is out of the question.'[39] The final stage of Émile's education begins at the age of 15 and is intended to prepare him to enter into the moral, social and political order by giving him a 'full knowledge of questions of government public morality and political philosophy of every kind'.[40] It initially involves a historical study of alternative societies and cultures, which is followed by extensive instruction in political philosophy, which culminates in Émile acknowledging that the view of good life exposed in *The Social Contract* is one for which he has been educated and which he now desires to pursue. In this sense, *Émile* offers an educational programme designed to create members of a society based on *The Social Contract*. As Perkinson says:

> The Émile that he [Rousseau] has created is to be an apostle and an exemplar . . . the prototype of those who will place themselves under the General Will – those who will make the social contract . . . Émile will

be a model for other men, teaching them by living what Rousseau had been trying to teach them by writing *The Social Contract*.[41]

It has recently been asserted that 'there are two and only two Great Educators: Plato and Rousseau. In a way, western education today is a battlefield between two groups of philosophical ideas evolved from these men.'[42] Whether or not this is true, it is certainly the case that the conceptions of education articulated by Plato and Rousseau have greatly influenced contemporary educational debate and still inform much modern educational policy and practice. Platonic ideas, in particular, continue to permeate many common-sense educational assumptions. They are, for example, evident in the conventional rationale for discriminating between pupils according to their age, aptitudes and abilities and they clearly underpin the justification for maintaining separate élite schools with responsibility for educating the future leaders of society.

Rousseau's *Émile* stands in relation to the modern or 'progressive' conception of education as Plato's *Republic* does to its 'traditional' counterpart. Both sought to characterize the kind of education appropriate to living the good life in the good society. For Plato, the good society is an aristocratic society ruled by an educated élite. For Rousseau, the practical consequence of implementing Plato's views was the creation of a corrupt society in which a conception of the good life was imposed on the uneducated and irrational majority by an educated intellectual minority. The inevitable result was a society characterized by inequality, oppression and the denial of human freedom: a society that could only be transformed by creating an alternative conception of the good society and by enacting the alternative conception of education this entailed.

Conclusion: revitalizing the educational debate

Although this chapter has sought to show why any serious debate about recent educational reforms has to address fundamental political questions about the conception of the good society that these reforms presuppose, it would be imprudent to circumscribe too dogmatically the parameters within which such a debate ought to proceed. To do so would severely underestimate the significance of one of this chapter's central arguments: that questions about how recent educational reforms should be debated are not abstract 'procedural' questions that have to be answered before the debate can begin but substantive political questions that are an indispensable part of the debate itself. However, if the arguments developed in this chapter are to be more than mere rhetoric, it is necessary to summarize some of the conclusions they entail about how the process of educational change ought to be examined and understood.

The first is simply a reiteration of an insight as old as Plato: that education is not something 'external' to society but a dynamic part of the general process which reproduces the cultural, economic and political life of society.

The second is that although education always has a tendency to reproduce the social life or society, it also simultaneously serves to transform existing patterns of social life so as to promote alternative views of the good life and the good society. Thus there is, at any one time, always an unavoidable tension in education between social reproduction and social transformation, reflecting the internal tension between social stability and social change. In this sense, educational change is an intrinsic part of the continuous process through which society is simultaneously reproduced and transformed.

Third, educational change is never simply a matter of implementing a set of educational principles or social ideals. What provides the dynamic of educational change is the process of contestation that emerges out of the conflicts, disagreements and differences that occur between individuals and social groups whose different conceptions of education reflect their different views about the good society and how it may be created.[43] Although these different views of the good society may initially have been articulated through the intricate arguments of political philosophers such as Plato and Rousseau, they are now to be found in the ideologically structured forms of consciousness through which individuals acquire their particular understanding of social life in general and of the relationship between education and society in particular. Thus it is that the conception of education dominant in a society at any given time always bears the marks of past and present political struggles between competing conceptions of the good society.

Fourth, since any analysis of educational change always involves a critical examination of the view of the good society that such change sustains, the language appropriate to this analysis is not that technical discourse characteristically employed to examine whether any educational change has effectively achieved some politically given end. It is instead a form of ethically informed political discourse in which questions about the role of education in promoting some version of the good society can be openly addressed. Once political ideals and ethical categories are eliminated from educational analysis, any evaluation of educational change will rapidly degenerate into a mundane technical exercise in which questions about their moral and political purposes can no longer find adequate expression.

To concede that any examination of educational change requires an assessment of its political purpose is to affirm that educational change can only be adequately understood if it is not detached from its historical roots. Thus, any assessment about the present condition or future development of education must be partially constituted by an understanding of its past. By counteracting the tendency to treat the past as a mere prelude to the present, such a requirement would help to dispel the illusion that there can be an uncontested and ahistorical conception of education. And by doing this, it would also help to ensure that any examination of recent educational change will not be confined to the agenda of educational problems which contemporary society has officially defined, or constrained by the particular conception of the good society which is sustained by the dominant political ideology.

The final conclusion to emerge is that any analysis of contemporary educational change will have to relate these changes to the broader historical context in which the political ideas they incorporate were initially formulated and expressed. Moreover, by connecting this kind of historical analysis to the specific political, cultural and economic contexts in which recent educational reforms have been implemented, it becomes possible to ask and answer questions about their democratic legitimacy in a more penetrating and critical way. Are the educational changes introduced in the 1980s and 1990s consistent with the aims and aspirations of a society which claims to embody democratic values and ideals? Is the democratic development of education now being impeded by non-democratic political ideologies inherited from the past? Under what political, economic and cultural conditions would an education for democracy be possible? What kind of education is constituted by, and constitutive of, a democratic form of social life? The purpose of the next chapter is to address these and related questions.

2   DEMOCRATIC THEORY AND DEMOCRATIC EDUCATION

> By slow steps not completed until the late 1920's Britain has become a
> democracy based on universal suffrage and this fact, by which the
> responsibility of deciding major social policy is transferred to the
> people as a whole, is obviously of central and inescapable relevance to
> education.
>
> (Raymond Williams)[1]

Introduction: the classical and contemporary conceptions of democracy

Britain, like most other western societies, is a democracy, and the belief that
democracy constitutes the good society is now sufficiently uncontested that
there seems to be no reason why educational policies should not be formulated on the basis of democratic principles and ideals. If the merits of democracy are, for all practical purposes, uncontested, the only outstanding task is
to assess the extent to which recent educational reforms embody the conception of education that would most effectively maintain and reproduce a
democratic society.

What, then, is a democracy? The concept of democracy derives from the
Greek words *demos* (the people) and *kratos* (rule), so that to claim that a
society is democratic is to claim that, unlike an oligarchy or a monarchy, it
is a society in which 'the people rule'. However, the notion of 'rule by the
people' is not unambiguous. Who are 'the people'? Are certain groups (women,
ethnic minorities, children) to be excluded? What is meant by 'rule'? Does

democracy mean that people actually rule themselves by participating equally in the exercise of political power? Or does it mean that political power is restricted to a small group of political experts chosen by, and accountable to, the people? It is because of the different and often conflicting ways in which these questions can be answered that there are different and often conflicting conceptions of how democracy is to be understood.

What this means is that the concept of democracy is, like the concept of education, an essentially contested concept whose history has been marked by political struggle and ideological conflict. Throughout this history, two broad conceptions of democracy have been advanced. One takes democracy to mean 'some kind of popular power (a form of life in which citizens are engaged in self-government and self-regulation)'; the other interprets it as 'an aid to decision-making (a means to legitimate the decisions of those voted into power as "representatives")'.[2]

These two conceptions of democracy – democracy as a form of popular power and democracy as a representative system of political decision-making – may, following common usage, be labelled the 'classical' and the 'contemporary' conceptions of democracy.[3] Although it is possible to see most interpretations of democracy as approximating to one or other of these two labels, it is important to treat them with some caution. 'Classical' and 'contemporary' conceptions of democracy do not refer to any particular democratic theories or correspond to any given political reality. They are best understood as 'ideal type' constructs: purely formal categories which help to classify various ideas about democracy in terms of their core values, their key features and their common assumptions.

As its name suggests, the classical conception of democracy has its origins in ancient Greece, where the concept was introduced to describe the emergence of Athens as a political society or *polis*: a city state in which citizens governed and ruled themselves. Thus, the ideal of Greek democracy was the maximum direct participation of all citizens in the common life of the community. In this community man (but not woman) was understood to be, by nature, a 'political animal' whose intellectual, social and moral capacities could only be adequately realized through participating freely and equally in the political life of the *polis*. In Athenian democracy the primary virtue of democratic participation was that it was constitutive of a form of society in which individuals could develop and realize their distinctively human capacities within the framework of a common life and on the basis of the common good. In this sense, democracy was essentially *educative*: it sought 'the education of an entire people to the point where their intellectual, emotional and moral capacities have reached their full potential and they are joined freely and actively in a genuine community'.[4]

A central feature of this classical conception of democracy, then, is that it is a *moral* concept identifying a form of social and political life which gives expression to the values of self-fulfilment, self-determination and equality – values constitutive of the kind of society in which all individuals can fulfil themselves by freely and equally determining the common good of their society. Few modern versions of classical democracy suggest that these moral

Table 2 The classical conception of democracy

Core principles:
Democracy is a form of social life constituted by the core values of 'positive' freedom and political equality. It is the way of life in which individuals are able to realize their human capacities by participating in the life of their society. A democratic society is thus an educative society whose citizens enjoy equal opportunities for self-development, self-fulfilment and self-determination.

Key features:
Democracy is a moral ideal and, as such, is never fully achieved. It requires continuously expanding opportunities for the direct participation of all citizens in public decision-making by bringing social, political and economic institutions under more genuine democratic control.

Main assumptions:
Human beings are essentially political and social animals who fulfil themselves by sharing in the common life of their community. Since involvement in the life of the community is a necessary condition of individual development, all should participate in deliberations about the good of their society. Any distinction between rulers and ruled is a distinction in degree rather than in kind.

Social conditions:
Democracy can only flourish in a society in which there is a knowledgeable and informed citizenry capable of participating in public decision-making and political debate on equal terms. It thus requires a society in which bureaucratic control over public life is minimal and in which decision-making is not treated as a professional expertise.

---

values have ever been, or ever could be, fully realized, and many of them recognize the major obstacles now preventing modern societies from developing more democratic institutions and practices. Nevertheless, its modern advocates argue that by offering an idealized vision of democracy, the classical conception provides a moral basis for evaluating the extent to which the existing political arrangements of modern democratic societies actually approximate to democratic values and ideals.

The classical conception of democracy informs a broad range of democratic theories ranging from the 'direct' democratic theory of Rousseau[5] and the 'developmental' theory of J.S. Mill[6] to the more modern participatory theories of MacPherson[7] and Pateman. This conception of democracy can be represented as shown in Table 2.

The second conception of democracy – the contemporary conception – is so called because it is a product of twentieth-century political theory and practice. At the beginning of this century, because of the sheer size and complexity of modern industrialized societies, the classical sense of democracy was increasingly regarded as 'utopian'. This eventually led to the classical conception being rejected and replaced by a more 'realistic' conception based on detailed studies of the political processes and institutions of advanced and long-established democratic societies (particularly Great Britain and the USA). These studies showed that any interpretation of 'rule by the people' as meaning that people actually rule themselves was not sustained by the facts of contemporary democratic life. What, in reality, is central to democracy is not participation by all, but competition between rival political parties for the right to exercise political power. On this contemporary conception, 'political equality' means an equal opportunity to vote for leaders and 'democratic participation' means exercising that vote at periodic elections. It thus takes competition between political élites – and not participation in decision-making – to be the essence of democracy and the criterion that allows the 'democratic method' to be distinguished from other methods of political decision-making.

This conception of democracy incorporates principles and methods that resonate closely with the principles and methods of a *laissez-faire* market economy. For example, in a democracy so understood, voters choose between the rival 'policies' offered by competing political parties in much the same way as they, as the customers and consumers of a market economy, make their choices of goods and services. Also, just as, in a market economy, extensive knowledge of and participation in the decision-making process by an informed workforce is regarded as economically inefficient, so extensive knowledge of and participation in the political decision-making process by an informed citizenry is regarded as a barrier to effective government. Advocates of this form of democracy claim not only that most people in modern western democracies do not possess the knowledge or expertise that political decision-making requires, but also that the political apathy and lack of interest of the majority play a positive role in maintaining the stability of democratic societies.

This contemporary conception of democracy informs 'élitist' theories,[9] 'pluralist' theories[10] 'realist' theories[11] and 'neo-liberal' theories[12] of democracy. Barbara Goodwin describes the common traits that distinguish these from classical theories in the following way:

> They deliberately omit the idealistic aspects and describe political activity in realistic, factual terms, reducing political motivation to self interest. Consequently, democracy is seen purely as procedure, a procedure justified as being the most efficient or the best utility-maximising method . . . The new theories often emphasise as goals the maintenance and stability of the system, rather than its . . . role in . . . educating citizens.[13]

This conception of democracy can be represented as shown in Table 3.

Conceptions of democracy and conceptions of education

This simple characterization of the classical and contemporary conceptions of democracy does little justice to the sophistication of the thinking that

Table 3   The contemporary conception of democracy

Core principles:
Democracy is justified as the political system which is most effective in securing
the core principle of 'negative' liberty. By providing a method for selecting
political leaders which curtails an excess or abuse of political power, it helps to
protect the freedom of individuals to pursue their private interests with minimal
state interference.

Key features:
Democracy is not a moral ideal but a value-neutral descriptive concept and its
achievement is synonymous with certain empirical conditions. These include:
regular elections, universal suffrage, the existence of rival political parties, a
representative system of government, a centralized political leadership, a free press
and an independent judiciary.

Main assumptions:
Human beings are primarily private individuals who form social relationships in
order to satisfy their own personal needs. They thus have no obligation to
participate in political decision-making and most ordinary people have no desire to
do so. A rigid distinction is, therefore, made between an active élite political
leadership and the passive majority of ordinary citizens.

Social conditions:
Democracy flourishes in an individualistic society with a competitive market
economy, minimal state intervention, a politically passive citizenry and a strong
active political leadership guided by liberal principles and circumscribed by the
rule of law.

---

informs them, and attention has been drawn to them only because they
allow the formulation of some initial questions about what the role of education in a democratic society should be. What different conceptions of education do the classical and contemporary conceptions of democracy entail?
What are the curriculum and pedagogical implications of such differences?

Since the classical conception of democracy is grounded in a way of life
in which all individuals can develop their distinctively human qualities and
capacities, it envisages a society which is itself intrinsically educative: a 'learning society' in which political socialization is a distinctively educational
process. In such a society, the primary aim of education is to initiate individuals into the values, attitudes and modes of behaviour appropriate to
democratic citizenship and conducive to active participation in democratic
institutions. Education in a classical democracy thus seeks to empower its
future members to participate collectively in the processes through which
their society is being shaped and reproduced.

Historically, the type of education deemed appropriate for enabling future
citizens to participate in the shaping of their society has been liberal education – a form of education first shaped in classical times to meet the
needs of free and equal citizens actively participating in the common life of
their community. The task of cultivating in pupils the knowledge, skills and

attitudes necessary for public participation requires a curriculum which fosters those forms of critical and explanatory knowledge which allow pupils to reappraise existing social norms and reflect critically on the dominant social, political and economic institutions of contemporary society. Pedagogically, it requires participatory rather than instructional teaching methods in order to cultivate the skills and attitudes which democratic deliberation requires.

The classical conception of democracy also sustains a distinctive view about the relationship between education and work. This is because the extent to which economic prosperity should be an overriding political and educational aim will be a contested issue, reflecting the views that citizens take about the significance of wealth creation in constituting the good life and the good society. Also, the conception of education associated with the classical conception of democracy can be usefully debated in terms of the 'needs of society' only in so far as what is covered by such a phrase refers primarily to the educational needs of democratic citizens.[14] Similarly, disagreements about the needs of society will themselves be resolved democratically, and questions about the conduct, content and organization of education will be answered in ways which reflect the concerns of the many social and political groups that have a legitimate interest in education.

The kind of education appropriate to the contemporary conception of democracy will be very different from that which the classical conception requires. For example, since it does not make any intrinsic connection between democracy and education, educational policy will primarily be formulated by political leaders rather than through public discussion and democratic debate. Also, in so far as the political ignorance and the apathy of the masses are regarded as essential to social stability, political education will always be narrowly defined and have a marginal status in the curriculum corresponding to the marginal status of political participation in most people's lives.

Because the contemporary conception of democracy results from, and reflects, the political requirements of a modern market economy, most of the central demands made on the educational system will be related to society's economic needs. The kind of education that most of the members of such a society will require is therefore one that prepares them for their future roles as producers, workers and consumers. Moreover, in a democracy so defined, there will always be a tendency towards a two-tier system of education: one offering a minority an education appropriate to future political leaders; the other preparing the mass of ordinary individuals for their primary social roles as producers, workers and consumers in a modern market economy. For the same reason, it is always likely that mass education will have a strong emphasis on preparation for the world of work and that curriculum content will be regarded as a body of knowledge and skills which have some market value. Pedagogical relationships will tend to be authoritarian and competition will, as in society generally, play an essential role. Finally, schools themselves will not be organized democratically and decision-making will be predominantly in the hands of headteachers who are themselves appointed on the basis of competition.

Although the education systems of most western democratic societies now tend to embody and endorse the contemporary conception of democracy, the claim that this represents the only 'realistic' conception of democracy that education can promote should not be taken too seriously. To define democracy by reference to the goals, institutions and practices of what are conventionally called 'democratic' societies involves a circularity of reasoning that begs the very question at issue. Also, any definition of democracy which simply identifies the main characteristics of a political system that is already assumed to possess that status will inevitably prejudge the answer in a way that favours the status quo. To understand the meaning of democracy in this way is simply to

> surrender the rich history of the idea of democracy to the existent. Questions about the appropriate extent of citizen participation, the proper scope of citizen rule and the most suitable spheres of democratic regulation questions that have been part of democratic theory from Athens to nineteenth century England . . . are answered merely by reference to current practice. The ideals and methods of democracy become, by default, the ideas and methods of the existing democratic systems.[15]

If this kind of parochialism is to be avoided, it is important to understand how the contemporary conception of democracy is the outcome of a historical process through which democracy was transformed from a moral concept that incorporated a vision of human nature and a commitment to a particular form of life, into a neutral concept that is devoid of both. What this implies, is that any further enquiry into the meaning of democracy and the view of education it sustains must, to a large extent, be a historical study concerned with exposing the cultural, political and ideological contexts in which the classical conception was displaced and out of which the contemporary conception of democracy was eventually to emerge. As Arblaster puts it:

> To suppose that this century can fix the definition of democracy, or even more arrogantly that it is in this century that democracy has been finally and definitively realised, is to be blind not only to the probabilities of the future but also to the certainties of the past.[16]

Interpreted as a request for historical intelligibility rather than as a description of contemporary practice, any further attempt to clarify the relationship between education and democracy will have to concern itself with the questions of why and how, in the eighteenth and the nineteenth centuries, two distinct and apparently conflicting political traditions – liberalism and democracy – combined to form the tradition of 'liberal democracy' within which the British system of education originated, developed and evolved.

The British liberal democratic tradition

Up to the eighteenth century, 'democracy' was regarded as synonymous with 'mob rule' and thus as one of the worst types of government possible. MacPherson makes the point clearly:

Democracy used to be a bad word. Everybody who was anybody knew that democracy . . . would be a bad thing fatal to individual freedom and to all the graces of civilized living. That was the position taken by pretty near all men of intelligence from the earliest historical times down to about a hundred years ago.[17]

It is thus unsurprising that the kind of democracy that first began to find favour in Britain in the eighteenth century was very different from the 'classical' conception of ancient Greece and was advocated and defended in terms of a view of the good life and the good society very different from those which the classical conception sought to promote. The reason for this is not hard to identify: the initial attraction of democracy was not that it promoted a desirable vision of the good society but rather that it offered a system of government which would allow an already established view of the good society – the liberal society – to work. In other words, the form of democracy that actually emerged in Britain in the nineteenth century was designed to meet the needs of a society that had already accepted the moral values and political principles of liberalism. As MacPherson put it, 'by the time the liberal state was democratised, the old idea of democracy had been liberalised'.[18]

'Liberalism' is notoriously difficult to define and it is probably best understood as an evolving political tradition held together by a coherent set of moral values and political ideals. One way to understand these values and ideals is to appreciate the overriding importance liberalism attaches to the notion of the individual. For liberals, the individual is always prior to society and has a higher moral value and political importance than any collective entity or social group.

> The individual is the fixed point of reference in the liberal world . . . Liberal individualism involves seeing the individual as primary, as more 'real' or fundamental than society . . . In this way of thinking, the individual comes *before* society in every sense . . . .[19]

Closely associated with this emphasis on the individual is the view that people are essentially atomistic and egoistic: atomistic in the sense that each individual is seen as existing in isolation from other individuals; egoistic in the sense that individuals are seen as fundamentally selfish and driven only by their own private interests and desires. Within the liberal tradition, it is the individual pursuit of self-interest that both motivates human action and justifies personal ambition. It is also taken as axiomatic that each individual's interests and desires are naturally given rather than socially formed and that only individuals' own understandings of their particular interests and desires are valid and true.

Given this view of the individual, it is not surprising that liberalism regards the notion of the 'national interest' or the 'good of society' as referring to nothing other than the sum total of the interests and 'goods' of its individual members. For liberals, society has no existence above or beyond that of individuals and can serve no purpose nor have any interests other than the purposes and interests of its individual members. It is for this reason that liberalism attaches overriding importance to the value of individual freedom. Indeed, what distinguishes liberalism from all other political traditions is the pre-eminence it gives to promoting political principles and political institutions that will ensure that the freedom of the individual can be guaranteed. As Lord Acton put it, for liberals 'freedom is not a means to a higher political end. It is itself the highest political end.'[20]

Although the value of individual freedom is a permanent feature of liberal thought, it was also a central value of classical democratic thinking. But, of course, for the Greeks human beings were essentially social and political animals who could only realize and achieve their freedom by participating in the public sphere. By contrast, for liberals, human beings are emphatically not social or political animals and their freedom can only be achieved if they are allowed to pursue their individual interests in a private sphere which is protected from any undue interference by either society or the state. It is for this reason that the liberal conception of freedom is 'normally defined negatively, as a condition in which one is *not* compelled, *not* restricted, *not* interfered with, *not* pressurised'.[21]

Within the liberal tradition, freedom from the constraints and compulsions of the state is seen as a necessary condition for individual self-fulfilment, social progress and economic development. For liberals the good society is a society whose members have the right to think, believe and act as they like, provided that they do not prevent others from exercising the same right. One consequence of this is that liberalism puts a high value on principles such as freedom of speech, tolerance, dignity and respect for others. Another is that liberalism promotes the ideal of individual autonomy as a fundamental political goal. Indeed, a distinguishing feature of any genuinely liberal society is its commitment to developing the capacity of individuals to think and act autonomously: the capacity to determine and pursue their own version of the 'good life' for themselves, free from manipulation by others or from external pressures and constraints.

Because 'individual autonomy lies at the heart of the values of liberal democratic societies',[22] it is unsurprising to find that it has always been a dominant theme within liberal educational theory as well.[23] Indeed, in many ways, the mobilizing principle behind most theoretical justifications for liberal education has been a commitment to the aims and values of 'rational autonomy' – aims and values that always reflect the liberal view that the freedom of individuals is always a matter of developing their capacity to think, act and choose on the basis of their own rational reflections. In his famous essay *On Liberty*, J.S. Mill describes this view of education in the following words:

the free development of individuality is one of the leading essentials of well-being. It is ... the proper condition of a human being ... to use and interpret experience in his own way ... To conform to custom, merely *as* custom, does not educate or develop in him any of the qualities which are the distinctive endowment of a human being. The human facilities of perception, judgement, discriminate feeling, mental activity and even moral preference, are exercised only in making a choice. . . .[24]

In the eighteenth century, the idea that a democratic system of government would best serve to protect and promote a liberal society was far from obvious. At that time it was believed that democracy would simply replace the old aristocratic systems of government by a new 'tyranny of the mob' which would more seriously threaten individual freedom precisely because it could legitimize its infringements on personal liberty by claiming to be enacting 'the will of the people'. Clearly, before democracy could become an acceptable form of government it would have to be stripped of all those features that made it potentially threatening to liberal values and reconstructed so as to enable it to function to protect the liberty of individuals from undue interference from those with political power. The most influential theoretical exposition of this kind of 'protective' democracy was provided by the utilitarian political philosophers Jeremy Bentham (1746–1832) and James Mill (1773–1836).

Central to Bentham's utilitarianism was a distinctive version of the liberal view of human nature which he set out with great clarity in the opening sentences of his *Introduction to the Principles of Morals and Legislation*:

Nature has placed mankind under the governance of two sovereign masters, *pain* and *pleasure*. It is for them alone to point out what we ought to do, as well as to determine what we shall do. On the one hand the standard of right and wrong, on the other the chain of causes and effects are fastened to their throne.[25]

For Bentham, then, human beings are exclusively driven by the desire to maximize their own happiness. He also accepted the basic liberal assumption that 'society' is 'a fictitious body composed of the individual persons who are considered as constituting, as it were, its members'.[26] From this view of human nature and society, Bentham concluded that the good life is one in which individuals can, without limits, pursue their own happiness and the good society is one governed by the basic utilitarian principle of the greatest happiness of the greatest number.

The political problem to which this gave rise was that of devising a form of government that would resolve the chaos and conflicts that would inevitably result if egoistic individuals were allowed to pursue their own desires without restraint. What was required was a system of government that would protect the freedom of individuals to pursue their own interests and desires and only prevent them from doing so if this would infringe the equal rights of others to pursue their interests and desires. Given his egoistic view of human nature, Bentham was quick to recognize that a government always operates to maximize its own interests rather than the interests and happiness of the governed. Indeed, since no politician would, as a matter of high principle, seek to promote the greatest happiness of the greatest number, it was necessary to introduce a political system which would create an 'identity of interest' between rulers and ruled. To this end Bentham's disciple, James

Mill, in his *Essay on Government* (1828), presented the utilitarian case in favour of 'representative democracy'. In it, he argued for a system of government based on universal suffrage, secret ballots and annual parliaments in which the people's representatives would be made directly accountable to a democratic electorate for any selfish abuse of their power.[27] Thus, as formulated by Jeremy Bentham and James Mill, democracy was to be simply an instrument for making government accountable to private individuals for securing their wants and protecting their freedom. As Bentham put it: 'a democracy has for its characteristic object and effect, the securing of its members against oppression and depredation at the hands of those functionaries which it employs for its defence.'[28]

By the 1820s many people thought it was possible to carry out the kind of political reforms that Bentham and Mill advocated. A new political party, the Philosophical Radicals, was established with this aim in mind and, by the 1830s, James Mill's son, J.S. Mill (1806–93), had become its leading spokesperson. But, by that time, J.S. Mill had realized that Bentham's 'protective' justification for liberal democracy was in need of revision and reconstruction. For example, he argued that though Bentham and James Mill had advocated representative democracy solely on the grounds that it offered a mechanism for protecting the liberty of individuals, this was not its sole purpose. Similarly, while he accepted the utilitarian principle of 'the greatest happiness of the greatest number' he rejected the Benthamite assumption that happiness can be crudely equated with the pursuit of pleasure and the absence of pain. The capacity to experience 'human happiness', argued J.S. Mill, depends on individuals' moral and intellectual development and the extent to which they are able rationally to understand and evaluate their own needs and desires, formulate their ends and goals and determine their own interests. For J.S. Mill, to promote 'the greatest happiness of the greatest number' was to promote the human capacity for autonomy and self-determination.

In his *Considerations on Representative Government*,[29] J.S. Mill argued that a liberal democracy is to be judged by the extent to which it develops and uses the intellectual and moral capacities of its members. By these standards, the good society is one in which individuals can, through active participation in democratic decision-making, develop their moral and intellectual capacities. However, although he was fully committed to the educative function of democratic participation, J.S. Mill also retained the traditional liberal fear of 'mob rule'. In particular, he was fearful of the threat to individual liberty and social progress if society was dominated by a mediocre body of public opinion. In a democracy, individual liberty must not only be protected from the despotic state; it must also be protected from the 'tyranny of the majority' and, in particular, from the dominance of the 'commercial spirit' of the new industrial middle classes. Because of his obsession with this problem, J.S. Mill moved away from the ideals of a participatory democracy and instead proposed a modified form of representative democracy constructed so as to ensure that political decisions were only made by 'right persons'. Thus, presenting a modern version of Plato's philosopher kings, Mill wrote:

The idea of a rational democracy is not that people themselves govern but that they have *security* for good government . . . the best government (need it be said?) must be the government of the wisest and these must always be the few. The people ought to be the masters, but they are masters who must employ servants more skilful than themselves . . . .[30]

For Mill the practical problem of ensuring that the elected leaders were always the 'wisest few' could not be resolved by an undemocratic restriction of the suffrage. Instead, he proposed that while, in a democracy, all should have the vote, the more intelligent and better educated should have a plural number of votes. 'It is hurtful', he wrote, 'that the constitution of the country should declare ignorance to be entitled as much political power as knowledge.'[31] This reluctance to allow people equally to exercise political power clearly creates a serious ambiguity in Mill's whole theory of democracy and he never effectively reconciled his 'classical' defence of democracy as a morally transformative educational force, with his concern for protecting individual liberty. On the one hand, he was a firm believer in the educative role of participatory democracy; on the other, he feared the 'brute ignorance' of the working classes and the dangers that this would create if democratic participation was not severely limited and qualified.

J.S. Mill is often described as 'the man who . . . founded modern liberalism',[32] and there is no doubt that his justification for representative democracy provided the classical defence for liberal democracy in the second half of the nineteenth century. It also gave rise to a fundamental educational question. If, as Mill suggested, special importance must be attached to the 'highly gifted and instructed few' who were to lead the democratic majority, how are they to be educated? The most influential answer to this question was provided by Matthew Arnold. In the Introduction to *Culture and Anarchy*, Arnold wrote 'I am a Liberal . . . and I am, above all, a believer in culture',[33] and much of the book is devoted to showing how classical liberalism was leading to the gradual erosion of civilized values and a slide into anarchy – a process made all the more inevitable by the growing trend towards greater democracy. For Arnold, the only way to avoid anarchy was through the revitalization of culture. Only a wider diffusion of culture throughout society could ensure that the new industrial middle classes were adequately prepared for positions of political influence and power. Arnold regarded the English middle class as 'the worst educated in the world', embracing a 'philistine' attitude to culture that was superficial and vulgar. The future of democracy, therefore, required extending to the new middle classes the kind of 'high culture' previously reserved for the aristocratic élite. For Arnold, the educational requirements of the political leaders of the democratic future were not significantly different from those of the political leaders of the aristocratic past.

During the 1860s and 1870s, enlargements to the electorate began to revive all the classical liberal fears of democracy: the demise of individual responsibility, the growth of state power and the threat to individual freedom. Also, despite the efforts of J.S. Mill to correct some of the obvious limitations of Bentham's political philosophy, it was clear that classical liberalism had not produced 'the greatest happiness of the greatest number' and was of no real benefit to the mass of ordinary people. As the nineteenth-century liberal historian, Lord Action, was to reflect:

> the old notion of civil liberty . . . did not benefit the mass of the people. The progress of knowledge left them in abject ignorance . . . Society . . . announced that the best thing for the poor is not to be born . . . Liberty, for the mass, is not happiness.[34]

By the 1880s, then, the major political problem was to reformulate liberalism so that it could effectively address issues concerning the condition of the 'masses', while at the same time preserving the core liberal value of individual freedom. At the heart of this problem was the need to reinterpret the classical liberal view of the relationship between the individual and the state. Although liberalism was fundamentally opposed to any extension of state power, liberal governments had, throughout the nineteenth century, introduced legislation designed to control and regulate large areas of economic and social life. This legislation – which included the various Factory Acts and Education Acts – clearly ran counter to liberal ideas and made it obvious that liberal governments were no longer practising what they preached. In this situation, it was clearly necessary to rethink the liberal concept of freedom and the liberal theory of the state. This task was initially undertaken during the 1880s by the Oxford philosopher T.H. Green, and eventually led to the emergence of the 'New Liberalism' that was to provide the intellectual basis for many late nineteenth-century and early twentieth-century social and educational reforms.

Drawing on classical Greek philosophy and culture, Green argued that the classic liberal view of the 'common good' as nothing more than the satisfaction of individual private wants and desires, failed to recognize that individuals' wants and desires are not simply given but are always formed within the framework of a common life. For Green, as for the Greeks, human beings are essentially social animals whose freedom can only flourish in a society that provides the conditions which will allow freedom to be exercised and enjoyed – a framework which Benthamite political philosophy had deliberately set out to destroy. For Green, freedom is not to be equated with freedom from state interference but with the opportunity for individuals to develop their human powers and realize their human capacities by contributing to the common good of their society. For Green, the role of the state is to enlarge the opportunities for freedom by providing the social and political conditions under which all individuals are able to realize their capacity to contribute to the common good.

Green developed this view in his lecture 'Liberal Legislation and Freedom of Contract' (1880). In this, he argued that though the Factory Acts had undoubtedly restricted the freedom of employers to use child labour, they were nevertheless appropriate and legitimate attempts to extend individual freedom. This is because 'freedom is not merely freedom from restraint or compulsion . . . freedom to do as we like irrespective of what it is that we like'.[35] Rather, as he wrote:

> When we speak of freedom . . . we mean a positive power or capacity of doing or enjoying something worth doing or enjoying, and that, too, something that we do or enjoy in common with others . . . When we measure the progress of society by its growth in freedom, we measure it by the increasing development and exercise on the whole of those powers of contributing to social good with which we believe the members of the society to be endowed . . . Thus . . . the mere enabling of a man to do as he likes is in itself no contribution to true freedom . . . if the ideal of true freedom is the maximum power for all members of human society alike, to make the best of themselves, we are right in refusing to ascribe the glory of freedom to a state in which the apparent elevation of the few is founded on the degradation of the many . . . .[36]

Green's view of individual freedom, then, differs from its classical predecessor in that it is no longer defined 'negatively' as the absence of compulsion or restraint, but 'positively' as the possession of the power to exercise and enjoy freedom. Further, if all people, and not just a privileged few, are to have the opportunity to possess this freedom, the active intervention of the state is both necessary and desirable. To demonstrate this, Green used the example of the Education Act of 1870 which, though it was a 'great system of restriction', nevertheless marked a major enhancement of individual freedom.

> Without a command of certain elementary arts and knowledge, the individual in modern society . . . is not free to develop his faculties. With a view to securing such freedom among its members it is . . . within the province of the state to prevent children growing up in that kind of ignorance which practically excludes them from a free career in life . . . .[37]

During the first decade of the twentieth century, the 'New Liberalism' as espoused by Green was taken up by other liberal political theorists such as Hobhouse and Toynbee and soon became the official doctrine of the Liberal Party. However, by the 1920s, it was becoming clear to many political philosophers and theorists that the classical conception of democracy was increasingly becoming untenable and that in most western democracies the principle of 'rule by the people' did not really apply. Although this state of affairs might have led to a fundamental critique of the failure of liberal democracies to live up to their self-proclaimed democratic ideals, it led instead to the concept of democracy being redefined so that it would more adequately articulate the facts of contemporary political life.

The starting point for this redefinition was a series of empirical studies, conducted in the 1920s, of the voting behaviour of citizens in liberal democracies. What these studies revealed was that most voters were politically ill informed, indifferent and apathetic and that, by its own standards, the classical theory of democracy was a myth. This view was popularized by the

American journalist Walter Lippmann, whose two books – *Public Opinion* (1922) and *The Phantom Public* (1925)[38] – offered a damning indictment of classical democratic theory both as a description of modern democracies and as a prescription for their future development. Classical democracy, Lippmann noted, was based on two assumptions: that all citizens had sufficient intelligence to form a rational understanding of political issues; and that all citizens had access to the knowledge and information necessary for them to make informed political decisions. But in reality, he argued, citizens' political perceptions were invariably based on misunderstandings and misapprehensions and their access to sophisticated political and economic knowledge was always severely limited. From this he concluded that the public opinion should play little part in democratic decision-making. Indeed, since the problems of a politically unenlightened and uninformed citizenry cannot be avoided, public participation in decision-making should be kept to a minimum.

It was against this background that 'classical' theories of democracy gradually began to be replaced by new 'contemporary' theories which redefined the concept of democracy in ways which would legitimize restricting political power to an élite group of 'experts' and giving public participation in political decision-making a minimal role. The most influential exponent of this theory was Joseph Schumpeter, who not only rejected the classical idea that an active informed citizenry was a precondition of democracy, but also insisted that democracy required citizens who were passive, apathetic, uninformed and uninvolved. Thus, in his seminal text *Capitalism, Socialism and Democracy*, he argued that the classical idea of democracy as 'rule by the people' ignored the innate political apathy and limited rationality of the people. The proper role of the people in a democracy, maintained Schumpeter, is not to participate in a process of self-rule, but to participate in the choice of their rulers by casting a vote at periodic elections. The people 'must understand that once they have elected an individual, political action is his business and not theirs'.[39] Thus Schumpeter arrives at his famous definition of democracy:

> . . . democracy does not and cannot mean that the people rule in any obvious sense of the terms 'people' and 'rule'. Democracy means only that the people have the opportunity of accepting or refusing the men who are to rule them.[40]

By redefining democracy so as to make it compatible with the ideology of modern industrial societies, twentieth-century realist and élitist theories of democracy effectively converted democracy from a critical concept incorporating a set of political ideals and a coherent vision of the good society, into a descriptive concept derived from observations of the political systems of western industrial societies. As a result, the idea of democracy 'ceased to be a norm or principle against which reality could be measured'.[41] But, by redefining democracy in a way which stripped it of its historical association with active political participation, realist and élitist theories were simply completing the historical process which began in the eighteenth century and through which democracy was gradually transformed from a political ideal that gave expression to a moral vision of the good life and the good society into a political method that was devoid of both. As Held puts it:

> Whether one takes as a benchmark the political philosophy of ancient Athens or the emergence of liberal democratic thought ... , it appears that democratic theory has come full circle: from a defence of a range of fairly tough grounds which might justify a commitment to a form of democratic life, to an argument which seems to cede almost everything to the opponents of democracy.[42]

Realist and élitist theories of democracy offered an image of democratic life in which the price to be paid for living in a modern industrial society was to recognize that the classical democratic ideal of equal political participation was based on an unrealistic view of ordinary people's intellectual limitations: limitations to which no amount of education could make any significant difference. The American philosopher John Dewey (1859–1952), however, argued the reverse. Like the realists and élitists, Dewey recognized that in order to grasp the contemporary significance and future potentiality of democracy it was necessary to understand the consequences of industrialization for social and economic life. He also conceded that the democratic realists had exposed many of the shortcomings of modern liberal democracies, and he described Lippmann's *Public Opinion* as 'perhaps the most effective indictment of democracy as currently conceived ever penned'.[43] But, unlike the realists and élitists, Dewey refused to accept that the failure of western liberal democracies to live up to classical democratic ideals meant that democracy had to be redefined so as to bring it into line with contemporary political reality. What it meant was that political reality had to be changed so as to bring it into line with classical democratic ideals. For Dewey, the essential condition for creating a society sustained by democratic values was a radical reform of education.

The book in which Dewey gave the most complete exposition of his ideas about the role of education in a democracy – *Democracy and Education* – is now frequently dismissed as obsolete: a book which was well suited to the intellectual climate of North American culture at the beginning of the twentieth century but which no longer needs to be read. But because most modern assessments of Dewey's educational philosophy take no account of his political and social philosophy they fail to appreciate the extent to which his educational ideas can only be adequately understood by first understanding his political and social philosophy and, in particular, his ideas about the future of liberal democratic societies.[44]

John Dewey: political and social philosophy

John Dewey is undoubtedly the most influential educational philosopher of the twentieth century. During his long life the western world underwent many fundamental cultural, economic and intellectual changes: America had emerged from its colonial status to become a major nation; science was developing as a major intellectual and cultural force; and the Industrial Revolution had made great progress. Although these changes help to explain the origins of many of Dewey's educational and political ideas, the starting point for much of his work was an intense hostility to the Platonic view that the role of political philosophy was to discover a realm of fixed truths on which the good society could be rationally grounded and towards which all political, social and educational reform could be directed. Because this view was so prevalent, political philosophy had become a sterile academic activity largely unrelated to the political and cultural problems of individuals and society. For Dewey, philosophy would only recover its cultural role when it 'ceases to be a device for dealing with the problems of philosophers and becomes a method, cultivated by philosophers for dealing with the problems of men'.[45]

The most important 'problems of men' at the beginning of the twentieth century concerned the future of the democratic institutions that had developed since the eighteenth century – problems about the relationship between freedom and equality which had been articulated in the New Liberalism of T.H. Green as well as problems about democratic participation that were being exposed through realist and élitist democratic theory. For Dewey, both of these theoretical developments simply confirmed the way in which philosophy always brings 'to consciousness in an intellectual form . . . the inherent troubles of complex and changing societies'.[46] For Dewey, the central task of contemporary political philosophy was to resolve those 'inherent troubles' by reconstructing the central concepts of liberal democratic theory in the context of contemporary social life. This he attempted to do in two books: *The Public and its Problems* and *Liberalism and Social Action*.[47]

In *The Public and its Problems*, Dewey readily acknowledged that the democratic realists had exposed many of the problems of modern liberal democracies and had reconstructed the meaning of democracy in a way that eliminated the gap between contemporary democratic reality and classical democratic ideals. But although he did not object to their description of the current state of liberal democracies, he regarded their response to the problem they identified as posing a serious threat to the future of democracy that could not go unanswered.

The realist prescription, noted Dewey, was based on a scepticism towards two of the central beliefs of classical democratic theory: the belief that ordinary people have the intellectual capacity for rational political judgement; and the belief that widespread public participation in all aspects of political and social life is desirable. Dewey regarded this scepticism as seriously misplaced. In opposition to realist claims that ordinary people lack the capacity to make political judgements he observed that, if ordinary citizens were as intellectually impoverished as democratic realists claimed, then rule by an intellectual élite could not work: 'The very ignorance . . . which [is] alleged to incapacitate them from share in political affairs, unfits them still more for passive submission to rule by intellectuals'.[48] He further argued that what people lacked was not intelligence but adequate information on which to base their political judgements: 'Until secrecy, prejudice, bias, misrepresentation and propaganda, as well as sheer ignorance are replaced by inquiry and publicity, we have no way of telling how apt for judgement of social policies, the existing intelligence of the masses may be.'[49]

Dewey also regarded the realist notion of intelligence as a fixed and innate personal endowment as 'the great conceit of the intellectual class' that had little relevance to democratic politics. What mattered for democracy was not the innate intelligence of individuals but the level of social intelligence operating in society: 'A more intelligent state of social affairs, one more informed with knowledge, more directed by intelligence, would not improve original endowment one whit, but it would raise the level upon which the intelligence of all operates.'[50] Moreover, Dewey argued that the lack of such knowledge was not due to the low intelligence of the average individual but to the inadequacies of existing educational provision:

> The indictments that are drawn against the intelligence of individuals are in truth indictments of a social order that does not permit the average individual to have access to the rich store of accumulated wealth of mankind in knowledge, ideas and purposes ... It is useless to talk about the future of democracy until the source of its failure has been grasped and steps are taken to bring about that type of social organisation that will encourage the socialised extension of intelligence.[51]

But Dewey regarded the chief weakness of the realist argument to be its rejection of the idea that democracy required the active participation of the public. Against this he argued that, though a genuinely democratic public required a kind of knowledge and a form of intelligence that did not exist, this should be interpreted as a criticism of the existing institutions and practices of liberal democracy rather than of the political aspirations and moral ideals that gave democracy its initial attraction and appeal. Thus he wrote:

> the old saying that the case for the ills of democracy is more democracy is not apt if it means that the evils may be remedied by introducing more machinery of the same kind as that which already exists or by refining or perfecting that machinery. But the phase may also indicate the need of returning to the idea itself, of clarifying and deepening our sense of its meaning to criticize and remake its political manifestations.[52]

For Dewey, then, the proper task of political philosophy at the beginning of the twentieth century was not to redefine democracy so much as to 'remake its political manifestations' by 'returning to the idea itself'. What, in particular, was required was a theoretical analysis aimed at revealing the obstacles to establishing the social, cultural and political conditions which would make genuine democratic participation possible.

The starting point for such an analysis was, noted Dewey, a realization that the existing political institutions of liberal democratic societies had not been initially introduced to expand democratic participation but to protect the individual freedom of the nineteenth-century middle classes, 'who were deeply suspicious of the state and whose interest in the ethical basis of democracy was minimal'.[53] What also has to be noted is the fact that the Industrial Revolution had transformed society in ways which made these political institutions virtually obsolete from the moment they were created. For as well as liberating individuals from many laborious tasks, the process of industrialization had also given rise to a form of 'mass society' which made it increasingly difficult for people with common interests to form social groups in which they could engage in co-operative activities aimed at discussing their common concerns. In pre-industrial society such groups – or 'publics' – came into existence as they were required and developed in response to specific social needs. As such, they occupied an autonomous 'public sphere' that was located between the state and the private individual – a sphere in which individuals could participate in public dialogue, formulate common goals and publicly legitimate their decisions on matters of general concern. Within the framework of liberal democracy, the interests of individuals had been increasingly privatized and depoliticized, 'public life' had been gradually eroded, and active participation in the public sphere was becoming increasingly obsolete. For Dewey it was the demise of public life that had provided the conditions for the emergence of democratic realism and gave credibility to its claim that an active public was not a necessary feature of a democracy. But the decline of the public sphere, argued Dewey, does not demonstrate that the existence of a public concerned with the formation of general social policies is democratically unnecessary. What it demonstrates is the extent to which the existing political institutions of liberal democracy are unable to serve the need of the public to organize itself for effective political participation. For Dewey, the revitalization of democratically organized public life was the most important requirement for the future development of democracy. The intellectual task to which this gave rise was that of reassessing the extent to which liberal values were any longer embedded in existing political institutions and were actually informing contemporary social and cultural life.

In *Liberalism and Social Action*, Dewey insisted that if liberal values were to continue to direct the progress of society, then it was necessary to uncover the historical conditions in which liberalism had initially developed and the particular political and social problems to which it was addressed. The first step in this enquiry was to show how the eighteenth-century political, cultural and economic conditions which had created a demand for people to be emancipated from the old hierarchical social order had, in the nineteenth century, led to the emergence of a tradition of liberal democracy in which the 'individual' was understood as someone who existed apart from society and 'society' was understood as nothing more than the aggregation of isolated individuals pursuing their private ends. This concept of the individual as a private person who enters society with given needs and interests, had initially emerged in the historical circumstances of the sixteenth and seventeenth centuries when the dominant political institutions and forms of social relationship restricted free commerce and impeded intellectual development. Those who opposed these restrictions did so by appealing to a theory of individual rights 'which endowed single persons in isolation from any association except those which they deliberately formed for their own ends'.[54] Throughout the nineteenth century this appeal to individuals' rights, together with the assumption that individuals are prior to, and not the product of, their social relations, continued to provide the common defence for liberal democracy and for justifying its institutions as the best means of protecting individual freedom.

Dewey insisted that if society was to continue to be guided by liberal values, it had to be conceded that this nineteenth-century interpretation of individual freedom was neither immutable nor fixed and that its preservation in the twentieth century simply meant that a theory of individual rights that had initially been a potent force for emancipating the middle classes from the arbitrary power of the state, had now degenerated into a conservative ideology which functioned to protect the privileges of a minority and limit the freedom of the majority. As a result, liberalism had been transformed from a demand for individual liberty and social change into a pseudo-liberalism which allows a dominant social group to use 'ideas that were once weapons of emancipation as instruments for keeping the power and wealth they have obtained'.[55] Clearly, if liberal values are to be upheld, the concept of the individual would have to be reinterpreted in the light of the very different intellectual and cultural conditions that existed at the beginning of the twentieth century.

In *Individualism, Old and New,*[56] Dewey argued that the nineteenth-century liberal distinction between the 'individual' and 'society' was a philosophical abstraction that nowhere exists. What the nineteenth-century history of liberal democratic societies had clearly revealed was that the individual, far from being some kind of preformed entity that existed prior to society, was always a product of its social relationships and that individual freedom was not a natural right with which all individuals were endowed at birth, but an end point that could only be achieved through a certain kind of social life. For Dewey the preservation of the illusion of a fixed, ready-made individual was one of the chief obstacles impeding the twentieth-century development of liberal democracy.

Like T.H. Green, one of his intellectual heroes, Dewey insisted that individual freedom was not simply an abstract principle but a concrete power, so that questions about the right to individual freedom were always questions about how and to whom this power was allocated. Dewey also agreed with Green that individual freedom and equality were mutually dependent values. The demand for freedom was a demand for a society which allowed equal opportunities to exercise freedom, and the demand for equality was a demand for the kind of society that would promote the freedom of all its members. Again echoing Green, Dewey insisted that the classical liberal 'identification of liberty with unrestrained individualistic action ... is as fatal to the realisation of liberty for all as it is to the realisation of equality'.[57]

Thus Dewey insisted that although the nineteenth-century theory of liberal democracy as developed by Bentham and J.S. Mill had been a force for radical reform, its association of liberty with 'negative' liberty was, in the twentieth century, seriously impeding the growth of individual freedom.

What was required for the twentieth century was not an *extension* of liberal democracy but a new *conception* of liberal democracy: one that would revitalize liberal values in a way that not only recognized that the traditional opposition between the individual and society and between liberalism and democracy was now obsolete, but also took account of the major intellectual, cultural and economic transformations that had occurred during the nineteenth century. Prominent among these were Darwin's theory of evolution, the growth of modern science and the process of industrialization.

The attraction to Dewey of Darwin's theory of evolution was that it allowed the atomistic liberal view of human nature to be replaced by a view that was non-individualistic and entirely social. Like Darwin, Dewey viewed human beings as organisms which had developed specific biological characteristics in order to eliminate conflicts between their innate needs and their natural environment. But as well as this process of natural evolution, human beings had also undergone a process of social evolution – a process through which the species had acquired various intellectual dispositions which enabled it to adjust to its cultural environment by dealing intelligently with the problems and conflicts of social life. By developing what Dewey called 'social intelligence', human beings had gradually developed the capacity collectively to enlarge their own freedom and to create a more desirable form of social life. But although Dewey understood freedom to be achieved by the progressive application of social intelligence to the problems of culture and society, he did not believe that there must be some fixed end towards which this process should move or any preconceived ideas about what course it should take. For Dewey, the 'good life' is simply one which allows individuals to realize their potentialities for 'social intelligence' by reconstructing their experiences in ways which are themselves conducive to the growth of their freedom. The good life is 'a life of self-transformation and change' in which 'the growing, enlarging, deliberate self ... goes forth to meet new demands and occasions, and readapts and remakes itself in the process'.[58]

Thus, for Dewey, both social progress and individual freedom are best understood as the growth of the social intelligence that is developed when individuals participate intelligently and co-operatively in the search for solutions to the problems created by social change. By participating in this process, individuals develop those intellectual dispositions which allow them to reconstruct themselves and their social institutions in ways which are conducive to the realization of their freedom and to the reshaping of their society. In this sense, the 'individual' and 'society' are neither separate nor distinct: they are both elements within a single process of 'growth': an endless spiral whereby individuals use their intelligence to reshape the society by which they themselves have been shaped in order to make it more conducive to the development of their individual freedom. 'Growth' is thus a dynamic and dialectical process of self-transformation and social change. It is the process whereby individuals, in the course of remaking their society, remake themselves.

For Dewey, a democracy is a society that aspires to contribute to the growth of all its members. At the beginning of the twentieth century, any genuinely democratic society should understand that modern science not only provided a sophisticated method for acquiring specialized knowledge but also a model of a community in which social intelligence was developed by resolving problems on the basis of shared experience, an egalitarian distribution of knowledge, open communication and co-operative action. A democratic society that aspires to promote the growth, and hence the individual freedom, of all its members will, therefore, be one which seeks to ensure that the procedural principles governing the activities of the scientific community – principles of open discussion, freedom of speech, tolerance and respect for the opinions of others – are diffused throughout its political institutions and social arrangements. 'The crisis in democracy', wrote Dewey, 'demands the substitution of intelligence that is exemplified in scientific procedures for the kind of intelligence that is now accepted'.[59]

For Dewey, then, a democracy is not simply a political mechanism or a set of individual rights. Still less is it the embodiment of a universal abstract principle. Rather, it is a society which has created the conditions under which its members can collectively determine the future of their society on the basis of their shared social intelligence. It is the form of social life which provides the opportunity for the full development of individual freedom by allowing all individuals to participate in the future shaping of their society. In a democracy

> all those who are affected by social institutions must have a share in producing and managing them. The two facts that each one is influenced in . . . what he becomes by the institutions under which he lives, and that therefore he shall have in a democracy a voice in shaping them, are the passive and active sides of the same fact.[60]

What made the emergence of this kind of democracy a real possibility at the beginning of the twentieth century was the process of industrialization: a process that was stimulated by – and itself served to stimulate – the growth of modern science. In *The School and Society*[61] – a series of lectures delivered in 1899 – Dewey described how industrialization had brought about the disintegration of traditional forms of community life. The division of labour and the division between home and work created by industrialization meant that the cultural environment in which people lived and worked was no longer conducive to the spirit or co-operative living that had characterized pre-industrial life. At the same time, however, by introducing modes of production in which science and technology controlled nature, industrialization had created the conditions in which people's personal capacities could be liberated and a form of society could be envisaged which facilitates 'the participation of every mature human being in formation of the values that regulate the living of men together'.[62] But, as well as providing the conditions for the emergence of this kind of democracy, industrialization could also lead to a class-divided society which would restrict the personal development of most of its members and exclude the majority from major areas of common concern. The only way to prevent this was by transforming mass schooling into a system of public education that would 'render nugatory the indictment of democracy drawn on the basis of the ignorance of the masses'.[63] Without a radical reform of public education aimed at promoting and revitalizing a democratic public, the democratic impulse implicit in industrial life could not be developed and the effective extension and expansion of liberal ideals would not occur. In *My Pedagogic Creed*, Dewey said: 'I believe that education is the fundamental method of social progress'.[64]

Dewey acknowledged that nineteenth-century liberals such as Matthew Arnold and J.S. Mill had recognized the close connection between democracy and education. But because they assumed that this entailed little more than extending to all the kinds of education previously restricted to the aristocratic élite, they failed to appreciate the social function of education in reproducing existing patterns of cultural, economic and political life. By believing that a form of education that had evolved to reproduce a pre-democratic and pre-industrial social order could also function to serve the needs of a modern, industrial democracy, they failed to acknowledge how the democratic transformation of society required a democratic transformation of education. This meant that their explanation of the connection between education and democracy was superficial:

> The superficial explanation is that a government resting upon popular suffrage cannot be successful unless those who elect and obey their governors are educated. Since a democratic society repudiates the principle of external authority it must find a substitute in voluntary disposition and interest: these can be created only by education. But there is a deeper explanation. A democracy is more than a form of government: it is primarily a mode of associated living, a conjoint communicated experience.[65]

If democracy is 'primarily a mode of associated living' embedded in the culture and social relationships of everyday life, then education cannot perform its democratic role simply by expanding the prevailing system of traditional schooling. The goal of traditional schooling, argued Dewey, was 'to adjust individuals ... to fit into present social arrangements and conditions'[66] and, to the extent that these continue, they support teaching methods which breed democratically undesirable social attitudes (such as obedience and self-interest) and encourage schools to rely on authoritarian methods (such as direct instruction and the inculcation of fixed beliefs). These traditional forms of education were legitimized by profoundly anti-democratic educational philosophies in which spurious distinctions between 'mind' and 'body', 'culture' and 'utility', 'theoretical knowledge' and 'practical knowledge' were used to justify the division between a 'liberal' education for a ruling élite and a 'vocational' education for the mass of ordinary working people. A prerequisite for the democratic reconstruction of education was the democratic reconstruction of educational philosophy, a task which Dewey undertook in his seminal text, *Democracy and Education*.

John Dewey: democracy and education

One of the first tasks Dewey set himself in *Democracy and Education* was to evaluate the strengths and weaknesses of educational philosophies which had been 'formulated in earlier social conditions but which still operate in societies nominally democratic, to hamper the adequate realization of the democratic ideal'.[67] The strength of one of these educational philosophies – the Platonic educational philosophy – was that it clearly recognized the role of education in creating and reproducing a particular kind of society. However, although Dewey freely acknowledged that 'it was Plato who first consciously taught the world . . . about the social import of education', it has to be recognized that 'the society in which the theory was propounded was so undemocratic that Plato could not work out a solution for the problem whose terms he clearly saw'.[68] For Dewey, what particularly vitiated the argument of *The Republic* is Plato's limited view of human development and his unwillingness to concede that a society may evolve and change and yet remain stable. Plato's 'bondage to state ideals' and his 'conviction that change or alteration was lawless flux' meant that 'he could not trust gradual improvements in education to bring about a better society, which should improve education and so on, indefinitely'.[69] It is this lack of any understanding of how education and society may transform and be transformed by each other, that Dewey cited as the main reason why Plato's educational philosophy offers an inadequate solution to the problem it so clearly identified.

When he turned to reconsider Rousseau's educational philosophy, Dewey was again concerned to identify both its weaknesses and its strengths. Its 'true significance' argued Dewey, was 'its impetus towards a wider and freer society'.[70] But if the strength of Rousseau's educational philosophy was its 'impassioned devotion to the emancipation of life' from the 'distorting and corrupting limitations imposed upon the free powers of man', its weaknesses lay in the way Rousseau's desire to replace 'an artificial corrupt and inequitable social order . . . found intellectual formulation in a worship of nature'.[71] By giving 'nature full swing' Rousseau's conception of education had the positive value of 'drawing attention to the wrongness of aims which do not have regard to the natural endowment of those educated'.[72] But his view of 'nature' as antithetical to 'society' had led him to regard the individual's 'natural endowments' as non-social and to view 'social arrangements as mere external expedients by which non-social individuals might secure a greater amount of private happiness'.[73] This image of the pre-social individual whose natural powers could somehow spontaneously flourish outside of society was 'pure mythology'. For Dewey, the natural powers of individuals can only develop through interaction with the social environment:

> That civil institutions and customs work almost automatically to give wrong education which the most careful schooling cannot offset is true enough, but the conclusion is not to educate apart from the environment, but to provide an environment in which native powers will be put to better uses.[74]

Thus, for Dewey, 'to leave everything to nature' is to 'negate the very idea of education'.[75] Education is essentially a social process that has to be grounded in the kind of environment in which the 'native powers' of individuals can develop. In the formation of democratic citizens, the most important native power of human beings is their social intelligence, and this can only be developed in an educational environment in which intelligence can be socialized through participation in co-operative deliberation, shared enquiries and collective decision-making. An educational environment which puts the power of social intelligence to full use is not one that prepares individuals for democracy but one that is itself democratically organized. 'Much of our present education fails', wrote Dewey, 'because it neglects the fundamental principle of the school as a form of community life'.[76]

For Dewey, therefore, the educational system of a democracy is one in which schools are themselves organized so as to promote the kind of social intelligence which is the prerequisite to individual freedom and growth. For Dewey, individuals can only learn to understand themselves as democratic individuals by becoming members of a community in which the problems of communal life are resolved through collective deliberation and a shared concern for the common good. For this reason, a democratic school is a common school providing a broad social community to which children of different race, class, gender and religion can belong. Democratic schools thus offer 'a mode of associated living' which would replicate the kind of educative environment provided by the social communities of pre-industrial society.

But unlike pre-industrial education, the primary aim of democratic education is to ensure that pupils' capacity to act intelligently in changing situations and circumstances can develop and grow. For Dewey, education in a democracy has no fixed aims or goals. As he famously asserted, '. . . the educational process has no end beyond itself; it is its own end; . . . Since in reality there is nothing to which growth is relative save more growth, there is nothing to which education is subordinate save more education'.[77] This kind of growth cannot be achieved by controlling or directing what pupils think. Rather, it requires schools to provide a democratic culture in which pupils are encouraged to resolve practical, moral and social problems through joint activities and collective decision-making. Since, in a democracy, decision-making is no longer the preserve of an aristocratic élite, schools must become embryonic societies providing all pupils with opportunities to develop the social attitudes, skills and dispositions that allow them to formulate and achieve their collective ends by confronting shared problems and common concerns. For Dewey, it is primarily by promoting the growth of social intelligence through co-operative problem-solving activities that schools can support and promote the evolution of a more democratic social order.

Dewey recognized that this kind of democratic education could only be realistically achieved if the existing separation of a 'liberal education' for an élite few from a 'vocational education' for the mass of ordinary people was abolished. 'The price that democratic societies will have to pay for their continuing health', he argued, 'is the elimination of an oligarchy . . . that attempts to monopolise the benefits of intelligence . . . for the profit of a few privileged ones'.[78] Historically, liberal education has been restricted to the education of a particular privileged class. But, in a democracy,

> liberal education becomes a name for the sort of education that every
> member of the community . . . should have: the education that will

liberate his capacities and thereby contribute both to his own happiness and his social usefulness . . . In short, a liberal education is one that liberates. Theoretically, any type of education may do this. As a matter of fact, all of them fall much short of accomplishing it.[79]

Given this kind of understanding, it is easy to understand why Dewey regarded the eradication of the distinction between liberal education and vocational education to be of crucial significance for the future of democracy. It is also easy to appreciate why he regarded most existing forms of vocational education as offering little more than a disguised form of class education that simply used 'the school as an agency for transferring the older division of labour and leisure, culture and service, mind and body, directed and directive class into a society nominally democratic'.[80] Only when the ideological function of these divisions had been recognized would it be possible to develop a form of democratic education that was both liberal and vocational: a form of education that would no longer 'separate training of employees from training for citizenship, training of intelligence and character from training for narrow industrial efficiency'.[81] Similarly, once the full political and social meaning of the concept of 'vocation' had been acknowledged then it would become clear that the function of vocational education was not 'to adapt workers to the existing industrial regime' but to develop 'such intelligent initiative, ingenuity and executive capacity as shall make workers . . . the masters of their own industrial fate'.[82] So understood, vocational education would not be concerned to offer training for a particular trade or occupation. Instead it would offer

> instruction in the historic background of present conditions; training in science to give intelligence and initiative in dealing with material and agencies of production; and the study of economics, civics and politics, to bring the future worker in touch with the problems of the day and the various methods proposed for its improvement.[83]

And by doing this, it would 'help on such a reorganisation of industry as will change it from a feudalistic to a democratic social order'.[84]

Dewey was no idealist. He recognized that a democratic reconstruction of society would not be achieved simply by reforming education. He also 'openly acknowledged that schools were inextricably tied to prevailing structures of power and therefore extremely difficult to transform into agencies of democratic reform'.[85] He knew that his educational proposals would have to face the opposition and resistance of powerful entrenched interests and would be detached from their political rationale and assessed in ways which largely ignored their role in initiating individuals into a democratic culture. It is therefore unsurprising to find that Dewey's educational principles – such as practical problem-solving and collaborative learning – have been reduced to pedagogical techniques whose relevance to the creation of a democratic society is no longer apparent. Nor is it surprising that Dewey's central educational concepts – such as 'growth', 'interest' and 'personal development' –

have been so thoroughly depoliticized that their moral, political and social significance has now become almost impossible to discern.

Conclusion: education and liberal democracy

For most of the twentieth century the educational proposals made in *Democracy and Education* have been implemented and evaluated without any reference to the political and social philosophy from which they emanate or to the view of democracy they were designed to promote. But once an understanding of Dewey's educational philosophy is informed by his ideas about politics and society, its relevance to any understanding of the role of education in a democratic society becomes increasingly clear. For example, it becomes clear that though Dewey was fully committed to the values of liberalism, he relinquished the pretence that these values had to remain grounded in the nineteenth-century concept of the atomistic pre-social individual. For Dewey, continuing adherence to the eighteenth-century assumption that democratic institutions had to be justified by appealing to the liberties and rights of individuals was, in the twentieth century, diverting attention from the real problem of making the future of democracy more secure. If democracy was to progress it has to be conceded that the problems facing liberal democratic societies in the twentieth century could not be resolved by reasserting the continuing validity of solutions that had originally arisen to resolve the political, cultural and economic problems of eighteenth- and nineteenth-century social life.

What, secondly, becomes clear is that the educational aim of rational autonomy cannot be effectively pursued through a form of liberal education that was initially designed to meet the needs of an aristocratic élite. It can only be achieved through a form of education aimed at the continuous growth and expansion of social intelligence: a form of practical reasoning that requires collective deliberation aimed at realizing the common good. Social intelligence is the form of reasoning that guides collective action in a democratic society – a society which has ceased to rely on the authoritative knowledge of a ruling élite and prefers instead to operate on the experience-based knowledge of ordinary men and women. In such a society the role of political and educational philosophy will no longer be to provide theoretically justified educational aims and political ideals. Instead it will be a form of 'public philosophy' which informs critical dialogue and public debate by exposing the tensions and contradictions that exist between democratic values and educational practices and by indicating how these practices may be reconstructed so that the central values of the liberal democratic tradition can be progressively pursued and enlarged.

Thus what, thirdly, becomes clear is that the purpose of *Democracy and Education* was not so much to demonstrate the superiority of the democratic way of life over any other, as to render explicable the philosophy of education appropriate to liberal democracies that are genuinely concerned to remain faithful to their own self-image. If liberal democracies lack this kind of commitment, the educational philosophy proposed in *Democracy and Education* would lack the necessary condition for its effective practical application. But this would not indicate a weakness in Dewey's educational philosophy so much as the extent to which modern liberal democracies were failing to live up to their own social principles and political ideals.

What, finally, becomes clear is that *Democracy and Education* can be read as an educational philosophy that recognizes how any future vision of the role of education in a liberal democracy has to be premised on very different assumptions than those supplied by classical liberalism and requires old certainties to be abandoned and new questions to be asked. What, in educational terms, follows from a realization that the liberal democratic tradition is open and indeterminate and hence subject to reinterpretation and reconstruction as it passes from one historical context to another? What are the educational implications of conceding that the traditional liberal notion of the individual has now become a hindrance to the future development of democratic institutions and practices? Does it any longer make sense to equate democratic aspirations with the idea of a non-vocational 'liberal education' imposed by the state and based on a common or 'national' curriculum?

One of the purposes of this chapter has been to indicate why any serious examination of contemporary educational reforms must engage with these – and other – questions that inevitably arise out of a philosophical and historical understanding of the relationship between education and democracy. Another has been to reveal why any attempt to confront these questions must be partially constituted by a historical account of the educational traditions in terms of which current understandings of the relationship between education and democracy have been formed. Yet another has been to make clear why this history will be incomplete if it does not adequately recognize that these educational traditions could not have evolved in the way that they did unless and until the classical conception of democracy as an educative form of social life had been replaced by the contemporary conception of democracy as a mechanism for selecting a political élite. In the course of this transition to a non-participatory and non-educative conception of democracy, understanding of the democratic role of education has been transformed. The only way to make this transformation explicit is through a historical narrative which connects the nineteenth-century educational traditions through which contemporary educational ideas, structures, policies and practices have been constructed, to the processes of political, cultural and economic change through which the liberal democratic tradition has evolved. It is only through such a history that it will be possible to assess the extent to which contemporary understanding of the role of education in a democratic society has degenerated. And it is only through this kind of historical awareness that it will be possible to assess whether contemporary educational reforms will either enhance or distort democratic life.

3 'GENTLING THE MASSES':
THE NINETEENTH-CENTURY
ORIGINS OF THE ENGLISH
EDUCATIONAL TRADITION

> But the effects of a long past during which it was the rule that the
> many should be schooled for the service and convenience of the few
> are not . . . easily to be thrown off, even if that past is no longer with
> us, as some would contend that it still is.
>
> (Fred Clarke)[1]

Introduction: politics and the historical imagination

One of the purposes of the last chapter was to show how England was a
market-orientated society long before it became democratic, how democracy
had to evolve in ways which were acceptable to the pre-existing structures
of liberalism, and how, in the early nineteenth century, the political philosophies of Bentham and James Mill provided the initial intellectual legitimation for a particularly English form of democracy – liberal democracy. Another
was to reveal how, in the second half of the century, J.S. Mill and Matthew
Arnold articulated some of the educational implications of this form of
democracy by emphasizing the need to educate a new élite so as to ensure
that the liberty of individuals would remain protected from the dangers
of an ignorant and uneducated majority. A further aim was to show how

other political theorists, most notably T.H. Green and John Dewey, offered trenchant criticisms of this view of liberal democracy and developed an alternative view that had different implications for the structure, content and organization of education.

In many ways these intellectual developments reflected, and were a response to, the profound cultural, economic and political changes that had been set in motion by the Industrial Revolution. These changes – urbanization, industrialization, democratization, and the formation of new social classes – not only provided the climate in which new political ideas and arguments emerged; they also defined the context within which the English educational tradition was formed and the parameters within which the intellectual debate about education had to take place. The purpose of this chapter is to examine the origins and history of English state education in order to show how the solutions to the problems of industrial change that were adopted in the nineteenth century helped to establish an educational tradition that was more appropriate to the needs of the old pre-industrial aristocratic political order than to an emerging democracy, and how the core values of that aristocratic order structured and defined the English educational tradition. By making explicit what Silver[2] calls the 'nineteenth-century contours' it becomes possible to appreciate why the French writer Taine commented in the 1860s on the 'sinewy quality of English institutions' and the 'animal, almost brutal, vigour of the English governing order'.[3]

These 'nineteenth-century contours' and 'sinewy qualities' have helped to establish an educational tradition which still makes it difficult to place on the political agenda questions about how the inherited structures and content of English education continue to inhibit the development of an educational system appropriate to a modern democratic society, and about how the continuing power of this tradition has facilitated its contemporary reassertion in new forms and under new guises. By tacitly appealing to this educational tradition, it is always possible to summon up the phantasmagoria of 'Britain's Golden Age' when the country was economically pre-eminent in the world; *laissez-faire* values and practices were dominant; state power was minimal and individual choice was greatest; schooling extolled basic skills and capabilities; and religious and moral values inculcated a respect for order, authority, stability and excellence. Since this symbiosis between the English educational tradition and the political successes of the New Right is central to an understanding of developments in English educational politics between 1979 and 1993, it is important to explore the links and connections between its origins and historical development and the liberal democratic tradition as it has evolved since the beginning of the nineteenth century. Using historical evidence to link educational developments to wider political and ideological issues helps to avoid not only the illusion of assuming that education can be separated from politics but also the naive pretence that it is possible to achieve major political advance through education alone. A historical perspective demonstrates, in addition, the complexity of educational issues and processes and the importance of balancing the specific and the unique against the general and the theoretical.[4]

The connections between a democratic society's political ideas and institutions and its educational tradition are always complex and often contradictory. A number of levels of relationship are involved. At the level of ideas the concern is with what democracy is taken to mean, how it is to be understood. At the cultural level it is about the degree to which the conception of democracy which a society formally follows actually permeates its culture, institutions and social practices and, in particular, how far its educational and other institutions celebrate democratic values and attitudes. Is it expected that a wide range of people should be answerable to public scrutiny? Does national democratic politics flow down to regions, towns and villages? Are the climate, tone and ambience of society and its institutions such that people, and the groups that represent them, are taken seriously? Do minorities count?

A further level is that of structures and traditions: who has the vote, how does the formal system of political representation work? How is power controlled, balanced, and delegated? Finally, there is the question of how education relates to these other levels. As Green points out:

> in England all major educational developments bore a close relation to shifts in political power ... the gradual emergence of democratic political forms was reflected in the spread of mass education, and was connected with it ... the relations were more complex than they may appear and there can be no simple equation between the extension of national education and the rise of liberal democratic forms.[5]

Getting the vote, having your interests, agenda and aspirations taken seriously by politicians, all have consequences for the quality of, and resources provided for, education. Historically, the 'frontier' of this political and educational debate was always where political, social and economic ambition came up against the old, exclusive and pre-democratic traditions, structures and processes. It started with the 'dissenting academies' (particularly University College, London, founded in 1828), which allowed non-Anglicans to take part in university education and which 'constituted a direct challenge' to the monopoly of 'learning and higher education' held by the ancient universities.[6] It then moved on to the higher-grade elementary schools which had evolved from ordinary elementary schools, and then on to secondary provision first in exclusive grammar schools, then in secondary modern schools, and finally in comprehensive schools. It entered further and higher education in the 1990s with the development of 'free-standing' colleges and 'new' universities.

Democratic representation, even at the formal level, was conceded slowly in England, and as a result when the English educational tradition was established the system was not designed for, or by, citizens in a democratic society, but for workers, servants and subjects. The English political tradition, even at the level of rhetoric, did not need to take the majority of the people or their education seriously. By 1884, when the electorate was around 5 million out of a population of 35 million, the educational tradition had been more or less already established.[7] This tradition, by enabling privileges appropriate to pre-democratic societies to be legitimated within the rhetorics and values of a democratic society, and by inhibiting the organization of the kind of consent and support required to sustain and support democratic changes and reforms, has had far-reaching consequences both for education and for contemporary democratic life.

A 'tradition' is always in part an argument about the good life and the good society – an argument embodied in the stories that we tell each other about the past. It is an 'argument' because the 'official' stories can be – and always are – disputed and undermined by other 'non-official' and more subversive stories of those who have not yet 'won' political power.[8] The educational 'tradition' is, then, a story we tell ourselves about educational institutions and structures which incorporate assumptions and taken-for-granted views about what it is to be educated; the nature of 'real' curriculum subjects; and the characteristics of 'proper' teaching and assessment. Teachers and pupils enter this tradition in circumstances not of their own making, and they have to work with the warp and weft of that tradition. When elementary schools 'evolved' into primary schools or secondary modern schools became comprehensive schools, or polytechnics metamorphosed into universities, the ideological and moral baggage of the old institutions did not disappear but continued in new and modified forms. Like all social change, the process of educational change is also a process of continuity.

Because human beings are essentially story-telling animals they can only answer the question 'what am I to do?' if they can answer the prior question 'of what stories do I find myself a part?'.[9] It is through historical narratives that we become tellers of 'stories that aspire to truth'. Some stories think forwards – 'what shall I do next?' – and some look backwards – 'how did we get into this mess in the first place?'. And, as Collingwood observed, 'we can only think forwards if we understand backwards'.[10]

History clarifies how education is related to wider social, economic and political conditions and contexts – it makes explicit the complexity of these relationships, and the need to 'engage with historical commonalties and diversities'.[11] It also develops an informed scepticism about what education can be expected to achieve when treated in isolation from cultural, political and economic factors by undermining claims that issues such as 'standards' and 'excellence' can be pulled away from a 'contamination with the social'.[12] Education and schooling cannot be disconnected from the social fabric in which they are embedded and treated as if they had a life of their own. History, likewise, makes it more difficult to sustain those radical critiques which assert that educational institutions are social arenas where the world can be changed in major ways. Because schooling is simultaneously both an 'agency of state-led social regulation' and a potential site of 'autonomous social change', any politically realistic analysis will always have to ensure that the balance between regulation and reproduction, on the one hand, and the possibilities of change, on the other, are kept firmly in mind.[13]

The great danger from the 'assassins of memory', from whatever political stable, is that they make utopian and simplistic 'solutions' sound attractive.

By ignoring the historical interconnections between schooling, education and the wider society, the complex and extensive changes that would be required to make education more democratic are not made explicit. As a result, fundamental issues remain unrecognized, and the questions to which they give rise remain unaddressed.

Many of these questions concern the nature of curriculum knowledge. What (and whose) knowledge should be taught? Why should it be taught? How should it be taught and assessed? Who should have access to this knowledge? How in a democracy should such knowledge be distributed and who should decide?[14] Does the claim of the radicals, in the 1790s, that *'any knowledge, was political knowledge'* – remain true today?[15] For Matthew Arnold, in the mid-nineteenth century, questions about curriculum knowledge were – as for Plato and Rousseau – ultimately questions about political authority and where it was to be found.[16] For Arnold, 'the fundamental social transformation of the nineteenth century was the ending of the traditional sources of authority in Church and State: religion was mortally wounded by science, aristocracy by democracy'. This meant that if the eighteenth-century world, based on civilized liberal values as understood and practised by an aristocratic minority, was not to be destroyed, it had to be extended to the new middle classes. This could only be done if culture replaced religion, and Arnold 'offered a notion of cultivating the nation by nationalising culture'. The culture was 'the best that has been known, and said' in the past, and he believed that through 'right reason' an educated minority would be able 'to decide for society as a whole what is good and what is bad'. That is why *Culture and Anarchy* 'was the prime social text of the new English ruling class of the later nineteenth century for it provided more persuasively than anything else the intellectual basis upon which aristocracy and bourgeoisie could adopt a common style'. This attempt to respond to democracy with a curriculum which 'nationalized culture' aroused old tensions and conflicts about the extent to which 'high culture' can provide an adequate basis for thinking about the democratization of education. T.S. Eliot expressed this fear in 1948 when he said:

> there is no doubt that in our headlong rush to educate everybody, we are lowering our standards and more and more abandoning the study of those subjects by which the essentials of our culture . . . are transmitted; destroying our ancient edifices to make ready the ground upon which the barbarian nomads of the future will encamp in their mechanised caravans.[17]

Another issue that is critical for understanding the timing, characteristics and development of state schooling is the process of state formation, which is the historical processes through which the modern state has been constructed. It includes the construction of 'the political and administrative apparatus of government and all government-controlled agencies', as well as 'the formation of ideologies and collective beliefs which legitimate state power and underpin concepts of nationhood and national "character"'.[18] In late Victorian England around 80 per cent of the 'private real estate' 'was controlled by 7,000 people, with some 360 magnates owning . . . a quarter of all land in England',[19] and the 'Victorian state' was

> exceptional in both the austerity of its means and the simplicity of its functions. In absolute figures, overall public expenditure registered nil growth between 1830 and 1850, actually falling in per capita terms. Thereafter it rose by a mere 20 per cent per capita over the next forty years, during a period when public spending more than doubled in France, and trebled in the U.S.A. and Germany.

In 1850 'the Victorian civil service numbered just under 40,000 and by 1861 it had fallen to 31,000', whereas in France 'at the same time it numbered 450,000'.[20]

This minimalist view of the state was bound up with particular events in British history. After the settlement of 1688 'individual liberties were highly regarded' and there was widespread scepticism about centralized state power which was seen to be in opposition to the maintenance of individual freedoms. There was a 'tradition of suspicion towards the government and its initiatives'. This view had reverberations across the entire class structure so that there was constant political pressure to limit state power. This developed a negative view of freedom which was opposed to arbitrary, absolutist, centralist power, but which made the development of a more open democratic culture and hence positive freedom more difficult to achieve. After the revolution in France, on the other hand, 'the state was seen by many Republicans, including radicals, as a bulwark against aristocratic privilege and clerical tyranny'. In England, the political philosophy of 'individualism and hostility to the state have constituted almost a whole way of life'.[21]

The English view of the state was obviously influenced by the fact that the first Industrial Revolution had occurred in England with little state intervention. The mechanisms of economic change had consisted almost entirely of private capital and uncontrolled market forces. Religion was another reason for the English preference for minimal state power. This was particularly important in educational provision where the Anglicans, and their Established Church, wanted to retain control over education. Between 1843 and 1867 Baptists and Congregationalists opposed 'all state aid for education on the grounds that such aid was principally designed to further the interests of the state church'.[22] Finally, although the middle classes had gained political power in the nineteenth century, they did not use this power to press the state to support widespread educational advance. The *laissez-faire* approach whereby the state merely 'filled the gaps' meant that independent and semi-independent schools could be established to advance the particular interests of the middle classes. Widening educational opportunities for all would be resisted as an attempt to undermine established privilege. Unlike the French bourgeoisie, their English equivalent 'saw the state as the source of all tyranny, whether in the form of oppressive legislation or extortionate taxation'.[23]

All historical accounts are, of course, partisan, selective and contested, and any question about how the story of English education is to be told is itself a political question. The account that follows focuses deliberately on those ideas and individuals which helped construct the dominant English educational tradition while also recognizing attempts to subvert, change, and democratize this same tradition.[24] The central aim is to show how the English educational tradition has been used in the 1980s and 1990s to undermine the embryonic democratic elements contained within the post-war settlement. As Hayek puts it, few people

> will deny that our views about the goodness or badness of different institutions are largely determined by what we believe to have been their effects in the past. There is scarcely a political ideal or concept which does not involve opinions about a whole series of past events, and there are few historical memories which do not serve as a symbol of some political aim.[25]

By providing an account of 'a whole series of past events' the intention is to provide an 'adequate sense of tradition' and so make it possible to grasp those future possibilities which the past has made available to the present.[26]

The peculiarities of English society and the establishment of state schooling

During the eighteenth century it was commonly assumed that individuals were 'by nature' unequal and that everyone had a pre-ordained position in the social order. Indeed, at that time most European societies were based on hierarchical systems of social relationships under which the uneducated lower orders were not required or encouraged to think for themselves. Soame Jenyns put the view forcefully when he wrote, in 1757, that ignorance 'is necessary to all born to poverty and the drudgeries of life . . . [since it is] the only opiate capable of . . . [enabling] them to endure the miseries of the one and the fatigues of the other'.[27]

In the second half of the eighteenth century this view of society was seriously undermined by a complex configuration of political and philosophical ideas which was eventually to become known as the Enlightenment project – a project which aimed to expose the inadequacies and injustices of the existing social order and to relieve the people of their economic exploitation and social bondage. For Enlightenment thinkers such as Voltaire and Rousseau, the idea of a 'natural order' in society was no more than a mythical device for denying freedom and dignity to the mass of ordinary people and confining them to a life of servitude. The aim of the Enlightenment project was not only to abolish the old forms of feudal absolutism but also to ensure that the individual's position in the world became more dependent on his/her own free rational activity. Once people were emancipated from the restraints of prejudice, dogma and tradition, humanity would have finally completed its long period of immaturity and individuals could become the autonomous subjects of their own development. It followed from this that the practical task of the Enlightenment project was, in key part, an educational task: to develop in all people the universal power of human reason and thereby enable them to create collectively a form of social life that would satisfy their aspirations and needs. It is thus unsurprising that Enlightenment thinkers recognized that their aims and aspirations required and implied the development of a more democratic form of life. The English radicals, such as Tom Paine, Mary Wollstonecraft, William Godwin and William Lovett were also part of this Enlightenment tradition and saw education 'as a tool of human emancipation and as a right of man'.[28] But, as we have seen, the Enlightenment philosopher who most clearly articulated the relationship between political democracy and public education was Jean-Jacques Rousseau.[29]

Rousseau, along with other Enlightenment philosophers, helped to create the intellectual climate that led to the French Revolution and the subsequent replacement of traditional aristocracy by modern democracy. But in Britain, the power and privileges of the aristocracy were more seriously undermined by the Industrial Revolution which began in the eighteenth century and continued throughout the nineteenth century. The Industrial Revolution dramatically changed the nature of the productive process and, in so doing, not only brought the factory into existence but also transformed the ways in which people understood themselves, their experiences and their place in society. During this period, the social relationships that had previously secured the power and privileges of the landed aristocracy began to disintegrate and were replaced by forms of relationship in which the distinction between the bourgeoisie and the working class became dominant. In addition, the informal and 'organic' forms of organization associated with traditional communities were replaced by impersonal and mechanical organizations in the form of factories and schools. The processes involved in the changes from pre-industrial to industrial social relationships and institutions are, of course, complex, and schooling had an important role to play in the transitions that took place.[30]

In Britain the economic, cultural and political changes caused by the Industrial Revolution were challenged and opposed by conservative forces demanding the restoration of pre-industrial values and beliefs. Nevertheless, the Industrial Revolution established the conditions for the profound transformations that were to occur in Britain in the second half of the nineteenth century and which created modern British society:

> The years between the 1860s and the First World War transformed Britain more swiftly and more profoundly than any other comparable era. British society became urbanised and suburbanised, secularised, democratised; general assumptions about social relationships and politically legitimate behaviour shifted from the basis of vertical hierarchic community groupings to stratified classes: in a word, it became modern.[31]

The general structure of economic, political, social and educational institutions was established during this period and 'the characteristic "Englishness" of the English culture was made then very much what it is now'. The quip 'that all the oldest English traditions were invented in the last quarter of the nineteenth century has great point'.[32]

The material and economic changes in this period were remarkable. Between 1861 and 1901, income per head of population more than doubled; the population nearly doubled between 1851 and 1911; the modern conurbations such as Manchester, the West Midlands and London were formed; and by 1861 more people lived in towns than in rural areas. In that year, London had a population of nearly 3 million, and Manchester, Liverpool and Birmingham had more than 250,000 people each.[33] When, in 1851, Matthew Arnold became an inspector, England was entering an era of unexampled economic prosperity,[34] and led the world of finance, trade and industry. From 1850 to 1873 Britain 'was the forge of the world, the world's carrier, the world's ship-builder, the world's banker, the world's workshop, the world's clearing-house, the world's entrepôt. The trade of the world . . . pivoted on Great Britain'.[35]

By 1860, perhaps the high point of Victorian capitalism, England 'enjoyed yet unchallenged economic supremacy, producing half the world's manufactures and a third of its cotton, iron and coal'. No 'country in history with the conceivable exception of the United States for the first ten years after . . . the Second World War ever enjoyed so near-hegemonic an industrial dominance as did mid-Victorian Britain'. For most 'yardsticks of industrial predominance' Britain 'produced more than all the other major European powers combined'. By 1870, and without any doubt by 1913, 'a very different picture had emerged', although even in 1913 Britain still consumed, for example, more raw cotton than France and Germany combined.[36] This was also the country which had been one of 'the most literate in Reformation Europe', but which had, by the 1860s, become one of 'the most illiterate and under-educated' societies in western Europe.[37]

The intellectual and cultural climate reflected this economic pre-eminence and had a number of characteristics.[38] One was the philosophical radicalism of Bentham and James Mill. Another was the emphasis on evangelicalism. The evangelicals, 'with their combination of social conscience and missionary zeal were a powerful reforming agency'. Their aim was to improve not just the lower orders but also the 'moral tone of the upper classes'. A further characteristic was that this was 'an age of rapid scientific and technological advance'. It was also an age of greatly increased social and geographical mobility and saw the beginnings of a more meritocratic view of social position and status. For some, the response to these changes was optimistic: that people could perfect themselves through their own efforts and from their own resources. For others, however, the speed of social change was seriously undermining traditional and established beliefs. Then, as now, the fear was that 'the values of the cultured few would be swamped by those of the semi-educated masses'. The work of Darwin added to this crisis about authority and knowledge as his theory claimed to explain the origins of human beings in purely biological and scientific terms.[39] It was out of this 'interwoven cultural fabric' that the educational thinking which led to the educational policies and practices of the twentieth century was to develop.[40]

One important element in this 'cultural fabric' was the nineteenth-century English Romantic movement which Mathieson and Bernbaum see as a reaction against the scientific, commercial and materialist temper of the Enlightenment. It was opposed to the disintegrative forces of the period: the French Revolution; Nonconformity; philosophical radicalism; industrialization; urbanization; the popular press; commercialism; and the utilitarian education of the labouring classes. They take Coleridge (1772–1834) as the most influential thinker in the development of these ideas for education, particularly his notion of a 'clerisy' and the ideal of 'gentlemanliness'.[41]

For Coleridge the 'clerisy' was an educated minority whose role was to 'discriminate a unifying religion throughout the nation' and 'who valued imagination over the lesser faculty of understanding'. It had to be at 'the fountain heads of the humanities' and 'guard the treasures of past civilisation'. The clerisy had to support 'superior, imaginative, literary sensitivity' against the 'merely practical and useful science'. Coleridge believed 'that authority should be an all-persuasive feature of social relationship' and that the focus of 'authority was the state'.[42]

The ideal of 'gentlemanliness' (as proposed in the Clarendon Report of 1864) claimed that public schools have 'the largest share in moulding the character of the English Gentleman'. The cultural and educational processes which formed this character included religion (that is, Christianity); the classics and their canonical texts (in particular Plato's *Republic*); prefects and those team games which 'fostered individual skills and co-operation as well as loyalty to one's house and school'. Under this conception of education, the central goal was not the development of intellect but of good character. As Arnold put it, 'what we look for . . . is first religion and moral scruples, secondly gentlemanly conduct, thirdly intellectual ability'. For Coleridge, the only true philosopher was Plato and the Bible was the only place to find 'a science of realities'. This dislike of science, useful knowledge and vocational education meant that the emphasis was on religion and morality, and that for the majority of ordinary children 'discipline and good behaviour became the dominant themes'. For a small minority intellectual achievement could be allowed, but that meant entry to the clerisy via the classics and literature. Through the bonding qualities of values the ideal of gentlemanliness could be realized and a powerful legacy was bequeathed to the twentieth century:

> the notion of a superior, gentlemanly curriculum based upon literary experiences, which was likely to be more deeply religious and improving than institutionalised religion; the nation's best hope of resisting the materialism and godlessness of science.

Coleridge's ideas about an educated minority were deeply immersed in the classical texts and religion, gave priority to imagination over intellect, and had considerable influence on Thomas Arnold, who said that he would gladly have his son 'think the sun went round the earth, and the stars were so many spangles set in the bright blue firmament. Surely the one thing needed for a Christian and Englishman to study is a Christian and moral philosophy.' These views also came to be shared, in different ways, by 'the leading figures of the British establishment throughout the nineteenth and twentieth centuries', in 'politics, the church, industry and the military'. In education, especially influential individuals 'whose opinions had been moulded in the cloisters, chapels and common rooms' of leading public schools, included Sir Robert Morant, J.W. MacKail, Sir Henry Hadow, Sir William Spens and Sir Cyril Norwood. Such people formed a 'cohesive group united by a single vision of education's purpose and associated with each other through a myriad of contacts across denomination, profession and generation'.[43] They helped to construct and develop the framework within which state schooling was established.

So, in the second half of the nineteenth century, when the main framework of its educational system was being created, England was experiencing enormous cultural, political, economic, religious and ideological change. It was hugely prosperous. The old order was being replaced by the new. The ideas of a liberal market economy, eulogizing free trade, minimal state power, and an environment in which individuals could pursue their own interests and happiness, was believed to be essential to creating and maintaining wealth and prosperity. Although state education had played little part in its initial stages, the Industrial Revolution was to set the context within which education gradually expanded during the late nineteenth century into a national system of compulsory schooling.

The development of English education in the nineteenth century

State schooling, as a formal process, had first arisen in the absolutist monarchies of eighteenth-century Europe, where it 'was recognised to be a powerful instrument for promoting political loyalty amongst the people and for creating a cohesive national culture after the image of the ruling class'.[44] In many countries, state education gradually

> came to assume a primary responsibility for the moral, cultural and political development of the nation. It became the secular church. It was variously called upon to assimilate immigrant cultures, to promote established religious doctrines, to spread the standard form of the appointed national language, to forge a national identity and a national culture, to generalise new habits of routine and rational calculation, to encourage patriotic values, to inculcate moral disciplines and, above all, to indoctrinate in the political and economic creeds of the dominant classes ... It formed the responsible citizen, the diligent worker, the willing tax-payer, the reliable juror, the conscientious parent, the dutiful wife, the patriotic soldier, and the dependable or deferential voter.[45]

Unlike America and France, England had not had a revolution to stimulate debate about the role of education in the modern state.[46] Uniquely, it had industrialized without a state-run education system and did not develop one until the twentieth century.[47] Its sense of national identity had been established in Tudor times and no longer seemed to be an urgent issue. During

the nineteenth century it exported rather than imported people, and therefore lacked the American problem of turning immigrants into good citizens.
Religious disputes and conflicts did not produce (as they did in Scotland and
the Netherlands) the Calvinist pressure for literacy. Throughout the first half
of the nineteenth century, attempts at educational reform had failed so that
'the great defect of English education' was the lack 'of a national organisation' which formed 'the one great exception to the civilised world'.[48] During
this period there was considerable consensus about the importance of schooling and what it should deliver, but there was little agreement about the
means which should be followed to bring about desirable ends.[49] By 1850,
when Holland, Switzerland, Germany and the northern states of America
had virtually universal education, England had barely half the age group in
school. In the same way, when England instituted state secondary schooling
in 1902, it was '100 years after Napoleon created the *lycées*' and 'almost as
long since the U.S.A. and the German states created public elementary
schools'.[50] As a result, 'it was not until 1918 that full-time education to the
age of 14 became the general rule in England and Wales'.[51]

It was only in the closing decades of the eighteenth century that issues
about the need to extend provision of education to the mass of the population began to be seriously entertained in England. Prior to this period, it
was commonly believed – particularly by members of the aristocracy – that
educating the children of the lower classes was both unnecessary and undesirable. It was unnecessary because they did not need to be educated in order
to take their predetermined place in the social order. It was undesirable
because it had the potential to be socially disruptive, a view clearly expressed
in 1807 in the famous speech made by Davies Giddy against the Parochial
Schools Bill:

> giving education to the labouring classes of the poor . . . would . . . be
> . . . prejudicial to their morals and happiness; it would teach them to
> despise their lot in life . . . instead of teaching them subordination, it
> would render them factious and refractory . . . it would enable them to
> read seditious pamphlets, vicious books, and publications against Chris-
> tianity; it would render them insolent to their superiors . . . if the bill
> were to pass into law, it would go to burden the country with the most
> enormous and incalculable expense, and to load the industrious orders
> with still heavier imposts.[52]

The expansion of education was also frustrated by the Anglican church,
which wanted to ensure that its religious control over the education of the
labouring classes was not undermined. The newly emerging manufacturing
classes likewise opposed educational provision because they were concerned
that the provision of education would affect the flow of cheap child labour
on which they had come to depend even though technological advances
were gradually reducing the need for children to work.[53] But Robert
Lowe, among others, proposed a more socially acceptable role for schooling
whereby:

The lower classes ought to be educated to discharge the duties cast upon them. They should also be educated that they may appreciate and defer to a higher cultivation when they meet it, and the higher classes ought to be educated in a very different manner in order that they may exhibit to the lower classes, that higher education to which, if it were shown to them they would bow down and defer.[54]

But as a general proposition, the view that education was a vitally important political instrument for combating the problems of social order that were beginning to emerge as a result of industrialization, became increasingly important. The population explosion that had occurred as a result of industrialization was creating vast slums in and around new urban centres such as Liverpool, Birmingham and Manchester which provided the conditions under which crime and mob rule could flourish. As de Tocqueville said about Manchester in the 1830s, out of the 'filthy sewer pure gold flows', and the town 'embodied an unprecedented juxtaposition of extremes of wealth and poverty and a graphic illustration of the growing division between classes'.[55]

At the same time, the spread among the working classes of the dangerous and subversive ideas that had fuelled the French Revolution, was seen as a potential cause of civil unrest. The protagonists of educational reform believed that threats to the existing social structure, and the dangers of subversive ideas, could best be resisted by providing working-class children with a form of education directly aimed at 'gentling the masses' by reconciling them to their station in life, teaching them to respect their betters and thus make them less likely to engage in civil disturbances or crime. These aims were clearly stated by Patrick Colquhoun, a London magistrate, in his *New and Appropriate system of Education for the Labouring Poor*:

The higher and noble aim of preventing those calamities which led to idleness and crime . . . by guiding and properly directing the early conduct of the lower orders . . . and giving a right bias to their minds, has not, as yet, generally attracted the notice of those who move in the more elevated walks of society. The prosperity of every state depends on the good habits, and the religious and moral instruction of the labouring people . . . it is not, however, proposed . . . that the children of the poor should be educated in a manner to elevate their minds above the rank they are destined to fill in society, or that an expense should be incurred beyond the lowest rate ever paid for instruction. Utopian schemes for an extensive diffusion of knowledge would be injurious and absurd.[56]

The development of political consciousness among the working classes gave rise to continued concern among the middle-class reformers. As E.P. Thompson has shown, the radical response from Tom Paine and William Lovett, the Luddites and the mass Chartism of the 1840s, required a serious ideological and political counter-attack.[57] Indeed, 'throughout the nineteenth century there was an alternative political perspective on education which was located outside the central and local government and the churches'. It proposed that schools should teach really useful knowledge which would enable pupils to 'overcome the iniquities of the existing social, economic and political system'.[58] It envisaged a free radical press and educational institutions free from state and Church control. Some radicals, such as William Lovett, criticized the curriculum and pedagogy of the time, arguing that 'this ... rote-learning, memory loading system is still dignified by the name of education; and those who are stored with the greatest lumber are esteemed its greatest scholars'.[59]

Despite these radical views, the official rationale for educational expansion was from the outset social control: to ensure that the children of the labouring classes would have the knowledge, values and attitudes which were necessary if they were to accept their future social and economic roles in the emerging industrialized and urban society. Education was to achieve this by instilling into working-class children their social duties; a modicum of useful knowledge; a respect for authority; and a belief in religion. Although these limited and self-interested views about the need for educational expansion were not uncontested, they were sufficient to provoke a widespread demand for educational change. Further, the kind of educational development that actually occurred was always constrained by the prevailing political theory of the time: the utilitarian theory articulated in the writings of Jeremy Bentham.[60] This political philosophy enjoyed widespread assent throughout most of the nineteenth century and remained the dominant influence over political and educational thinking during the period. Several features of this philosophy are central to understanding both the protracted delay in achieving a national system of education and the character and organization of the system that was eventually to emerge.

One such feature is its excessive individualism and its view of society as nothing other than a collection of individuals pursuing their own interests and desires. This kind of individualism was deeply engrained in nineteenth-century thinking and served to impede the development of a national system of education by legitimizing the belief that state-provided education would undermine the moral responsibility of individual parents for the education of their children and so replace self-reliance by state dependency. In addition, it supported the claim that the role of the state should be confined to national defence, the protection of private property and the maintenance of law and order. Since, from this standpoint, a national system of state education was inevitably seen as a hallmark of tyranny, it was only to be expected that educational expansion would occur through the initiatives of individuals and private or religious organizations.

Another feature of this political philosophy that had important implications for the process of educational expansion was its utilitarianism: its constant insistence that the contribution of any public institution to the common good had to be calculated and quantified in terms of its productive usefulness. When combined with the *laissez-faire* economic doctrines of the time, this inevitably led to the view that any social or welfare service provided out of public taxation should give 'value for money'. The best-known and most vivid expression of this kind of political thinking was the Poor Law system introduced in 1834. Following the emphasis given to individual responsibility, it was firmly based on the belief that life inside the workhouse should be only marginally preferable to a life of destitution and poverty outside. And following the emphasis given to *laissez-faire* economic doctrines, it was taken to be self-evident that the burden on the taxpayer of providing assistance to those in distress should be kept as low as possible. It was only a short step from this view to the belief that any state-funded education system should be inferior to that provided privately by individuals and that it should be cheap.

At the beginning of the nineteenth century, the climate of opinion created by utilitarian political thinking defined the problems in such a manner that any attempt by the state to expand education was likely to be seen as an affront to individual liberty. Educational expansion, therefore, had to be accomplished through the efforts of voluntary organizations and philanthropic societies. In addition, the reluctance to use taxpayers' money to increase the number of teachers and schools meant that any voluntary initiatives had to devise ways of expanding educational provision by devising economical ways of organizing schools. In short, state involvement in education had to be kept to an absolute minimum. Excessive expenditure might lead to freedom of thought being undermined, a decline in industrial competitiveness, and discourage parents from taking personal responsibility for their children.[61]

The two voluntary organizations which proposed successful solutions to the problem of educational expansion were the *Anglican National Society for Promoting the Education of the Poor in the Principles of the Established Church* (which was founded in 1811), and the non-denominational and Nonconformist *British and Foreign School Society* (which was formed during the period 1808–14). Soon, 'National' and 'British' schools began to appear all over England and by the middle of the 1830s over a million children were attending them. The Anglican schools preached deference, the importance of hierarchy and the virtue of adjusting to one's allotted station in life which was no doubt an outcome of the 'stultifying condescension' of such schools, 'deriving from the ritual conservative belief in rank and status, [which] was to help to alienate the working classes from education'.[62] The Nonconformist schools, on the other hand, stressed humility, discipline, obedience and self-improvement. Although the founders of these two societies – Andrew Bell and Joseph Lancaster – were antagonistic towards each other, together they pioneered a system of schooling which provided a form of mass education that was highly consistent with the political and economic ideas of the time. This system – the 'monitorial' or 'mutual' system of schooling – was to become the most common system of mass schooling for the next half century.

The essence of the monitorial system was that it was economic and mechanical. It was economic because it did not require experienced teachers to do any direct teaching. Instead, they instructed older pupils or 'monitors' who then became responsible for instructing a small group of pupils – normally about ten – while the teacher acted as a supervisor, examiner and disciplinarian. In this way, it was common for a monitorial school with one teacher to have 500 pupils – though Joseph Lancaster boasted that under his plan it was perfectly possible for a teacher to teach a thousand pupils. Green describes one such school, the Spicer Street school in Spitalfields in London, as an 'educational battery farm'. The school room was 106 feet by 39 feet and it could 'accommodate 660 children in 33 rows of desks each designed for 20 boys'. One teacher could, with his monitors, teach 600 children for the cost of five shillings per year. The curriculum was very much about basics (the 'three Rs' plus Christian religion) and a 1840 Reading Series (for the British and Foreign Schools Society) had a section on political economy, which warned pupils about 'the dangers of challenging the economic order'.[63]

Teaching and learning in monitorial schools was wholly mechanical and relied entirely on the rote learning and memorization of factual knowledge and information. There was generally little opportunity for pupils to ask questions or display any individual initiative. Pupils were simply drilled by monitors who had themselves been drilled by the teacher.

Although, in the political climate of the period, the monitorial system effectively met the demand for an expansion to mass education, it is clear with hindsight that it was also laying the foundations for the mechanical methods, low standards and large classes that came to characterize large parts of English elementary education for the remainder of the nineteenth century. But at the time, it was regarded as an economical and efficient piece of social machinery that coincided exactly with the industrial spirit of the age. Indeed, it

> was the factory put into an educational setting. Every characteristic was there: minute division of labour; the assembly line, with children passed on from monitor to monitor . . . ; a complicated system of incentives to good work; an impersonal system of inspection; and finally an attention to cost efficiency and the economic use of plant which was carried to far greater lengths, than even its most modern advocates would recommend.[64]

By the 1830s it was becoming increasingly clear that voluntary efforts of the British and National societies' monitorial schools were incapable of keeping pace with the growing demands for elementary education and that some form of state intervention was necessary. In 1833, the government recognized this by voting the sum of £20,000 towards the cost of erecting school buildings 'for the Education of the Children of the Poorer Classes'. This grant was paid over to the British and National societies on condition that half the cost of providing new schools was met from voluntary contributions. In 1839, just by way of comparison, £70,000 was voted for the repair of the stables at Windsor Castle.[65]

The modest expenditure on education in the 1830s gave rise to a demand for a system of accountability. In 1839 an Education Committee of the Privy Council was established, with James Kay-Shuttleworth as its head.[66] The committee was made up of four politicians and presided over by the Lord President of the Council. This committee was set up 'without full parliamentary sanction and developed by administrative sleight of hand', and it was 'one of the weirdest pieces of government machinery England has ever known'.[67]

Kay-Shuttleworth was to become an 'elder statesman' of British education, and 'his name has become synonymous with the first years of state intervention in education in this country and with the foundations of our national system'.[68] He was aware of how the working classes were beginning to 'attribute their suffering to political causes', and his remedy was to offer an education which would make them understand the 'true causes which determine their physical condition and regulate the distribution of wealth'. For him, the working classes had to learn that 'they are destined to earn their livelihood by the sweat of their brow'.[69] Industrialization had resulted in partial breakdown of the traditional patriarchal family, and the family could no longer 'educate and socialise children' in the old ways. State schooling was seen as one way of modifying and controlling these changes and Kay-Shuttleworth was a propagandist for this approach.[70]

In his analysis of the thought of Kay-Shuttleworth, Johnson[71] exposes the social assumptions underpinning his educational views, connects them to the general intellectual and political context of the time, and suggests a number of important themes running through his thinking. These assumptions reveal a 'contingent optimism' about industrial society which led him to believe that whatever evils did exist were due to 'foreign and accidental causes'. His writings also denounce working-class decadence. By holding the poor responsible for their own poverty 'the educationalist was *enabled to believe* that his was a humane ... response to potentially removable evils'. The working-class family was inadequate, and suffered from 'provincial dialect and an indistinct articulation, coarse provincial accents, and faults and vulgarities of expression'. Parents, on the other hand, 'would almost starve themselves to give their children bread but would make *no sacrifice whatever* to give them food for their minds'.[72]

This simplified view is, of course, at variance with the variety and complexity of working-class culture. Some of these complexities are evident in the attachment to, and use of, private schools by some sections of that class. As Gardner shows, the working-class private school was a 'ubiquitous presence, both in town and country at least up to the 1870s', and allowed ordinary working-class parents to have some 'degree of power and control over both the content and organisation of education, which was entirely absent in the publicly provided alternative'. Middle-class education and inspectors had to explain why what publicly funded schools had to offer was being rejected and why, also, parents supported the alternative. They did this by assigning to working-class parents the characteristics of apathy (failure of motivation); ignorance (as their culture was brutalized, deficient and dangerous, true knowledge could not be expected); and status seeking (preferring, like the middle classes, something whose value came partly from the fact that not everyone could have it).[73] Kay-Shuttleworth made a lot of these cultural conflicts and disputes explicit.

Another of Kay-Shuttleworth's assumptions was that the school (and the teacher) should become parental substitutes. The actual parents of the poor were inadequate, and 'pauperism could be seen as a sort of moral contamination transmitted through the parent'. The problem was, that the influence of teachers and schools was often 'counteracted by the evil example of parent and neighbours'. Borrowing from European reformers such as Pestalozzi, Kay-Shuttleworth argued that teachers should develop personal relationships with pupils because natural parents were 'held to be disqualified or incapacitated from fulfilling their natural role'. From this viewpoint the school is seen as 'an essentially foreign implantation within a commonly barbarized population'.

The final theme permeating Kay-Shuttleworth's thinking was about how teachers should be selected and schools organized and managed. Teachers had to be 'emancipated from the local community', 'closely linked to local élites ... particularly the clergy', and 'raised, but not too far, out of their own class'. A 'good' school had to be correctly managed and supervised. As the Minutes of the Council on Education put it, there must be a 'clergyman, esquire, or members of their families' to keep 'the most important ends constantly in view' and to 'infuse that spirit which cannot be looked for from our present race of teachers'. As one inspector put it: 'We cannot let farmers or labourers, miners or mechanics, be judges of our educational work. It is part of that work to educate them all into a sense of what true education is.' This would, among other things, exclude private schools funded by such parents and partly responsive to their aspirations.

One way of looking at the thought of Kay-Shuttleworth is as a system of social control, as part of the Victorian obsession with authority and power when dealing with the education of the poor. The belief was that through the control of schooling (and teacher education) it would be possible to determine 'the patterns of thought, sentiment and behaviour of the working class. Supervised by its trusty teachers, surrounded by its playground wall, the school was to raise a new race of working people – respectful, cheerful, hard-working, loyal, pacific and religious.'[74]

In 1846 the issue of how to finance state education had been resolved by the system of annual grants inaugurated by Kay-Shuttleworth. As a result, the cost of exchequer grants for education had increased from £20,000 in 1833, to £250,000 in 1853, and to well over £750,000 in 1859.[75] Prussia, by comparison, in the 1830s, was already spending £600,000 on education.[76] By 1860, the Education Department 'had become one of the largest civil establishments of the state', with a staff of 127.[77] This gave rise to two issues: the administrative problem of bringing schools under political control and the economic problem of reducing expenditure and providing better 'value for money'. As a result a Royal Commission was set up, in 1858, to 'inquire into the Present State of Popular Education in England and to consider what measures are required for the Extension of Sound and Cheap Elementary Instruction'. In inquiring into 'the present state' of elementary education, the Commission found that it was beset by two major problems: irregular attendance and low levels of learning.

In its Report of 1861, the Newcastle Commission, as it came to be known, paid tribute to the work of Kay-Shuttleworth in developing elementary education in England. However, it proposed that if an 'administrative break-down was to be averted' his 'system of grants had to be overhauled and simplified'.[78] In order to recommend 'sound and cheap' solutions to these problems it proposed that state payments should depend on the attendance record of pupils and their performance in examinations. In the words of the Report, the managers

> of all schools fulfilling the conditions specified . . . shall be entitled to be paid out of the country rate a sum varying from twenty two shillings and sixpence to twenty one shillings for every child who has attended the school during the one hundred and forty days in the year preceding . . . and who passes an examination.[79]

This system of 'payment by results' was introduced by Robert Lowe in the form of the Revised Code which he presented to the House of Commons in 1861. During the next few months the Education Department 'received over a thousand petitions and letters of protest'. Under the Revised Code of 1862 teachers' salaries, and the grants to schools for equipment and apparatus, were to be distributed according to the grant-raising potential of pupils. What was 'new about the Revised Code was that success in the basic subjects now constituted the main, though not the sole, determinant of the size of a school's grant'.[80] 'Hitherto', said Lowe, 'we have been living under a system of bounties and protection. Now we propose to have a little free trade.'[81]

The aim of this system of payment by results was to ensure that all working-class children should be given the minimum elementary education as cheaply and as effectively as possible. The intention was made explicit by Robert Lowe in his speech commending the Revised Code to the House of Commons:

> We do not profess to give these children an education that will raise them above their station and business in life; that is not our object, but to give them an education that may fit them for that business. We are bound to take a clear and definite view of the position of the class that is to receive instruction; and, having obtained that view, we are bound to make up our minds as to how much instruction that class requires, and is capable of receiving, and we are then bound to have evidence that it has received such instruction.[82]

The 'evidence' required to demonstrate that working-class pupils had 'received' the desired 'instruction' was to be based on attendance and on examination performance in the 'three Rs'. The syllabus of work laid down by the Revised Code was graded according to six standards.[83] In 1862 a pupil who achieved the required standard in an examination conducted by an inspector would earn eight shillings for the school (the 'result' grant). Failure in any one of the 'three Rs' would mean that the grant was reduced by 2s. 8d. per subject. A grant of 4s. was also paid for each child attending school for a minimum of 200 half-day sessions (the 'attendance' grant).[84] Lowe, in recommending the Code to the House of Commons, famously remarked that 'if it is not cheap it shall be efficient; if it is not efficient it shall be cheap'.[85]

As Matthew Arnold pointed out, in 'a country where everyone is prone to rely too much on mechanical process and too little on intelligence' the new regulations would give a 'mechanical turn to school teaching, a mechanical turn to inspection, and must be most trying to the intellectual life of a school'. Further, 'by tying two-thirds of government aid to tested results in a limited range of subjects, it had made learning' rigid and narrow, 'reduced teachers to ciphers, and turned educational administration into a vast exercise in accountancy'.[86]

Certainly the introduction of payment by results produced economies. Between 1861 and 1865 the education grant was reduced from £813,441 to £636,806,[87] and between 1862 and 1870 school attendance rose from 857,000 to 1,400,000.[88] But its educational consequences for teaching and the curriculum were disastrous. For example, the effect of treating each pupil as what Morant called a 'grant-serving unit' not only fostered a mercenary and calculating attitude to the curriculum, but also ensured that the syllabus of the Code was rigidly observed. As E.G.A. Holmes was to remark in 1912, the system of payment by results

> did all his thinking for the teacher. It told him in precise detail what he was to do each year in each 'standard', how he was to handle each subject, and how far he was to go in it; what width of ground he was to cover; what amount of knowledge, what degree of accuracy was required for a 'pass'.[89]

This mechanical conformity to the requirement of the Code ensured that the curriculum of the elementary school was almost exclusively confined to the 'three Rs' and that all other kinds of work were virtually abandoned. By forcing teachers to concentrate on the grant-awarding potential of their pupils, any ideas about curriculum innovation were quickly suppressed: in these circumstances, 'something ventured was something lost'. Similarly, by penalizing teachers whose pupils failed to obtain the required examination results, payment by results inevitably reinforced the monitorial tradition of mechanical teaching concerned solely with ensuring that pupils could produce the correct response at a given time. By equating the memorization of facts and information with the acquisition of knowledge and understanding, it rendered the results of the examination virtually meaningless in educational terms. Matthew Arnold drew attention to this consequence of the Revised Code in the following way:

> The great fault of the ... famous plan of *payment by results* is that it fosters teaching by rote ... the teacher limits his subject as much as he can and ... tries to cram his pupils with details enough to enable him to say, when they produce them, that they have fulfilled the Departmental requirements, and fairly earned their grant.[90]

Payment by results lasted, with modifications, for nearly forty years. Its main purpose was to provide working-class children with the minimum rudiments of instruction as cheaply as possible. Although it was condemned by most contemporary educationalists of the period, it nevertheless helped to establish an educational tradition – never completely eradicated – whose negative influence still permeates educational thinking about teaching, curriculum and assessment. In 1911, reflecting on how the effects of the Revised Code lingered on long after its formal abolition (in 1897), E.G.A. Holmes, who had been Chief Inspector of schools, recalled how teachers had to try and dominate the child,

> to leave nothing to his nature, nothing to his spontaneous life, nothing to his free activity . . . The teacher's professional welfare 'depends upon the examiners' verdict' so the teacher holds himself responsible for 'every stroke and dot that the pupil makes'. The child has to 'think what his teacher tells him to think, to feel what his teacher tells him to feel, to see what his teacher tells him to see, to say what his teacher tells him to say, to do what his teacher tells him to do'. The code seems to be an 'ingenious instrument for arresting the mental growth of the child and deadening all his higher faculties'. The system of payment by results 'has never had, and I hope will never have, an equal'.[91]

Although the Revised Code did much harm to the curriculum and teaching methods of elementary schools, it did little to increase the provision of education. By the end of the 1860s the population of Great Britain had increased enormously and the demand for more schools became urgent. At the same time, the case for a centrally co-ordinated national education system began to gain ground. One argument for this was economic. Britain's industrial superiority was being threatened by other growing economies and it was believed that this could only be resisted by an extension of elementary education. Another argument was political and pointed to the need to educate the lower orders about how to exercise the vote which had been gradually extended since the Reform Act of 1832. Robert Lowe's oft-quoted response to the Reform Act of 1867, which gave the vote to artisans in large industrial towns, concisely expressed the argument: 'I believe it will be absolutely necessary that you should prevail upon our future masters to learn their letters.'[92]

But apart from economic pressure and political expedience, the case for a national system of education was also being advanced by those whom Raymond Williams has labelled the 'public educators': a group of nineteenth-century intellectuals such as Carlyle, Ruskin, Huxley, J.S. Mill and Matthew Arnold, who were sympathetic to the idea of democracy and who were prepared to argue that a democratic society had the duty and obligation to educate all its members. In a famous passage in his *Science and Education*, T.H. Huxley contrasted his democratic vision of the role of education with the kind of impoverished thinking that had invariably informed the provision of elementary education:

> The politicians tell us, 'You must educate the masses because they are going to be masters'. The clergy join in the cry for education, for they affirm that the people are drifting away from the church and chapel into the broadest infidelity. The manufacturers and capitalists swell the

chorus lustily. They declare that ignorance makes bad workmen; that England will soon be unable to turn out cotton goods, or steam engines, cheaper than other people; and then, Ichabod! the glory will be departed from us. And a few voices are lifted up in favour of the doctrine that the masses should be educated because they are men and women with unlimited capacities of being, doing and suffering, and that it is as true now as ever it was, that the people perish for lack of knowledge.[93]

Needless to say, these democratic aspirations were not reflected in the way that government dealt with education. In 1864 another Royal Commission – the Taunton Commission – was established to inquire into the education given in schools not covered by either the Newcastle Report (1861) which had dealt with elementary schools, or the Clarendon Report (1864) which had covered public schools. Its report, published in 1868, was 'guided by its terms of reference towards a narrowly hierarchical view of English education'.[94]

The Taunton Report proposed three grades of endowed schools. One would be for 'sons of men with considerable incomes independent of their own exertions': such schools would concentrate on classical studies. A second would be for 'tradesmen, shopkeepers and all who live by trade': these would cover the 'modern' curriculum based on mathematics, science and modern languages. The final type would 'be for a class distinctly lower in the scale ... the smaller tenant farmers, the small tradesmen, the superior artisans': these schools would cover basic literacy and numbers.[95] The report was highly critical of the majority of private and grammar schools which employed untrained teachers and whose pedagogy was poor. It proposed greater state-controlled supervision of secondary schools and examinations.

The Endowed Schools Act, which followed the Report in 1869, ignored most of the Report's proposals. The government did, however, encourage three tiers of schools which reduced working-class access to secondary education and increased the class differentiation of educational provision.[96] The Act of 1869 resulted in the appointment of three commissioners responsible for supervising and, if required, reorganizing all the trusts related to endowed schools.[97] By 1887, they had reconstituted over a thousand endowments and 'they revivified English secondary education' and 'reinforced the national ordering of society'. The explicit class basis of the changes was demonstrated in Liverpool where in 1877, the Francis Xavier School moved to new premises and reorganized as two schools. One had a large central hall for the classical school for boys who would go on to universities or professional life. The commercial school was at the other end of the building and 'offered a severely practical curriculum and evening classes to facilitate an early departure into local employment'.[98]

There are numerous other examples of how, under the Endowed Schools Act, some important grammar schools, 'which had originated as common schools serving their locality', were 'transformed into residential schools, serving a single class'. Local influence and control of these new schools was removed. The same process of removing local influence and control was also applied to the public schools which freed them from 'control by any elected body whatsoever'. As Simon points out, the fact that these processes of 'independence' took place at precisely the time when 'political democracy was being extended', underlines the position attained by the public school as a cornerstone of a class society, and as part of a 'system both reflecting and perpetuating deep social divisions but beyond the reach of the normal democratic process'.[99] The Headmasters' Conference was also founded in 1869, to ensure that public schools 'should be free from any form of guidance or control'. Such schools were 'the most aristocratic institutions of their kind in Europe' and were quite unlike a thoroughly bourgeois institution such as the French *lycée*.[100]

In the year that the Taunton Report was published (1868), Gladstone's Liberal government was elected to power. In 1870 W.E. Forster introduced his Elementary Education Act, which was designed 'to complete the present voluntary system, to fill the gaps, sparing the public money where it can be done without, procuring as much as we can the assistance of parents'.[101] The Act established for the first time that central government took responsibility for the provision of basic elementary education. It set up locally elected school boards which had the power to levy rates to fund elementary schools. But it still only 'filled the gaps' of voluntary provision: in 1882 it was still the case that twice as many children attended voluntary as board schools. Even by 1902 there were still twice as many voluntary schools as state schools.[102]

But the 1870 Act did achieve its purpose of increasing the provision of state elementary schools. In 1872 there were 8,700 children in board schools; by 1883 this had grown to over 1 million, and by 1896 over 2 million. In 1870 there had been over 1 million children in voluntary schools, and this had grown to $2\frac{1}{2}$ million by 1896.[103]

Secondary education remained outside the state system throughout the nineteenth century. By 1880 attendance at elementary schools was made, more or less, compulsory, and in 1918 the school leaving age was raised to 14. By the beginning of the twentieth century the foundations for a national system of elementary education had been established.

Conclusion: the educational consequences of the nineteenth-century inheritance

During the nineteenth century, when the English educational system was being established, Britain had become industrialized and, by the 1860s, was the leading industrial country in the world. Enormous wealth had been created, and great social, political and economic changes had taken place. This great wealth was not reflected in educational provision. At the beginning of the nineteenth century (in 1818) a Parliamentary Select Committee had described England as 'the worst educated country in Europe'. At the beginning of the twentieth century (in 1902) Balfour had asserted that England was 'behind all continental rivals in education'. In England in 1868 about one in 1,000 was in full-time secondary education, whereas in France one in every 260 French children was at a *lycée* or college.[104]

Accurate qualitative and quantitative comparisons are speculative, but what is undoubtedly true is that the English educational system that was to emerge in the twentieth century still retained most of the characteristics of the attitudes and vision that had informed its nineteenth-century origins. In keeping with the *laissez-faire* attitudes of the early nineteenth century, the system was still predominantly under the control of voluntary agencies and Church organizations. Also, because a political framework in which education could be treated as a democratic entitlement was never established, state intervention in education continued to be seen as a threat to individual liberty and something that had to be advocated in negative terms. It also made it virtually impossible to give any serious attention to questions about the role of education in the new emerging democratic society. Those who had opposed the extension of democracy by arousing apprehensions about mob rule had also opposed the extension of education by creating a fear of the working class developing aspirations beyond its station. The prevalence of this kind of thinking not only delayed the introduction of a national education system; it also ensured that the system that eventually emerged at the end of the nineteenth century was not an integrated system of public education but a fragmented and divisive system of mass elementary schooling, offering the minimal standard of instruction necessary to prepare a specific social class for specific occupational roles.

Of course, in a society which had adopted a form of democracy that placed such heavy emphasis on individual freedom, minimal state intervention and a *laissez-faire* market economy, the division of society into a wealthy capital-owning class and a poor labouring class, each requiring very different kinds of education, seemed obvious and natural. It is thus unsurprising that at the end of the nineteenth century secondary education still remained the exclusive preserve of the middle and upper classes. Nor is it surprising that the distinction between 'elementary' and 'secondary' education was not perceived as a distinction between two levels of education but as a social distinction reflecting the belief that only children of the upper and middle classes could benefit from an education which went beyond the rudiments of elementary provision.

But the pressure for educational advance was difficult to stop. After the 1870 Act, a new type of secondary school – the higher-grade elementary school – emerged in response to the demand for more knowledgeable and better-trained artisans. These schools were located mainly in urban centres and offered a form of secondary education that was essentially practical, technical and vocational. The spread of higher-grade elementary schools meant that there was, for the first time, a form of state-provided secondary schools with the potential to rival grammar schools. The threat posed by these schools to the established tradition of secondary education was explicitly recognized by the Rev. de C. Laffen:

The tradition of Arnold and Thring is, . . . a very precious inheritance of the secondary schools of England. To cut off the children of the people from this great tradition . . . is to do them a . . . wrong. The wrong is not lessened because something is given to them instead which bears the outward aspect of this secondary education without being inspired by its inward spirit.[105]

But the emergence of higher-grade elementary schools, together with changes in the political climate, led to questions being raised about whether secondary education could remain almost exclusively dependent on private effort, and by the end of the century the concept of 'secondary education for all' appeared for the first time on the political agenda. Because of the way in which educational provision had been established in the nineteenth century it was inevitable that the ensuing political and educational debate would be structured by the taken-for-granted nineteenth-century assumptions about what 'real' education should be like and that new educational institutions, structures and processes would continue to embody these assumptions. These included: a limited view of democracy; a minimalist view of the state; a view of individual freedom as negative liberty; and the absence of any tradition of using political power either to reduce hereditary privilege or to support the development of a more open, pluralist and democratic society. Because it was also believed that economic advance depended on a minimal role for the state, it was taken for granted that state education always had to be controlled, limited and provided at the lowest possible cost. It was also accepted that the power of parents to hand on privileges to their children was an uncontested political right. The result of this nineteenth-century inheritance was the emergence in the twentieth century of a system of schooling which defended, extended and legitimated already existing patterns of economic, political and geographical privilege; which confirmed children in the light of their parents' social position; and which only marginally encouraged mobility, equality and openness. In this sense, the educational system that was to emerge at the beginning of the twentieth century reflected, and was interlinked with, the limited system of representative democracy which had been developed in England during the nineteenth century. This nineteenth-century inheritance was to define the context within which both education and democracy were to develop in England in the first half of the twentieth century. The story of this development provides the subject of the next chapter.

4 'SECONDARY EDUCATION FOR ALL': THE STRUGGLE FOR DEMOCRATIC EDUCATION IN TWENTIETH-CENTURY ENGLAND

> The powerful still do not favour the cultivation among the lower orders of the scepticism and critical intelligence that is valued among their betters . . . the decline in investment and support for public education in this country is . . . a vindictive rather than a prudent economy. At stake is more than a hundred years of adventure beyond the mere basics, a span in which schools . . . have tried to make people independent thinkers capable of participation in the democratic process and of deciding what the future of their own society shall be like . . . We must now find ways of ensuring that a defensive, and more apprehensive, establishment in the context of a contracting economy does not make a critical education an education reserved for privilege.
>
> (Lawrence Stenhouse)[1]

Introduction: English education, 1894–1944

By the end of the nineteenth century, the social conditions created by the Industrial Revolution had effectively produced what Disraeli called 'the Two Nations': a society which was culturally, economically, and education- ally divided in terms of class. To many intellectuals, politicians and social reformers it was becoming increasingly clear that the Industrial Revolution had created economic conditions which inevitably supported the wealth, status and power of one group while relegating another much larger group to social inferiority and economic poverty. Although, in theory, liberal democracy incorporated the ideals of freedom and equality, in practice, the opportunities to enjoy or exercise freedom were, for most ordinary people, virtually non-existent. It was this basic contradiction between democratic ideals, on the one hand, and the combined effects of unbridled individualism and an unconstrained market economy, on the other, that provided the basis for the gradual erosion of the classical conception of liberal democracy. This erosion prepared the ground for the emergence of a conception of democracy in which excessive individualism could be tempered by the demands of social justice and under which the inequalities resulting from unconstrained economic competition could be mitigated by the intervention of the state. As this conception of democracy – social democracy – began to gain more widespread support, so the positive role of education in preparing individuals to participate more actively in the civic, political and cultural life of their society began to be emphasized.[2]

It was in this political environment that the Bryce Commission was established in 1894 'to consider what are the best methods of establishing a well organised system of secondary education in England'. In its report, published in 1895, the Commission defined 'secondary' education as a term used to describe three 'grades' of school. 'First grade' schools, which included famous public schools, were those whose main purpose was to prepare pupils 'to become members of the professional or cultured class'. They were expensive, socially exclusive, male-only boarding schools which offered a 'classical' curriculum. 'Second grade' schools, which included some endowed grammar schools, aimed at preparing pupils 'for some form of commercial or industrial life'. Many had a scientific or technical curriculum but some simply offered an inferior version of the first-grade curriculum. 'Third grade' schools included endowed schools, private schools and high-grade elementary schools whose 'special function is the training of boys and girls for the higher handicrafts or the commerce of the shop and town'.

These three grades of secondary school were clearly seen by the Bryce Commission as preparing pupils for different occupational roles in a class-divided society. First-grade schools prepared pupils for entry, via the universities, into the major professions; second-grade schools for entry to middle-class occupations; and third-grade schools for entry to lower middle-class work. Although the Commission rejected any idea that secondary education should be provided free or made available to all, there was nevertheless a conflict in the Report between, on the one hand, its meritocratic desire for higher education to be 'more open and accessible to capable and promising minds from every social class' and, on the other, its awareness of the dangers of social mixing: 'a parent who has reason to think that his children, if sent to a certain school, will run the risk of acquiring habits of speech or behaviour which might be disadvantageous to them afterwards is entitled to decline such a risk.'[3] The Report, therefore, proposed increased opportunities for secondary education but not common, free, secondary education for all.

The Commission also recommended that the three separate central agencies

– the Education Department, the Science and Art Department, and the Charity Commission – be merged into a single department with a minister responsible to Parliament. This was achieved in the 1899 Education Act which established a Board of Education with an administrative structure of a president, a permanent secretary, and three branches – elementary, secondary and technological. One of these permanent secretaries was Robert Morant, who was to play a key role in the implementation of the Bryce Report, and the 1902 Education Act which followed it. Morant was educated at Winchester and New College, Oxford, where he read theology. In a famous article on Swiss education, which he wrote in 1898, he set out a view of democracy similar to that held by J.S. Mill and Matthew Arnold:

> . . . the only hope for the continued existence of a democratic state [is] to be found in an increasing recognition, *by* the democracy, of the increasing need of voluntarily submitting the impulses of the many ignorant to the guidance and control of the few wise, and thus to the willing establishment and maintenance, *by* the democracy, of special expert governors or guides or leaders, . . . the more we develop our Society on democratic lines, *without* this scrupulous safe-guarding of the 'guidance of brains' in each and every sphere of national life, the more surely will the democratic State be beaten . . . in the international struggle for existence . . . disintegrated utterly by the blind impulses of mere numerical majorities.[4]

Given this affinity to the ideas of J.S. Mill and Matthew Arnold, it is unsurprising that Morant believed in 'the classical literary tradition of secondary education' with the public school as its prototype. Nor is it surprising that he attacked pupil teacher centres for their failure to disseminate the 'culture of Winchester and Oxford'.[5] It is for this reason, also, that state secondary schools always seemed to Morant to lack the essentials of a 'corporate life' – playing fields, rifle ranges, and fives courts – and did not possess 'uniform, badges and Latin mottoes' which were the essential characteristics of a 'true' secondary school. In curriculum terms such state schools neglected Latin and the arts and tended to give more significance to science, commercial subjects and games.[6] Morant used the Cockerton judgements (1900–1) to make the distinction between elementary schools and secondary schools explicit and to stop higher-grade schools from developing an alternative secondary education from that provided by the public school tradition.[7] He saw the role of the school as working with parents to allow children 'to become upright and useful members of the community in which they live and worthy sons and daughters of the country to which they belong'.[8]

In 1904 Morant brought in the Regulations for Secondary Schools with the deliberate intention of ensuring that the development of secondary education remained traditional and exclusive. He was relieved when, in 1906, he received a report from the Consultative Committee 'which enabled him to sustain and even reinforce the distinctiveness' of secondary education.

Although the National Union of Teachers accused the Board of Education of 'naked and unabashed antagonism to a popular system of secondary schools', Morant continued to create a recognizable and distinct system of secondary education which emphasized 'the exclusiveness, as well as the homogeneity, of secondary education'.[9] In a highly class-segmented society this was bound to disadvantage the poor and the excluded, and reinforce distinctions based on class, gender and other factors. It also ensured that an important precondition for democratic participation by ordinary people – access to education – was not available and so they would have to remain bound to the guidance and control of what Morant, like Matthew Arnold, called 'the few wise'.

Given Morant's views, it was only to be expected that although the 1902 Act provided a clear administrative structure within which a secondary system of education could develop, it would do very little to eradicate the class basis of education. Secondary schools remained socially divisive institutions, logically distinct from elementary schools. The bulk of the pupils in secondary schools were the children of middle-class parents, fee-paying, and following a non-vocational liberal education. Similarly, although the 1902 Act led to a massive expansion of secondary education, the new secondary schools were largely created in the image of the old public and grammar schools. The house system, sixth forms, emphasis on compulsory games and other features of the public school tradition were all quickly adopted. As a result, secondary education continued to be based on a strong sense of social hierarchy, and a widespread assumption that the masses lacked the abilities to benefit from it.[10]

Nothing exemplifies more clearly how the characteristics, style and values of élite education came to be embedded in state secondary schooling than the introduction of the sixth form as an institutional category. The sixth form had its origins in the eighteenth century in a 'small number of independent boarding schools'. It was the first 'form' to develop a definite identity, and at Winchester it contained the 'best' pupils who were taught by the 'best' master – the headmaster. It provided an institutional and ideological framework where, among other things, 'the deference of the people to the spectacle of power [could] . . . be secured by the inconspicuous collaboration of the middle class'. Its organizing values included Christianity (in its muscular form), loyalty and devotion to duty, solidarity and consensus. These became the educational rhetorics of manliness, gentlemanly conduct and intellectual excellence. 'Manliness' was gradually translated into manliness on the games field whose characteristics included 'honour, loyalty, skill at games, and a certain stoical acceptance of pain'. Under this conception of education, the teacher provides an *exemplar* rather than a source of knowledge or skills: 'to become educated is to imitate and internalise the manners, tastes, enthusiasms, and preferences of the teacher'. Much of this rhetoric was, of course, 'clustered around Arnold's Rugby' and a critical text in the popularization of these educational values was the novel *Tom Brown's Schooldays* by Thomas Hughes (1858).[11] The *Boys Own Paper*, launched in 1870, continued the process of bringing public school yarns before a much wider audience, so making it possible for those who were unlikely ever to attend such schools to have an idea of what such schools might be like.[12]

Before the 1902 Act, there were two potential patterns for the development of secondary education. The first was the model of the higher-grade schools, which would have ensured that

> what was offered was relevant to the needs of local communities and appropriate to the character and resources of day schooling. If this model had been adopted the system would have grown organically in response to local demand and could have been based on styles of organization which were flexible enough to accommodate a variety of curricula.

The other model was based on the public school and saw secondary education as essentially middle-class, stressed the importance of powerful heads, was centred around the sixth form, and followed a classical curriculum. Schools created on this model would be unlikely to have much experience of linking educational provision to complex cultural and social communities.[13] Morant played a vital role in ensuring that the second model triumphed and by so doing reinforced an important characteristic of the English tradition: treating significant *political* issues about education not as legitimate matters for explicit public debate but as technical issues which administrators could resolve behind closed doors. The issues included the following:

> should upper secondary education be on the pattern of the curriculum of the higher grade school or of the independent public school? Should the curriculum provide choices between specialisms or a general range of studies? Should secondary education rest on the foundation of the elementary school or should it represent a different but parallel educational experience?

The sixth form, and all it stood for, became a Trojan horse whereby these issues could remain unaddressed and the pre-democratic traditions could extend and consolidate their educational empire.[14]

The first significant challenge to this view of secondary education was marked by the return to power in 1906 of a reconstructed Liberal Party with a view of liberal democracy built on the notions of positive freedom and social justice. In pursuing this 'new liberalism', the Liberal government embarked upon a programme of educational reform aimed at breaking down the barriers between elementary and secondary education. As the Board of Education put it: 'A class education in compartments after the fashion of Plato's *Republic* is contrary to the essence of democracy.'[15] However, despite this rhetoric, the educational policy of the Board did not reject the definition of the aims and content of secondary education laid down in the 1904 Regulations. Nor did it embrace the concept of secondary education for all. Instead, Reginald McKenna, the President of the Board, announced in 1907 that the Board's policy was 'to democratise the secondary schools in the sense of securing for the humblest in the land the opportunity of education for their children in really good schools'.[16]

This was to be achieved by the introduction of the free places system by which grants to secondary schools were made dependent on their keeping 25 per cent of their places 'free' for elementary school pupils. McKenna reassured a deputation from the Incorporated Association of Headmasters that only scholars from public elementary schools would have to take the examination and that it was not 'his intention that the standard of the secondary school should be lowered in order to admit a different type of intelligence'.[17] The methods of selection for secondary schools varied enormously but gradually came to be based on mental testing. This usually included English, Arithmetic and 'intelligence' tests that had been derived from the work of Binet, developed by Cyril Burt (later Sir) and by Godfrey Thomson, who saw these tests 'as an instrument of social justice' which would 'give more opportunities to working-class children'.[18]

Although the free places scheme was widely praised, it was not uncontested. The Conservative opposition argued that elementary schools could not provide a sufficient number of pupils to make up 25 per cent of the secondary school population and hence that the policy would inevitably lead to a lowering of educational standards. Moreover, as the demand for free places began to outstrip supply, the allocation came to depend increasingly on competition, rather than on ability, and the pressure on elementary schools to prepare their pupils for the secondary school 'scholarship' examinations increased. One consequence of this pressure was to put basic questions about the wider purposes and aims of secondary education back on the public agenda. In 1916, the Board of Education argued that the success of a democratic society depended upon improved educational opportunities, a 'wide diffusion of a sense of responsibility', and 'the intelligent participation in public affairs by the rank and file of the population'.[19] In a similar view, Kenneth Lindsay, in *Social Progress and Educational Waste* (1926), argued that:

> The results of elementary education and the ladder idea are important but the future of a democracy is even more important ... secondary education may become unrelated to the present world ... unless there is a philosophy of democracy on which it is based.[20]

In the 1920s the search for this 'philosophy of democracy' developed under the slogan 'secondary education for all' and led to a concerted demand for an end to the parallel system of elementary and secondary education and its replacement by an 'end-on' system of primary–secondary education.[21] The argument that a democratic society could not be advanced by an education system organized upon élitist principles was a central feature of R.H. Tawney's policy document, *Secondary Education for All*, written for the Labour Party in 1922.[22] In this, he suggested that 'the only policy which is at once educationally sound and suited to a democratic community is one under which primary and secondary education are organized as two stages in a single continuous process'. 'Ability', he proposed, 'is probably dispersed more or less at random over the whole population ... The potential scientist or poet or inventor or statesman is as likely to be born in West Ham as in Westminster.'[23]

Tawney had dominated the advisory committee of the Labour Party which had produced *Secondary Education for All* and *Education: the Socialist Policy*

(1924), and these two documents 'remained the basis for Labour Party policy until after the Second World War'.[24] In them, Tawney argued that 'the hereditary curse of English education ... was its organisation on social-class lines. The public schoolboy was encouraged to regard himself as one of the ruling class and acquired the aristocratic vices of arrogance and intellectual laziness.' The assumption 'of the upper classes' was that 'a workman should be primarily a good productive tool. He is always judged from this point of view, from the assumption that all he wants or ought to want, is not to live but to work.' Tawney hoped that education would lead to 'the formation of an intelligent public opinion on educational matters by the dissemination of full and accurate information'.[25]

During the inter-war period there was also a 'flourishing of ideas' about curriculum, pedagogy and the organization of education. One source of this momentum had been the publication, in 1911, of Edmond Holmes's book, *What Is and What Might Be*, and it was around this time, too, that a few schools began to consider the somewhat radical idea that they might ask 'students what *they* felt about ... the artefacts put in front of them for their edification ... "what do *you* see?" being balanced against "See it like this" or ... "Talk about it like this"'.[26]

The argument that secondary education should no longer be restricted to a small proportion of the population was gaining support for a variety of reasons. Chief among these was the recognition that the selective principle of secondary education – based on the 'ladder' provided by the free places system – meant that the transfer of working-class children from elementary school to secondary school was still seen as a privilege rather than a right. This meant that selection was taking place through a process of elimination which reflected the social and economic backgrounds of pupils rather than their abilities. These criticisms could only be adequately met by eliminating the distinction between 'elementary' and 'secondary' education and creating a universal system of education freely available to all up to the age of 16.

Partly as a result of the Labour Party's policy of putting 'secondary education for all' on the public agenda, the Consultative Committee of the Board of Education produced the Hadow Report, which was published in December 1926, and which had as its terms of reference 'to report upon the organization, objectives and curriculum ... for children in full-time attendance at schools, other than secondary schools, up to the age of 15'. The Report was immediately heralded as an educational landmark. It argued that the types of schooling inherited from the nineteenth century were not adequate to the needs of a twentieth-century democratic society and that a major transformation was required in the content and structure of the education system. 'The schools whose first intention was to teach children how to read', said the Report, 'have to broaden their aims until it might now be said that they have to teach children how to live.'[27]

The Hadow Committee argued that because the new secondary schools created since the 1902 Act had developed patterns of curriculum and organization along the lines of the old-established endowed grammar schools, the elementary schools and secondary schools remained both socially and pedagogically divided. It therefore proposed that the distinction should be abolished and that secondary schooling should no longer be confined to the current academically orientated schools whose teaching and curriculum were moulded by the public school ethos. 'Between the age of 11 and [if possible] 15', argued Hadow, 'all who do not go forward to "secondary education" in the present and narrow sense . . . should go forward . . . to a form of second-ary education in the truer and broader sense'.[28] To achieve this, the Hadow Committee recommended that the two parallel systems – one of high status (secondary) and one of low status (elementary) – should be replaced by a single system consisting of two stages – primary and secondary – between which status differentiation would be irrelevant. At the secondary stage, schools should be of two types – selective grammar schools and non-selec-tive 'modern' schools available for all children.

By the 1930s the political pressure for a more democratic and egalitarian form of secondary education, partly created by the Hadow Report, cleared the ground for the Spens Committee in 1938 to propose that the term 'elementary' be abolished and that a tripartite system of secondary education consisting of grammar, modern and technical schools be established. The Spens Committee also officially conceded that the 'ladder' offered by the free places system operated on the basis of class and that the major determinant of success in winning scholarships was the social and cultural background of pupils. It rejected the view that the role of the secondary school should be 'vocational', arguing instead that its curriculum should offer a liberal education.

Concern about the actual organization of secondary schooling led to the setting up of the Norwood Committee which reported in 1943. Its Chair-man, Sir Cyril Norwood, another key figure in the development of the Eng-lish educational system, had read classics at Oxford and been headmaster of Bristol Grammar School, Marlborough College and Harrow School. He be-came President at St John's, Oxford, and was Chairman of the Secondary School Examination Council from 1921 to 1946.[29] Norwood was 'an un-yielding advocate of the ideology of education represented by the public schools of the late nineteenth century' who thought that a school should be the headmaster 'writ large', and that the state had to see that none but 'great and good men are given high command' since 'the little people of the realm are in the tribal stage which demands a chieftain to be followed'. For him, as for Plato, the world was divided into 'men who know and . . . men who don't know', and democracy was simply a process for ensuring that the individual accepts the 'view of the expert'.[30] Norwood acclaimed the 'late-nineteenth-century notions of social hierarchy, conscience, morality and community', and his report insisted that 'education cannot stop short of recognising the ideals of truth, beauty and goodness as final and binding for all times and in all places, as ultimate values'.[31]

The Norwood report gave official backing to these views. It proposed three sorts of school corresponding to three types of pupil. First, there was the 'grammar school type' who is 'interested in learning for its own sake, who can grasp an argument or follow a piece of connected reasoning'. Second, the 'technical school type' whose interests and abilities lie markedly in the field of applied science or applied art' and for whom an appropriate curriculum would be 'bounded by a near horizon clearly envisaged'. Finally, the 'secondary modern type' who 'deals more easily with concrete things than with ideas'; he is 'interested in things as they are; he finds little attraction in the past or in the slow disentanglement of causes and movements. His horizon is near and within a limited area his movement is generally slow'. Such pupils need a 'training' of mind and body to enable them 'to take up the work of life'.[32]

Norwood's Platonic classification of 'types' of pupil provided a cultural and psychological legitimation for maintaining the way of thinking about state education that had originally been shaped by the political and economic conditions of the nineteenth century, and which had been formed around the concept of social class. It was, therefore, to be expected that fears were widely expressed that the tripartite system proposed by Spens and Norwood would increase rather than reduce the social differences between 'types' of pupil and their different schools. Norwood himself (perhaps because of his great personal knowledge of the English educational system) was sceptical about 'parity of esteem' between the three types of school. His report handed this problem over to the schools, saying parity 'cannot be conferred by administrative decree nor by equality of cost per pupil; it can only be won by the school itself'. This gave secondary modern schools the impossible task of subverting the entire English educational tradition.[33]

Public schools were, to some extent, protected from the economic problems of the inter-war period and were not subjected to detailed public examination. But they did not want to become isolated in a period of radical social change, and their leaders supported the Fleming inquiry established in 1942 'to consider means whereby the association between the Public Schools ... and the general educational system of the country could be developed and extended'.[34] In its evidence to the Fleming Committee the Workers' Educational Association maintained that 'the position of the Public Schools is anomalous in a modern democratic society'. In *The Problem of the Public School*, R.H. Tawney argued that the issue is whether

> the existence of a group of schools reserved for the children of the comparatively prosperous ... is or is not, as the world is today, in the best interests of the nation. It cannot be decided by the venerable device of describing privileges as liberties.[35]

The main proposal of the Fleming Committee – that 25 per cent of public school places should be made available to boys and girls capable of profiting irrespective of the income of their parents – was fiercely contested from all sides. The public schools themselves resented this kind of 'political interference' in their affairs, while those who saw the public schools as bastions of élitism and privilege regarded the Fleming Committee proposal as falling far short of what was required. The conflicting views were outlined in a Nuffield College Report published in 1943: 'At one extreme ... are those who hold that the public schools belong to a past age and that in a democracy there is no place for private expenditure on education'. At the other extreme were those who 'hold that any step taken to widen the entry to the public schools will destroy their character'.[36]

By the beginning of the Second World War the English educational system had come a long way from its pre-democratic nineteenth-century origins. But it was still a system segmented and differentiated on class lines which, recalling Tawney's words, meant that the educational provision in West Ham was quite different from that in Westminster. For him it was one of the tragedies of English history that when, between 1850 and 1890, 'wealth was growing by leaps and bounds ... the opportunity of creating a really effective educational system was missed, [and] because riches came so easily ... education seemed unimportant'.[37] Tawney's claim that class bias was the dominant factor in English education is examined by Savage in her study of social class and policy between the wars. In this, she takes Tawney's argument that educational policy was made by men 'few of whom have attended the schools principally affected by' that policy 'or would dream of allowing their children to attend them' as a claim that civil servants were not neutral. She suggests that the cultural, educational and social origins of civil servants are especially important to understanding how the character of state-supported education was constructed and shaped. Of the 179 administrative-class male officials who worked in the Board of Education between 1919 and 1939, 60 per cent had attended Oxford or Cambridge and half had attended a Headmasters' Conference school. (In 1938, 1.7% of the appropriate age group attended university in Britain.) Probably the most interesting assumptions made by the civil servants who worked in the Board were those which made it unproblematic to believe that the characteristics of 'real' secondary education were based on the public school ideal.[38]

These civil servants played a key role in supporting policies and practices which produced 'an educational system geared for the selection and sustenance of a small, meritocratic élite remarkably similar to the small, aristocratic élite that had successfully governed England for so long'. They did this by supporting a view of education as 'an academic, non-vocational course of study that would mould the character as well as train the mind'. The idea that widening access to education would inevitably raise questions about the kind of education on offer was not on their agenda. The officials' own education at élite institutions did, of course, itself have a 'vocational' element as an entry qualification for the civil service. But, more importantly, it gave them the 'framing concepts' that they used in their work. In this way, social, cultural and professional identities became 'inextricably intertwined' and provided the mechanism that Tawney had identified as central to English education: its unexamined class bias.[39]

The egalitarian ideal: English education, 1944–76

One of the many consequences of the Second World War was a public demand for the post-war world to be better than the pre-war world. As part of the post-war reconstruction, the state took the view that full citizenship demanded the social rights of employment, health, housing and education. As Archbishop Temple put it: 'There exists a mental form of slavery that is as real as any economic form. We are pledged to destroy it. If you want human liberty you must have educated people.' The central moral value of these concerns was egalitarianism: 'justice as fairness: the foundation stone of common citizenship'.[40]

The 1944 Education Act arose out of these ideals and aspirations. It was produced by the war-time coalition government and implemented by the Labour government which had been elected in 1945. Like the educational reforms of the Liberals in 1906, the 1944 Education Act has to be seen as part of a broader programme of social reconstruction. It lasted for 40 years primarily because it had 'a sophisticated understanding of power' and was able to take seriously a whole range of 'values and interests which were perceived as legitimate and achieved a consensus across society which lasted a generation'. The outcome was that 'Whitehall was to promote education, Town and County Hall was to plan and provide, [and] teachers were to nurture the learning process so as to meet the needs of children and the wishes of parents'. The Act established, for the first time, 'the universal right to personal development through education'.[41] Under the terms of the Act, the education system was to be organized in three progressive stages to be known as primary education, secondary education and further education. Local education authorities were required to provide secondary schools 'which would afford for all pupils opportunities for education ... as may be desirable in view of their different ages, aptitudes and abilities'. The school leaving age was to be raised to 15, and the Board of Education was turned into a Ministry of Education with the power to influence local authorities and develop a coherent national educational policy. The Act gave county borough councils responsibility for organizing education in their areas. Primary schools were to have managers and secondary schools governors. An important concession to the religious lobby 'was the introduction of religious worship and instruction as a compulsory element in all schools'.[42]

Although the Act did not lay down any particular system of secondary school organization, the main political parties interpreted the requirement for schools to take account of 'ages, aptitudes and abilities' in terms of the tripartite proposals of the Spens and Norwood Committees. At that time, the Labour Party did not regard the tripartite system as socially divisive, and the belief that selection procedures would give working-class pupils equal opportunity to benefit from a grammar school education was an integral part of its programme of democratic reform: in 1946 'for many school education authorities, the "real" secondary school was the grammar school'.[43]

There were, of course, differences and arguments within the Labour Party which were clearly evident in the thinking of Ellen Wilkinson, who was Minister of Education from 1945 to 1947. Although she was determined 'that all children should have a better choice than she and her generation had' and was critical of the pre-war elementary school tradition, she nevertheless asked in a half-mocking memorandum: 'what shall we have to do to get miners and agricultural workers if 100% of the children who were able to profit are offered real secondary education? Answer: give the real stuff to the select 25%; steer 75% away from the humanities, pure science, even history.'[44] She also thought that children awarded higher IQs would 'become intolerable little wretches if they are stamped from the age of 11 as superior beings'.[45] However, she made clear her intuitive awareness of the dominance, and political significance, of the English educational tradition when she said:

> People have said that by talking in terms of three types of school we are promulgating a wrong social philosophy. I do not agree. By abolishing fees in maintained schools we have ensured that entry to these schools shall be on the basis of merit. I am glad to say that we are not all born the same.[46]

George Tomlinson, who succeeded Ellen Wilkinson in 1947, gave even greater emphasis to the tripartite system. In 1950 he warned the Labour Party that 'they are kidding themselves if they think that the comprehensive idea has any popular appeal' and his Parliamentary Private Secretary (O.R. Hardman) wrote that priority was to be given to grammar schools so as 'to maintain the highest possible academic tradition' and ensure that Britain would benefit from 'the finest trained brains it possesses, from whichever class of society those brains come'.[47] In 1948 the age of transfer from primary to secondary school was lowered from 11 to 10 for 'exceptionally brainy and intellectual children'. In the Parliamentary debate, Hardman said how important it was to safeguard these children,

> because we have to safeguard the nation. Brainy children developing into brainy intellectual adults make a great contribution to the life of the nation; and without them ... the nation will find itself in a very perilous condition in the decades which lie ahead.[48]

This 'meritocratic' view of secondary education had been outlined in a Ministry of Education pamphlet, *The New School Secondary Education*, published in 1947. This asserted that 'different types of secondary schools will be needed to meet differences that exist between children', and throughout the 1950s the official Labour Party continued to defend the tripartite system and the retention of grammar schools. It is an interesting illustration of the power of the English political and educational traditions that selective secondary schooling, which effectively excluded three-quarters of all children from higher education, was a taken-for-granted part of the mainstream of political life until the early 1960s.[49] It is also worth noting how the tripartite system represented an example of how educational discrimination can arise from structural factors outside the control of those actually working in schools. Under this system, children selected for grammar schools had the opportunity to take examinations (from 1951 the General Certificate of Education) which had value as a school leaving certificate and as an entry qualification for higher education. Secondary modern children, who generally left school at 15, had no examinations. In addition, standards were raised: in 1951 the standard of GCE O level was between 'pass and credit in the old School

Certificate', but by 1952 the aim was to raise it to that of the old credit and so place the standard of the new certificate 'well above' the old. The new examination was 'not an examination primarily designed for school leavers as such. It looks forward rather than back ... It has particular reference to university and professional qualifications'.[50] When, eventually, secondary modern children did get an examination it was controlled by teachers and clearly of a lower status than GCE. Thus the majority of children had no national examination at the end of their school days, and when they did get one it was plainly inferior. GCE continued the tradition of 'real' secondary education being suitable for only a small number of children.[51]

By the middle of the 1950s, the tripartite system was beginning to lose credibility for a number of reasons. One was the growing complaints of primary school teachers that the eleven-plus examination, by forcing them to 'coach for the test', was having a disastrous effect on the primary school curriculum. Another was the increasing doubts about the validity of intelligence testing as a basis for selection. Psychologists began to question whether the tests could measure general intelligence in a way which avoided cultural bias or remained divorced from social influences. By 1957, the British Psychological Society had to concede that it was not possible to predict accurately the educational potential of pupils by measuring their intelligence at the age of 11. In their view 'intelligence' was not static and fixed, but could develop through education. Intelligence tests reflected previous educational experience rather than innate intellectual endowment.[52]

These psychological criticisms were reinforced by a series of sociological studies which brought to light the extent to which the tripartite system was itself enmeshed in social factors and had done less than was thought to promote more equal educational opportunities for working-class pupils in it. For example, *Early Learning*, published in 1954, found that there was an over-representation of middle-class children in grammar schools and of unskilled working-class children in secondary modern schools. In the grammar school sample examined by the *Early Learning* inquiry, there should have been 927 unskilled working-class pupils. In fact there were only 436 and, of these, two-thirds left with less than three O-level passes.[53] These findings were reinforced and extended by other influential studies: *Social Class and Educational Opportunity*, conducted by Floud, Halsey and Martin (1957); Hoggart's *The Uses of Literacy* (1957); Bernstein's work on language and class (1958); Jackson and Marsden's *Education and the Working Class* (1962); and Douglas's *The Home and the School* (1964).[54] These studies not only demonstrated the failure of grammar schools to benefit children from working-class backgrounds, but also began to raise questions about the complexity of the interaction between home culture and school culture and the ways in which educational achievement was still mediated through the 'grammar school tradition' that derived from the nineteenth-century class-based educational system. The Floud study, for example, revealed that opportunities for working-class boys were not 'strikingly different from what they were before 1945'. Douglas's work, which demonstrated 'the effects of a variety of domestic influences upon children's school performance',[55] was used by Crosland in his book,

The Future of Socialism (1956), and influenced his policy when he became Minister for Education in the 1964 Labour government.[56]

By the end of the 1950s the scientific 'objectivity' of intelligence tests could no longer be seriously defended and the political legitimacy of the tripartite system of secondary education began to crumble. What had, in 1944, been a relatively unquestioned way of furthering the democratizing trend towards 'secondary education for all' had itself become highly questionable, and it was no longer self-evident that a meritocratic system of education was any more democratic than the class-based aristocratic system that it had replaced. In this climate, the movement to do away with all forms of 'separatism' and 'differentiation' and to reorganize secondary schools in accordance with the 'comprehensive' principle of single non-selective schools offering a common educational experience to all pupils began to gather force. In the 1960s the Labour Party, and then the Labour government, announced plans to end selection at age 11, and in July 1965 it set this policy in motion by issuing the famous Circular 10/65 which requested all local authorities to submit plans for reorganizing secondary schools on comprehensive lines. Despite the fact that it had no direct legal force, the impact of the Circular was considerable, and a large number of local authorities of all political persuasions and from all regions of England and Wales adopted and implemented comprehensive plans. But although, by the end of the 1970s, the comprehensive reform of secondary education was well advanced, this process was increasingly accompanied by a background of bitter controversy and organized protest. Under the slogan of 'save our grammar schools', opponents of comprehensivization argued that by removing their 'choice' of secondary schools, the democratic freedom of the individual was being seriously undermined and that selective grammar schools tradition of academic excellence was being destroyed.

If the period from 1944 to the mid-1960s can be characterized as a time of partnership, consensus, and relative optimism about the future development of education, the emergence of the demand for comprehensive education and the attack on the grammar school signalled the end of this truce. In addition, by the end of the 1970s, it was clear that, though the process of comprehensive reform had been in operation for over a decade, it was having only a limited success. Although comprehensive reforms promised to increase the educational opportunities of working-class pupils, in reality the expansions in opportunities that were created – particularly the opportunity to enter higher education – were primarily taken by the children of professional and middle-class parents. Similarly, although it was self-evident that comprehensive education could only operate successfully if it became a universal system of secondary education, it was never totally adopted. In 1978, 70 out of 104 local education authorities still retained forms of secondary education based on selective principles. Independent schools were also not part of the system.[57] It was also clear that, within the comprehensive schools that had been established, selective principles were still being applied. Despite the fact that the old tripartite system of grammar, technical and modern schools had largely been abolished, the internal organization of

comprehensive schools was rarely determined by the comprehensive principle. The 'noise' of educational change was quite loud but at the level of
practice less was going on. In addition, the national system of public examinations remained unchanged as did the organization, control and style of
higher education.[58]

Against the background of these failures to translate comprehensive principles successfully into practice, the democratic values and assumptions that
had influenced official educational policy since 1944 began to be questioned.
By the mid-1970s the educational debate increasingly became concerned
with decline in the British economy, the rise in unemployment, the massive
rise in inflation and unprecedented industrial unrest. In this context, the
tone of educational debate began to reflect a growing sense of disillusion-
ment with the comprehensive reforms, which was articulated in a series of
Black Papers written between 1969 and 1977.[59] In the main the *Black Papers*
consisted of polemical attacks on recent educational developments in general and their egalitarian philosophy in particular. According to the *Black
Paper* writers, comprehensive reorganization had led to a decline in educational standards and prevented schools from effectively pursuing the traditional aim of 'academic excellence', failures that could only be rectified by
re-establishing the old 'grammar schools' and reasserting the validity of traditional methods of streaming, selection, pedagogy and assessment.

One of the main aims of the *Black Papers* was to show how the 'ideology
of egalitarianism' was a threat to the stability of the political and social
order. In true Platonic fashion, they argued that society was arranged into
social classes because people were born with different levels of intelligence
which the educational process could not affect. Given that intelligence was
hereditary and corresponded to social class, a hierarchical structure of society
was unavoidable and a tripartite system of education was in accordance with
'human nature'. Any efforts to ensure greater educational equality would
achieve nothing but a diminution of quality: 'more meant worse'. What the
Black Paper writers wanted to see, therefore, was a restoration of traditional
teaching, traditional standards, traditional methods of streaming and selection, and traditional schools. Although their arguments were rarely substan-
tiated by evidence or logically compelling, the *Black Papers* probably reflected
a good deal of public opinion and by the end of the 1970s their claims –
about the adverse educational effects of 'equality', about the need to maintain 'standards', and about the need to preserve 'excellence' – began to
dominate the educational debate.

Another important publication of this period was the 'officially' secret
'Yellow Book', called *School Education in England: Problems and Initiatives*, which
had been prepared in 1976 by Department of Education and Science officials
as a confidential briefing document for the Prime Minister, James Callaghan.
The document proposed that the Department of Education and Science should
give a firmer lead in matters of educational policy and 'should firmly refute
any argument . . . that no one except teachers has any right to any say in
what goes on in schools'. It suggested that the time had come to establish
a core curriculum and 'generally accepted principles for the composition of

the secondary curriculum for all pupils'. In 1976 a new permanent secretary, Sir James Hamilton, was appointed to the Department of Education and Science who shared these concerns about the curriculum and who was described as an 'unrepentant centralist'. On appointment he said that 'the key to the secret garden of the curriculum has to be found and turned'.

In his Ruskin speech of 1976 Callaghan built on the claims made in the 'Yellow Book' and on the opinions of leading industrialists that education could be characterized as being run by 'unaccountable teachers, teaching an irrelevant curriculum to young workers who were poorly motivated, illiterate and innumerate'. His speech suggested that there should be greater central control of the educational system and that education should be subordinated more closely to the needs of the economy.[60] As Callaghan said, 'there is no virtue in producing socially well-adjusted members of society who are unemployed because they do not have the skills'.[61] These views, put forward by a Labour prime minister, could easily be interpreted as an attack on the democratic social principles that had dominated educational policy since 1944. The veiled attacks on 'informal methods of teaching', on teachers' power, on the 'irrelevance' of much of the curriculum, on the lack of importance given to science and technology, on examination standards and parent power, all echoed growing public concerns. After the Ruskin speech, Callaghan, launched a 'Great Debate' aimed at reappraising all aspects of the current education system, including those identified by the *Black Paper* writers.[62] Three years after the Ruskin speech Labour suffered a major electoral defeat and the Conservative Party was returned to power. A new government, with its free-market economic ideology, and its *laissez-faire* social philosophy, had arrived, and the stage was set for a reconstruction of education.

The idiosyncrasies of the English and their educational tradition

From this general, schematic and selective account of the evolution of the English educational system, it is clear that the expansion of English education in the twentieth century has not reduced the 'deep social cleavages' which characterized the nineteenth-century English educational inheritance.[63] This is partly because English society never experienced the kind of political revolutions that had occurred in France and America in the eighteenth century and therefore has never felt the need to reflect seriously and publicly on the type of educational system which would be appropriate to a democratic society. As a result cultural, economic and social change in England has often been used not as an opportunity to radically rethink educational policy, but rather as an excuse for a retreat into the spirits, fantasies, vocabularies and dreams of the past.

What people believe about the past is shaped by tradition. As well as telling stories about the past's 'treasured memories,' traditions also provide a framework within which ideals, policies, practices and changes are implemented. Educational traditions contain ideas about what constitutes 'real' education and 'real' schools and they guide peoples instincts about what can and should be done, and about what cannot or should not be done. They provide languages, vocabularies and political repertoires which both make possible new ways of thinking and act as boundaries beyond which it is dangerous to go.[64] For this reason it is important to connect the English educational system to the particular historical 'peculiarities' of England, a term used by de Tocqueville in the 1830s to highlight the unique character- istics of English society and culture.[65] In order to imagine what might be done in education, it is first necessary to understand how what *has* been done creates a powerful and dominant political, cultural and ideological tradition which cannot simply be abolished and always has to be tackled as part of a much wider agenda of political change.

The most obvious characteristic of the English educational system is its lack of coherence. It has developed in a fragmented, voluntarist and unco- ordinated manner so that at no time in its history has the force of political circumstances required an explicit and public answer to the question: 'what should be the main characteristics, structure and form of the educational system if it is to meet the requirements of a fully developed democracy?' Educational reforms, like the political changes which often preceded them, have been more preoccupied with limiting and constraining change to a necessary minimum and to make changes as cheaply as possible. So higher elementary schools, grammar schools, comprehensive schools and polytech- nics have developed, while the nineteenth-century citadels of exclusion and exclusiveness – public schools and the ancient universities – have remained almost untouched by democratic and egalitarian ideals. *Voluntarism* has been the socially and politically acceptable mechanism through which structural, social and economic inequalities have been reinforced and legitimized through educational processes and institutions.[66] One consequence of this is that questions about how, in a democracy, educational institutions should be controlled and organized have never been adequately addressed. Further, the nineteenth-century view that social class should quite explicitly determine the type and quality of education that children are given, has, in the twen- tieth century, helped to reinforce the idea that individual differences be- tween children should be the main selective mechanism operating between and within schools. As a result, questions about genuine individual unique- ness, and contested views about cultural differences, are converted into legitimations for 'educational failure' that merely reflect the structural in- equalities of class, gender and ethnicity. Because England was, and remains, a deeply segmented and divided society, this emphasis on voluntarism, diversity and *laissez-faire*, results in education magnifying and legitimating cultural differences and social inequalities. In societies characterized by marked inequalities, education of this type will generally confirm inequality rather than modify it.[67]

This experience, especially at the level of rhetoric and ideas, is quite dif- ferent from that of France and America. In France, education has been seen as a way of breaking with the old superstitions and ideologies. For Condorcet, 'inequality of instruction, is one of the main sources of tyranny', and the purpose of education is to 'bring classes closer together'. In America the advancement of the Republic required active participation by citizens 'whose intelligence and virtue were the bedrock of the republican order'.[68] This does not mean, of course, that France and America do not have élite systems of education. The political point is the significance and consequence of the élite system for the content, style and organization of the embryonic democratic system of mass education. In England the élite system played, and continues to play, a decisive role.[69] Further, in England state power was used not to tackle actively the inherited structures and bastions of privilege, but to hold the ring as it were, and to allow variety, diversity and voluntary action to flourish. A major characteristic of the period has been 'permissive legislation' – legislation which allowed central government to request, but not to require – reform.[70] This can be seen in the 1870 Act (where attendance was left to local discretion); the 1902 Act (which did not require local authorities to create grammar schools); and Circular 10/65 which, in 1965, requested but did not require, local authorities to submit plans for secondary reorganization. This meant that the cultural changes brought about through public schooling had less sense of urgency and were 'less deliberate and far reaching' than in other countries.[71]

The schizophrenic and fragmented nature of institutional provision can be seen at all levels of education: institutions, curriculum, teachers and their education, and examinations. The tradition clearly contains quite distinct curriculum perspectives: 'liberal' education for the élite, technical instruction for skilled workers, and the 'basics' plus codes of behaviour and the work ethic for the majority. The curriculum, far from providing a cohesive tendency was – and remains – full of opposites and contradictions: the useful versus the academic; education versus training; liberal versus vocational; arts versus science; pure versus applied science; classic texts versus modern studies; old history versus new history; creative writing versus literary criticism; fine art versus craft; and theory versus practice. Different segments of the educational 'system' also had quite distinct traditions of teacher training, education and qualifications: those who had attended the ancient universities and who had subject knowledge were quite separate from those teaching 'the people' who had a more basic apprentice-type training. This was continued into the twentieth century when secondary modern schools tended to have non-graduate teachers and generally inherited the old elementary school approach, while grammar schools had graduate teachers in the style of the élite public schools. Examinations were also different for different classes: the Revised Code, the Certificate of Secondary Education and General National Vocational Qualifications (GNVQs) for those not selected for élite higher education; 'local' external examinations (for Oxford and Cambridge universities), the School Certificate, entrance examinations for Oxford and Cambridge colleges, and A-level General Certificate of Education for those aiming at élite or semi-élite status. The school attended, therefore, decided the sort of teacher likely to teach, the type of examination likely to be taken, and the curriculum likely to be followed. The social destination of the child almost inevitably followed from these 'choices' and the school attended was closely related to the area in which the child lived. As Matthew Arnold put it, civilization, and its values, could only be defended by the 'highly in- structed few' rather than 'the scantily instructed many'. The elementary school tradition handled the latter, and the élite schools the former.[72]

One important consequence of this lack of coherence was that the 'status' of an English school was often inversely related to its closeness to the state: the more 'independent' and 'voluntary' it was, the higher was its status. In 1900 voluntary schools provided about half of the provision[73] and even in the 1980s they made up one-third of all primary schools and a fifth of secondary schools.[74] These schools survived into the twentieth century as a result of an arrangement made in 1902 under which voluntary schools obtained state aid in return for more local authority control over the non- religious curriculum. The managers of such schools continued to be respons- ible for the appointment of teachers and the teaching of religious education. Such schools can provide covert and subtle forms of selection, based on 'religious tests' and justified by 'parental choice', and have been able to resist moves towards comprehensive provision. They can also be seen as a 'half- way' house between private schooling and standard state provision.

A second, and somewhat paradoxical, characteristic of the English educa- tional system is that *pari passu* with this *laissez-faire*, voluntarist and unco- ordinated approach goes a central surveillance of 'standards'. Historically, the power, authority and resources of the state have been used not to modify or change existing patterns of inequality, but to allow them to flourish in an educational framework which ensures that children, teachers and schools are monitored and assessed according to explicit, 'objective' tests and criteria. This began in the nineteenth century with the Revised Code and has con- tinued in the twentieth century with the secondary School Regulations of 1904; with the eleven-plus selection for secondary schooling; and with ex- aminations such as General Certificate of Education, where the demands of universities became a key factor in deciding the form, content, and defini- tion of 'standards'. The educational and political consequences of a central- ized definition of 'standards' is quite different in a country such as Sweden where social and economic policy has (historically) been directed at reducing inequality, and where 'the creation of a comprehensive structure was accom- panied by related reforms in curriculum and evaluation'. In England, which has 'one of the most inegalitarian systems of education in the western world', centralized surveillance reinforces the 'standards' and status of its élite insti- tutions and encourages the view that highly complex judgements about educational processes and achievements can be translated into simplistic scores, tests and examination results.[75]

The third characteristic of the English tradition is the critical role of the 'political' or 'moral' curriculum. Unlike the American high school, or the French *lycée*, English schools have, historically, placed great emphasis on community values, religion, authority and learning one's place, and on the regalia of the public schools: 'school songs, caps, hats, foundation day cer- emonies and speeches'. This is particularly the case in secondary schools. To come into contact with the formal and academic curriculum – the cognitive, intellectual and artistic areas of experience – English working-class children have always had to 'pass through' another symbolic universe of uniforms; honours boards; prize days and speech days; prefects; religious beliefs, values and ceremonies; character training exercises and sport; and authority structures and hierarchies. The moral, political and ideological baggage institutionalized in the 'political curriculum' is not at the margins of schools life in England but at its centre. To succeed children have to accept it, or at least genuflect instrumentally towards it. The 'formal' curriculum selects, classifies and labels; the 'political' curriculum excludes, reconstructs or modifies children's values and behaviour.[76]

Within this 'political' curriculum central roles are played by religion, the 'gentlemanly ideal', and community values. In England, a major factor in the growth of popular education has been the 'struggle between the various religious groups for thought control over the poor'[77] and even today voluntary and Church schools still represent a crucial element in educational provision. In all the major Education Acts of the nineteenth and twentieth centuries, religion has played an important, if not central role, quite out of proportion to its significance in the wider, largely secular, society.[78]

The institutional and political role of public and then grammar schools, in circulating, legitimating, and applying these ideas and values to ever wider sections of the population, is critical. A useful distinction can be made between sixth-form education in schools, and the same education in tertiary colleges, through Tönnies' conceptions of *Gemeinschaft* and *Gesellschaft*. The former represents an approach to social order and cohesion based on 'communities' where relationships are 'intimate, affective, enduring and involuntary . . . and thought to be ends in themselves'. The latter is based on associations which find social cohesion through 'voluntary, partial relationships, entered into . . . for some specific, instrumental purpose'. Reid and Filby demonstrate how the 'institutional category' of the sixth form, as developed in the nineteenth century by Thomas Arnold (and others) is saturated with community-type values. Young people have to identify with the institution and accept judgements about games, dress, manners, language, attendance and attitudes to authority, as a condition of being allowed on the 'inside' of the formal curriculum. The community (*Gemeinschaft*) values centred on defining schools as *communities* where older pupils are co-opted into controlling younger pupils by exchanging privileges for responsibility. Such schools had strong views about 'correct community values' and those who did not share them were removed. As Arnold said, 'the first, second and third duty of a schoolmaster is to get rid of unpromising subjects'. The vital importance of Christianity and leadership, the critical role of the school head, the need for classical texts which provide enduring standards, and the importance of athleticism, are all values which continue in state secondary schools.[79] Under this model of what a school should be like, teachers are seen as substitute parents and schools as 'foreign implantations within a commonly urbanised population'. Once views such as these are combined with a stereotyped, simple and partial account of the complexities of working-class culture, the educational consequences are not difficult to predict.[80]

Cyril Norwood likewise regarded the grammar school as a key institutional category for bringing 'public school values' about education to the middle classes. As he said:

> The business of the schools is to teach that goodness, truth and beauty are absolute values, and every course of study in the school should be designed and lived as something governed by these standards ... There is a very great moral significance in maintaining the idea of the better type of grammar school.

His aim was to see that the public school ideals of discipline, chapel, culture, athletics and service were socially diffused by the grammar school. He also, like Matthew Arnold, gave great emphasis to 'Englishness' and took the view that the core of the school curriculum should be a foundation in English culture. 'At present pupils tend to leave school with a very slight knowledge of the history and manners of the country in which they live'. In a passage which relates obedience to national greatness (and which might even be a motto for the contemporary 'better' type of grammar or grant-maintained school), Norwood said that the ideals of the school should be:

> [t]hat you must show yourself capable of obedience if you are ever to be fit to rule, capable of loyalty if you are to be trusted, that in every responsibility you must think of others before yourself, and that in any position of trust the one unforgivable sin is to fail in the task which has been given you to do. This code of conduct ... is steadily spreading, to the immeasurable good of the country, from the older schools to all the secondary schools of the country.[81]

It was, and is, in élite educational institutions that these ideas, beliefs and ideologies developed and flourished. Such institutions include public schools, other prestigious independent schools and the ancient universities of Oxford and Cambridge, and their continuing existence represents the fourth characteristic of the English educational system. Public schools are the 'most notorious of Britain's old institutional anachronisms' and have remained uniquely powerful and independent.[82] In such schools generations of upper-class youths have been instructed

> by a group of bachelors in the mysteries of the tribe and the wisdom of ancestors, expressed in a dead secret language, the mastery of which took years of diligent, dreary practice; sexual and peer-group segregation in an isolated compound ... ; heroic (but quite futile) efforts to enforce total sexual abstinence; submission to deliberately inflicted cruelties ... ; a regime of physical exercise, cold baths, spartan diet, primitive living conditions, severe routinized discipline, regular moral and religious exhortation, all devised to produce qualities of endurance, courage, and a sense of leadership.[83]

Stone argues that the 'nineteenth-century English public school was (and still is) a highly successful device for the preservation in an industrialized society of aristocratic values, institutions and distribution of power and wealth.[84] They are the educational equivalent of the rotten boroughs of the nineteenth century, where privilege and status can be bought on the open market. Although, in the nineteenth century, there was public concern about the quality of their teaching and pedagogy and the relevance of their curriculum, public schools have almost completely avoided any formal state control. During this period they stressed

> tradition rather than supporting intellectual criticism and imagination. They chose to make themselves an anchor of stability, a guardian of conservatism, in such a way that they were unable to . . . serve the cause of intellectual enlightenment . . . [T]hey produced leaders . . . whose insularity and complacency matched . . . the insularity and complacency of their island people.

Public schools have managed to evade regulation 'at every crucial stage in education legislation throughout the century. The 1944 Butler Act left them intact and unaffected and comprehensive reform occurred as if they did not exist.'[85]

Unlike many other societies where 'private schools exist in the main to satisfy minority and mainly religious groups', in England they 'provide an intensive education for the children of the upper middle class' and give 'far better access to positions of influence, power and affluence than do other schools'.[86] Not only do such schools have various charitable and taxation advantages, they also subvert the state system by ensuring that their criteria and standards become the criteria and standards by which state schools are judged. Ability to gain high grades at A level and obtain entry to the ancient universities became the aim of grammar schools, and then comprehensive schools, and the criteria by which they were judged. The maintenance of traditional assessment and selection procedures therefore is central to the future of élite schools. Once assessment becomes more open, and more consistent with the needs and aspirations of a pluralist democratic society, it becomes vital to defend traditional methods and to undermine those modes of assessment which open up opportunities for an increasing number of pupils.

Over the centuries, like the educational system of which they are a key part, public schools have adapted to, and controlled, the modernizing and democratizing tendencies in society. While such schools educate around 7 per cent of all children, their products make up nearly half of all the students at Oxford and Cambridge. They are protected and defended by a complex web of legal, charitable and taxation benefits, but their role and position have largely remained outside the arena of serious public debate about education and its role in a modern democratic society.[87] It sometimes even seems to be claimed that such schools, and the universities of Oxford and Cambridge, are the sole 'custodians and transmitters of English culture'.[88]

The fifth characteristic follows from the previous two: the English obsession with differentiating, grading, sorting, classifying and testing pupils from an early age. In the nineteenth century the class basis of selection was taken for granted and the Newcastle, Clarendon and Taunton Commissions reflect this view. In the twentieth century the basis of educational segregation had shifted from elimination to differentiation, from social class to individual intellectual ability, from aristocracy to meritocracy, and from selection between schools to selection within schools. But the residual idea of different types of school with different types of curriculum for different types of pupil remains relatively untouched.

The English educational system is, therefore, a very subtle and complex social mechanism which can modernize and reform while at the same time preserving and conserving traditional values and processes. It finds new improved and politically correct ways to differentiate, classify, sort, grade and test which can replace what have become morally unjustifiable and politically dubious mechanisms.

The sixth characteristic of the English educational system is that it is a 'sponsored' rather than a 'contest' one.[89] 'Contest mobility' is like a sporting event where, theoretically at least,

> all the players compete on an equal footing. Victory must be won solely by one's own efforts. The most satisfactory outcome is not necessarily a victory of the most able, but of the most deserving. 'Sponsored mobility' rejects the pattern of the contest and substitutes instead a controlled selection process in which an élite or their agents, who are best qualified to judge merit, *call* those individuals to élite status who have the appropriate qualities.

Under a contest system of education, the criteria of élite status are public and popular, and selection is left open as long as possible. Under a sponsored system early recognition of talent is vital and requires 'insider knowledge' to recognize it. Social control under the sponsored system 'is by training the masses to regard themselves as relatively incompetent to manage society, by restricting access to the skills and manners of the élite, and by cultivating belief in the superior competence of the élite'. The American educational system probably most closely relates to the contest system, and the English to the sponsored system. Under the sponsored system 'schooling is valued for its cultivation of élite culture . . . [E]ducation of the non-élite . . . tends to be half-hearted . . . [and] educational resources are concentrated on "those who can benefit most from them"'.

A sponsored system of education has a number of important tasks. It has to identify talented individuals early and to make sure that, from as early an age as possible, they are given the correct education. It also has to use methods for defining talent that are generally regarded as beyond serious public debate. Finally, and perhaps most important, it has to make sure that not too much talent is created, because otherwise the system would not be able to cope. A sponsored system, therefore, has to identify, define and limit ability and then to train those selected, separately and as soon as practical. The English tradition has always given great emphasis to providing opportunities for children of 'ability' to have access to forms of education, and educational institutions, from which they were previously excluded. Metaphors of 'ladders' are to be found everywhere. As Sir John Gorst said:

It is in the interest of the commonwealth at large that every boy and girl showing capacities above the average should be caught and given the best opportunities for developing these capacities. It is not [in] its interest to scatter or broadcast a huge system of higher instruction for any one who chooses to take advantage of it, however unfit to receive it.[90]

Under the English sponsored system the 'absolute standards' of the élite require that many will be called but few will be chosen. The early identification of talent is a priority, as is the requirement to have separate tracks, routes, curricula and institutions, through which the potential élite members can be given a separate and better education. Further, it is essential that the requirements needed to meet the 'standard' are changed when it looks as if a disproportionate number of children and young people are about to meet them.

The seventh characteristic of the English tradition is the myth of the (often male) 'great head' and the significance attached to the head in the success of a school. This tradition of the 'great head' originated in public schools, with Thomas Arnold and his propagandist son Matthew, for whom the head 'was the chief representative' of the social élite and who had to maintain 'three great Imperatives: learn to obey, learn to exert yourself, and learn to deny yourself and overcome your desires'. Through 'intellectual discipleship' (which came from the head teaching the sixth form) true 'sweetness and light' could reign. The ability to accept the authority of the head was essential, because students who had submitted to authority of the head could 'aspire to be rulers themselves'.[91] All this, of course, resonates closely with Plato's *Republic* which was a key text in the curriculum. It is therefore unexceptional to find that 'English education has often seemed to constitute a life size working model of Plato's educational ideas'.[92] Further, what Popper says of Plato could equally be applied to the power of the head: 'The greatest principle of all is that nobody should be without a leader.'[93] It was in the sixth form of public schools that the important rhetoric of 'manliness', 'gentlemanly conduct' and 'intellectual excellence' was developed and it was the 'great head' who played a pivotal role in this process as a social 'character' whose role could be emulated far outside the confines of Rugby, Eton and Winchester.

In the area of elementary education where schooling was viewed as an instrument of social control, it was natural for heads of schools to be seen as heads of enterprises and held personally responsible for results. One reason for the 'transcendence of the head' may have been the desire for school teachers to have some 'ultimate power behind them when dealing with pupils and parents'. Equally, children, parents, local authorities and other groups find it easier to 'have a single person to speak to on any matter that interests them, so all combine to confirm the power of the head'.[94] Also, there was a close link between heads and the governors and managers of state schools. Heads had to demonstrate that they were competent and proper people to have power over the day-to-day running of schools. 'Institutional leadership', in the sense of 'setting the goals, ethos and values' of the school, could 'not be trusted to a mere elementary school head teacher', it was a matter for the superior classes. But 'pedagogic' and 'moral' leadership could be expected, and this could lead to more autonomy and control.[95] As a pedagogic leader, the head had to demonstrate 'efficient and effective whole class teaching to the requirements of the prescribed curriculum' and in organizing and encouraging other teachers. Moral leadership meant that the head had to be a 'personal exemplar of certain religious and moral values' and be 'the chief agent for their transmission in the schooling process'. Such leadership had to be a 'bulwark against anarchy'. During the social democratic changes which took place between 1940 and the 1960s state headteachers gradually took over from governors and managers the institutional leadership of state schools. They acquired, as it were, something of the 'aura, respect and power of the head teachers of the great English public schools'.

This growth in autonomy and power was another example of how the English tradition was able to influence the way in which state schools developed. During the period of democratic development such schools acquired a model and role definition of a head which had evolved in the nineteenth century and was appropriate to a pre-democratic age. The autonomous model clearly emphasized traditional, conservative values, and the main beneficiaries of the class and cultural changes of the period were 'male graduate head teachers. School leadership in practice was strongly constituted in hierarchical, patriarchal and professionally dominant ways.' This meant that schools, which for most children are the first institution that they experience, acclaim the values of authority, hierarchy, patriarchy and discipline, rather than those of openness, plurality and democratic debate. These are important lessons for children and parents (as well as teachers) to learn.[96]

The final characteristic of the English educational tradition is the low status and significance awarded to teachers and to their education. From the outset, the emphasis was always on moral training, and teacher education has been an arena of conflict between the state and religious groups over who should control the process. Kay-Shuttleworth saw teachers as 'Christian missionaries', whose training had to be 'rooted in religion': 'no skill can compensate adequately for the absence of a pervading religious influence on the character and conduct of schoolmasters'.[97] As one student put it: 'training college life ... was one round of chapel, lectures and study ... the library was curious enough to be negligible ... no educational treatise encumbered the shelves'.[98] The centralized system of education built around the Revised Code of 1862 was an attempt to reduce the power and status of elementary school teachers and to retain control by the state. This was to be done by

a vigorous application of market principles to elementary schooling. The mechanism would be the Code and the agents of assessment would be the Inspectorate ... Teacher competence would be apparently a matter of mechanical efficiency – of meeting the requirements of the Code ... The dominant principle was now to be that of efficient pedagogic work production with an emphasis upon basics.

The settlement was contested by teachers who 'began their long struggle to have themselves evaluated as professionals and not as pedagogic technicians'.[99] The contestation took place in individual schools, through individual teachers, as well as through more collective action. In the mid-nineteenth century it was the fear of over-educated elementary teachers (and over-educated pupils) that led Robert Lowe to warn the House of Commons that the control of education was moving out of the 'hands of the Privy Council and of the House of Commons into the hands of the persons working the educational system'.

Because, from the beginning of mass schooling, there has always been an obsession with authority, power and control, the competence of teachers to control children has always been placed at the centre of the agenda. During the nineteenth century, when there were worries about crime, pauperism, and lack of religious practice, the 'trusty teacher' had a crucial role to play in the political and moral reformation. This notion of a 'trusty' teacher had a number of elements. One was ideological reliability, 'expressed initially in notions of religious and moral character of the teacher and in notions of his or her respectability'. Goodness was preferred to mere cleverness. As Kay-Shuttleworth put it, the elementary teacher should be 'the gentle and pious guide of the children of the poor' and not 'a hireling into whose mind had sunk the doubts of the sceptic and in whose heart was the worm of social discontent'. It was hoped that ideological reliability would be facilitated by careful 'screening upon entrance' to the training colleges, a 'high degree of surveillance' during the course and a 'closely controlled curriculum'. This was made easier by making most of the colleges residential. Teachers also had to be competent and efficient in social control 'expressed in notions of management, discipline and good order'. As the Newcastle Commission (1861) argued, the success of teachers required 'the role of maintaining exact order and ready and active attention as the first necessity and after that as much kindness to the children as is compatible with a habit of entire obedience'. The existence of large groups of pupils and poor facilities ensured that teachers 'could not educate . . . only subjugate'; with 'large classes, cramped space, and an arid curriculum, the strategy of a survivor-teacher had to involve dominance, hierarchy and respect'.[100]

Teachers' status and position declined during the late nineteenth century. From 1880 to 1900 teachers' pay 'increased more slowly than those of other occupations'. Further, apart from one 'minor fluctuation, teachers' incomes declined as a percentage of the net national *per capita* income in the period from 1880–1920', which meant a 'worsening economic position for teachers relative to the gains being made in other occupations'. When the 1902 Education Act replaced the local school boards with local education authorities secondary education could be separated from elementary education, and set on 'its separate and élitist course'. Because of this the aim of the elementary teachers to create 'a single, unified and closed teaching profession' was effectively defeated.[101] In the 1908 'Regulations for the Training of Teachers in Secondary Schools', Morant stipulated that day training departments should establish secondary departments for graduates only who would study a single curriculum subject and undertake 60 days' teaching practice. Those taking the four-year training course had to take 'the pledge', which was a commitment to undertake teaching as a career. It was not abolished until 1951.

In 1925 regional Joint Examining Boards were set up to oversee teacher education. They were made up of representations from local education authorities, universities and training colleges, and they 'represented a diminution of central control in education'.[102] At the same time the Board of Education removed all the remaining elements of the Revised Code and 'the modern principle of curriculum autonomy and teacher autonomy' was established. The 'decisive factor was political: the 1920s marked a high point of Conservative fears about the growth of socialism in Britain and particularly about the political role of education as an instrument of socialism'. The fears were that teachers would become more politicized and allied to more militant sections in the labour movement, and that centralized power over education could be used by 'an elected Labour government and turned to socialist ends'. The result was to view education as 'non-political'. This led to 'licensed autonomy' and to the growth of a form of professionalism which teachers regarded as a defence against centralized state power. During the period characterized by this ideology, from the 1930s to the 1960s, 'most teachers found themselves distanced from a formal apparatus of control and surveillance'.[103] After the Second World War it was agreed that HMI would only inspect teacher training courses in universities if 'invited' to do so. As G.B. Jeffrey (Director of University of London Institute of Education) put it:

> If ever it was my sad lot to tell the University that its work was not an acceptable guarantee of academic quality unless it was supported by the verdict of HMI, the days of co-operation between the University and the Ministry would be numbered.

In 1960 the three-year training course came in, and as a result of the Robbins Report (1963) teaching moved towards becoming an all-graduate profession.[104] The economic expansion, and democratic advances, of the 1950s and 1960s consolidated the view that teaching and teacher education were important enough to be autonomous from formal state control. Education was believed to have a positive role to play in the economic, political and social advance of society.

This history has given rise to two very disparate strands in the traditions of teacher education in England: one derived from the élite schools, and the other from the 'teachers of the people'.[105] Teachers in élite schools, and those modelled on them, have a number of important characteristics. Their status and position are built around subjects, and until recently this meant the study of the classics. The headmaster of Eton, the Rev. C.O. Goodford, 'when asked point-blank for his rating of the relative value of classics, mathematics and modern languages, rather unsurprisingly put his thoughts into mathematical form and answered with the proportion, 15:3:1'. As more subjects came to be seen as important the curriculum expanded, but élite school teachers were still defined as teachers of subjects, and their status came from their knowledge of the subject, and its rank order in the curriculum.

As teachers in élite schools normally went to Oxford or Cambridge, the schools and their curriculum were closely linked to the demands and requirements of those universities. In the nineteenth century, to obtain a teaching post at the Clarendon Nine (the nine public schools covered by the Clarendon Report of 1864) 'an Oxford or Cambridge degree was all but essential, with a bias for each individual school towards one university or the other'.[106] So the importance of these universities was not so much the content of their courses but the simple fact that the staff had attended them. They were not just teachers of a subject, but teachers of a subject who had a degree from an ancient university.

It was assumed that such teachers had little need of any formal teacher training. When the Headmasters' Conference asked Oxford and Cambridge universities to 'consider providing facilities for training secondary school teachers Oxford declined but in 1879 Cambridge agreed'.[107] One of the key reasons for the lack of any need to train élite teachers is that, within the framework of the schools in which they teach, the notion of 'education' is uncontested and simply reflects the political, cultural and economic aspirations of the classes who use them. There is no pressure for deliberation about the aims, content, structure, pedagogy and history of education.

For teachers of the people, on the other hand, the nineteenth and twentieth centuries have been a long struggle for qualifications and some sort of professional status. The advancement of these teachers depended upon society taking the quality of the education of the children that they taught seriously, and providing the resources to enable it to be undertaken. This required opportunities, space, and time for such teachers to become educated themselves. For them education is always a highly contested terrain which constantly gives rise to enduring and perennial problems about how in a modern society an increasing proportion of children can become educated. That requires a sensitivity towards the culture, values and attitudes of those they teach; a knowledge of the dominant established culture; and a perennial critical debate about the role of education in a modern democratic society. Such issues do not arise in an acute form for teachers in the élite tradition.

Conclusion: democracy and the English educational tradition

At the end of the nineteenth century the proposition that only a minority of the population needed to be educated, and that the masses only required a minimal elementary education, was still widely regarded as being consistent with the idea of a democratic society. But in the period between the Education Act of 1902 and the Ruskin speech of 1976, a cluster of political and educational principles emerged concerning the role and organization of education in a democracy and gradually evolved into policy. From 1944, elementary education was abolished, and the ideal of 'secondary education for all' was accepted. By the 1960s the general principle that a democracy is obliged to educate all its members began to become the cornerstone of educational policy and practice.

Of course, it would be misguided and idealistic to believe that this situation was the outcome of a deliberate programme consciously designed to promote democratic ideals. What the history of the English education system over the past two centuries clearly reveals is that it has evolved in an unco-ordinated and fragmented way, creating new educational structures on the basis of existing structures without any clear or unifying conception of what the role of education in a democratic society should be. The fragmented development of the education system has not only meant that it is more the result of pragmatic compromise than any principled democratic vision. It has also meant that there has been no concerted effort to repudiate the non-democratic educational assumptions and political ideas out of which the system originally emerged. As a result, any democratic conception of education has always had to be advanced in the context of educational traditions and practices that were produced by – and themselves serve to reproduce – the undemocratic political and educational thinking of the nineteenth century. One consequence of this is that the concept of an educated public, which Dewey and others saw as so central to the modern development and progress of a democratic society, has rarely been forcefully advocated. As Green puts it:

> the notion of education as a 'right' and a civic 'virtue', a matter for which there is a collective public responsibility has been traditionally weak in a country noted for its individualist and *laissez-faire* culture. Although the idea of corporate or public responsibility has been considerably strengthened ... [and] has been central to the politics of social democracy, there has continued to be a sense in which the concept of the 'public realm' has been attenuated and impoverished by the power of an antecedent liberal philosophy which puts the individual above the community and opposes the use of the state as a developmental force.[108]

The residual power of this 'antecedent philosophy' is firmly embedded in the English educational tradition and remains a potent weapon for those who wish to oppose the implementation of a more democratic educational system. It is for this reason that nineteenth-century arguments about the 'freedom of the individual' continue to have considerable force when used to counter attacks on the privilege and élitism of public schools; why attempts to construct a more democratic approach to teaching and the school curriculum can still be opposed by arguments about the need for schools to be responsive to the employment needs of an expanding and changing economy; and why efforts to strip the narrow nineteenth-century interpretation of liberal education of its aristocratic features can still be resisted on the grounds that the extension of liberal education to the masses would vulgarize its content and lead to a lowering of academic standards. It is for this reason, too, that England still lacks participatory institutional social and political structures, in which people can determine the educational policies and practices necessary for democratic advance.

By the middle of the 1970s the English educational system had acquired many of the characteristics of a modernized democratic educational system: comprehensive schools; more open access to higher education; and more progressive forms of curriculum, pedagogy and assessment. But these democratizing advances were part of a very fragile tradition and always had to be bolted on to the non-democratic educational traditions that had been formed in the nineteenth century. This tradition continues to limit what can be done in education towards the end of the twentieth century and ensures that there is still in popular consciousness a view that 'real' education is what takes place in élite institutions. This failure to shift the agenda, policy and practice of education into the realm of democratic politics, meant that continued political support for democratic educational reforms could not be automatically assumed. As Britain moved into the 1980s and the 1990s this support crumbled and disintegrated under the impact of a prolonged and pronounced political onslaught by the 'New Right'. It is the story of how and why this happened that is examined in the next chapter.

5 THE BATTLE OF IDEAS

AND THE RISE OF THE

NEW RIGHT COALITION

IN BRITAIN

In late Medieval times, a few decades of confrontation with alien world-views and 'open' sceptical thinking tended to be succeeded by decades of persecution of those responsible for disturbing established orthodoxy and by a general 'closing-up' of thought ... the moving, shifting thought-world produced by the 'open' predicament creates its own sense of insecurity. Many people find this shifting world intolerable. Some adjust to their fears by developing an inordinate faith in progress towards a future in which 'the Truth' will be finally known. But others long nostalgically for the fixed, unquestionable beliefs of the 'closed' culture. They call for authoritarian establishment and control of dogma, and for persecution of those who have managed to be at ease in a world of ever-shifting ideas. Clearly, the 'open' predicament is a precarious, fragile thing.

(Robin Horton)[1]

Introduction: democracy and the English educational system

The last three chapters have examined the broad social, political, economic and intellectual contexts within which the English educational system has evolved during the past 200 years. One of the reasons for doing this was to show how the English educational system and the English system of democracy have developed dialectically through an appeal to traditional nineteenth-century liberalism and how this helps to explain not only the peculiarities of British democracy, but also the idiosyncratic characteristics of the English educational system as well. These characteristics not only contribute to an understanding of modern educational structures and institutions, but also enable us to appreciate what Raymond Williams calls 'the structure of feeling' that permeates our particular way of life, shapes our 'common-sense' ways of seeing problems and provides the bedrock for the meanings and values infecting our everyday attitudes and behaviour. The significance of this 'structure of feeling' is profound and, is 'self-perpetuating and resistant to change'.[2] One of the purposes of the last three chapters was to show how the 'structure of feeling' that was formed in the nineteenth century profoundly affected the development of English schooling, and continued to influence schooling long after the society that gave birth to it disappeared. Another was to show how it sustained key features of English education which prevent the development of a coherent *system* relevant to a democratic society: an emphasis on voluntarism combined with centralized surveillance of standards; a critical role for the 'political' curriculum with a considerable emphasis on formal religion; a sponsored rather than a contest system; an obsession with grading, differentiating, sorting and classifying of pupils; the central importance of élite institutions; the tradition of the 'great head'; and a low importance attached to the education, training and status of teachers.

The aim of this chapter is to show how, over the past 20 years, this 'structure of feeling' has been exploited in order to revive many of the central tenets of nineteenth-century liberalism and replace the post-war social democratic consensus on education with the political and educational doctrines of what has become known as the 'New Right'. In order to achieve this aim, the chapter focuses on a series of questions. What were the fundamental problems facing British society in the 1970s? How did the economic, political, social and ideological context differ from that of the mid-nineteenth century when state schooling was established? Why did the definition of the political and educational 'problems' as well as the 'solutions' offered by the New Right coalition seem to be politically attractive? What was the role of intellectuals in the emergence of the New Right and how did the ideas they proposed relate to the conservative political tradition? How did the New Right coalition put their ideas to work in the political arena?

British society in the 1970s: crisis in the West

When the English state schooling system was being established in the middle of the nineteenth century, Britain was a world power: pre-eminent in finance, commerce, manufacturing and transport, and ruler of a world empire. In terms of most industrial yardsticks, 'Britain produced more than all the other major European powers combined'.[3] However, the world of the 1970s was very different, and there is no doubt that from the 1870s Britain experienced 'one of the largest declines in economic strength ever recorded'.[4] Although this comparative decline is important, Britain had, from 1945, experienced almost 'thirty years of uninterrupted growth', with low unemployment and inflation. The event which was to change this was the fourfold increase in oil prices in 1973 which led to large increases in unemployment and to price inflation on a scale not seen before in Britain. In the '1980s unemployment rose to at least five times the highest level in the 1960s, and a level about as high as was ever experienced in the 1930s'.[5]

Cairncross argues that it is impossible 'to identify some single factor that can by itself provide a complete explanation of Britain's relatively poor economic performance. Even if one could, the explanation would be unlikely to have the same force throughout the past hundred years.'[6] However, the complexity of the reasons for Britain's economic decline did not inhibit simplistic 'explanations' from gaining political currency. The most fashionable of these were cultural: the diversion of talent away from business and manufacturing into academic life and the civil service; the failure of the educational system to inspire the values and teach the skills which employers require; and the lack of professional status for engineers. Probably the most renowned studies of these 'cultural critique' explanations of Britain's economic decline have been Sampson's *Anatomy of Britain*, Barnett's *Audit of War* and *The Collapse of British Power*, and Wiener's *English Culture and the Decline of the Industrial Spirit 1850–1980*.[7] Economic factors were also thought to be important, particularly the failure to restructure British industry; a concern with short-term profits rather than long-term growth; industrial disputes; weak management; well-organized unions; and an inability on the part of management to hasten technical change.[8]

Education could fairly easily be seen to have a role in each of these 'causes of decline', particularly as it was consuming an increasing proportion of national wealth. For example, in 1965–6 total expenditure on education in Britain was £1.6 billion (which represented 4.5% of GNP); by 1975–6 this had risen to £7 billion (6.2% of GNP).[9] Doubts were also being expressed by leading industrialists about how far schooling was fulfilling its historic role of producing a labour force which had respect for tradition and authority. Michael Bury, for example, said that school leavers in 1975 'were badly handicapped for most forms of employment by the lack of elementary skills in reading, writing and arithmetic and communication'. One 'solution' to these problems was to integrate educational institutions more closely with the world of work. As the *Mail on Sunday* put it: 'There's nothing wrong with the British people. It's our institutions like our universities that are letting us down.'[10]

Britain in the 1970s was a society under stress, and had to rethink its place in the world. Following the acceleration of inflation, and the steep rise in unemployment after oil prices quadrupled in 1973, 'it was recognised that managing the economy successfully was going to be much more complicated than in the previous two decades'.[11] One response was to argue that radical reappraisal was not required: that all that was needed was a return to the traditional values and beliefs of the past. From this viewpoint, it would follow that the reinstatement of traditional approaches to economics, industrial organization, schooling and social life was more likely to result in a 'return to greatness' than the introduction of more radical alternatives. The safety and nostalgia of the past were to be preferred to untried experiments with the future. In the 1970s there were a number of foci ready for this kind of analysis and treatment.

One of these was social democracy itself. In the nineteenth century increased demands for political rights were often opposed on the grounds that they enabled groups without power (the working class, women, ethnic groups) to start the long process of demanding the status of full citizenship. This meant that newly enfranchised groups could, in time, demand better schools and education; improved conditions and pay at work; pensions and security against illness, old age and death; and adequate health care and leisure facilities. These economic and social demands – the demands for the 'social rights' of citizenship – presented a potential threat to the status, power and wealth of already established and privileged groups by requiring the state 'to mitigate the pressures towards inequality stemming from the way that markets operate'. As the process continued, a universal franchise 'allowing freedom of speech, association and assembly created powerful pressures for further extensions of rights and the remedying of abuses and disadvantages through government action'.[12] Those who had resisted extending the franchise were aware of these dangers. For them, social democracy itself was an easier and more politically acceptable target than the complexity of Britain's changing role in the world economy, or the arcane and archaic nature of British institutions and culture.

As more and more of the population became incorporated into 'the nation', through the various Reform Acts, a new type of state had to be constructed which would sustain these new political and social forces. Through social and welfare reforms, like those of William Beveridge, the state took a more active role in preventing ignorance, poverty and unemployment. New categories and social identities were created ('such as old age pensioner') and each category 'required a whole battery of state and/or voluntary agencies in order to ameliorate the effects of each particular "disorder"'. All this resulted in a 'broadening of the theories of social, as against individual rights and resulted in the poor, the homeless, the disabled, women and the unemployed' all laying 'claims to a more equal share in the social goods to which citizenship entitled them'. This led to an expansion of citizenship 'from the sphere of legal and political to economic and social rights'.[13] Such rights 'reduce inequalities in the political, social and economic spheres of society, and move towards a genuinely egalitarian social order'.[14]

These demands and developments led to the view, from the political right, that social democracy itself was a major cause of the loss of British greatness and of Britain's economic decline. The argument had several strands. It was argued that social democracy, by creating a widespread demand for rights, was undermining the authority of the state. Because of this, there was a concerted effort to 'discredit the social democratic concept of universal citizenship rights guaranteed and enforced through public agencies and to replace it with a concept of citizenship rights achieved through public ownership and participation in markets'. Another challenge to the authority of the state concerned the way in which it mobilized consent. Increasingly, in the 1960s and 1970s this was done through the system of corporatism by which interest groups (such as trade unions and professional associations) were consulted by governments about what should be done. Critics of corporatism argued that what was needed was 'a strong new state, which did not need to bargain with organised interests' because it stood above and beyond mere sectional interests.

Finally, the Keynesian economic theories with which social democracy had become entwined, were increasingly seen as the cause of high inflation, unemployment and economic decline. The economic theory of monetarism, which placed 'sound money' and a reduction in overall public spending at the centre of its agenda, became the answer to the failure of traditional theories of economic management. But monetarism was not just a technical economic theory but also a political doctrine, aimed at reducing the power of the state, trade unions and other interest groups and eschewing the notion of national economic planning in favour of celebrating the role of 'the market' in economic growth. New Right economics was not about economics but about politics. It 'marks the rediscovery and reinvigoration of a crusading liberal political economy ... as well as [being an] explicit attempt to associate economics as an academic discipline with a new consensus on key policy issues'. Indeed,

> monetarism would have remained a technical debate among economists if conditions in the world economy had not altered so dramatically in the 1970s[15] ... The failure to maintain full employment and the principle of an expanding public sector greatly damaged confidence in social democratic governments and cast doubts on whether social democracy as an ideal was any longer either achievable or desirable. In the 1970s there were many prepared to argue that it was neither.[16]

As well as these criticisms of social democracy, the structure and organization of industrial and financial institutions were undergoing acute change. These developments are particularly important for education because they raise questions about how educational organizations should be managed, and what forms of education (curriculum, pedagogy and assessment) are most likely to prepare young people for the world of work. In the late 1960s and 1970s the old Fordist and Taylorist models of industrial organization began to be challenged by what became known as the 'flexible accumulation' model. Taylorism, named after the American Frederick Taylor (1856–1915), was based on the idea of 'scientific management' and had considerable influence on education. It has a number of elements: separating the process of thinking about and organizing work from the process of actually doing it, with management undertaking the former and workers (or operatives) the latter; finding out the most effective ways to undertake the work and specifying how it is to be done in great detail; selecting the correct people for the job; training the workers; and finally, monitoring the performance of the workers to see that the work has been done efficiently.

Fordism was named after Henry Ford (1863–1947) who founded the Ford Motor Company in 1903, and pioneered mass-production assembly line techniques.[17] The Fordist model is rigid and has difficulty in responding to changes in demand. The workers see themselves as alienated from issues about quality, development and organization, and as goods become more complex this has consequences for efficiency. The financial and industrial crises of the late 1970s acted as a catalyst for these difficulties and for the emergence of alternative ways of organizing production, which Harvey calls 'flexible accumulation'. This celebrates the 'flexibility of labour processes, labour markets, products, and patterns of consumption' and is characterized by 'greatly intensified rates of commercial, technological, and organisation innovation'. High rates of unemployment in most advanced industrial societies enabled employers to demand, and get, flexible working practices. Increasingly there were 'core' workers and 'peripheral' workers who were often 'part-time, temporary or sub-contracted'. Such a mode of production is found in new industries in locations such as 'third Italy', Flanders, 'silicon valleys and glens', and in countries like the Philippines, South Korea and Brazil. On the consumption side, the relatively stable 'aesthetic of Fordist modernism has given way to all the ferment, instability, and fleeting qualities of a post modernist aesthetic that celebrates difference, ephemerality, spectacle, fashion and the commodification of cultural forms'.

In the financial world similar processes took place, creating 'a single world market for money and credit supply'. This made information and technical knowledge 'an essential aspect of successful and profitable decision-making'. Increasingly 'paper entrepreneurs' emerged who could make more money by using the processes of world high finance than by becoming involved in actual production – 'stateless' money amounts to nearly as much as the sum total of money aggregates in the USA. These wide-ranging changes create economic insecurity which can lead to a 'desire for stable values' and 'a heightened emphasis upon the authority of basic institutions – the family, religion, the state'.[18]

These moves to more flexible and less stable modes of production have had the consequences of moving economic advantages to those cultures most able to adapt to them, particularly Japan, Hong Kong, Singapore, Taiwan, China and South Korea. They also raise economic, educational and political questions. In education the issues are particularly sharp: should society continue to have one sort of education for the thinkers and 'ideas people' and quite another sort for operatives, or should it support a common education for more collective and co-operative forms of economic activity? Should it concentrate on making children and young people as different from each other as possible or on making them more similar to each other? What kind of education and training is appropriate for those young people who may never work? In the area of politics, how far can a society organized on Fordist and Taylorist principles be democratic? Is it compatible with a developed democratic theory to have thinkers and 'ideas people' in charge, and the rest of the population treated as operatives whose role it is to carry out other people's orders?

Partly as a result of these economic and political changes, the social fabric of British society was also undergoing changes in the 1960s and 1970s. Social life was entering a world where certainty, authority, confidence and predictability were being questioned by variety, contestability, lack of certainty and new forms of relationships. These changes could be seen in family life with the decline of the 'traditional' marriage and the growth of new patterns of relationships and child-rearing; the questioning of traditional gender roles; and explicit support for different forms of sexual orientation and practice. Many of the social factors influencing family life had been established in the late 1950s and included family planning and lower birth rates; increased employment for women; higher living standards, and some decline in the 'absolute authority of the father-husband'. In the 1960s, when what Gamble calls the 'cultural explosion' took place, one of its consequences was to create 'a powerful feminist challenge to the patriarchal family and to the continued subordination of women throughout society'.[19]

Traditional values were outraged by these developments and in some circles the 'ideal of Christian marriage and the Christian family' came to be identified as a bedrock of morality. These changes were then interpreted as a 'breakdown in family life', and the official statistics were seen to echo this with increases in divorce, a trend towards cohabitation, increases in teenage pregnancy and abortion, and a growth in 'lone parents'. The decline in economic growth, after 1973–4, made the social and economic costs of these changes in family life central to the political agenda.

The family, and related traditional values, have always been important in conservative thinking in which authority, allegiance and tradition have been core concepts. For conservatives, the family is vital to the maintenance of the state and it is 'the main social institution in which the habits of allegiance are acquired'. As Burke put it

> to love the little platoon we belong to in society, is the first principle, the germ as it were, of public affection. It is the first link in the series by which we proceed towards a love of our country and to mankind.

This view is echoed in more contemporary accounts. Berry proposes that the family is 'necessarily a hierarchic authority structure' and its 'naturalness inclines conservatives to translate this model into other institutions'. The process is intuitive for, as Scruton argues, '[t]here is a natural instinct in the unthinking man to accept and endorse through his actions the institutions and practices into which he is born'.[20] He proposes that the family is central to understanding authority in politics. The child 'must be acted upon by its parents' power' which is an 'established power'. The bond between children and parents is 'transferred by the citizen from hearth and home to place, people and country'. The 'transcendent bonds' which arise in families dispose people to 'bestow authority upon the existing order' and it is within the family that 'habits of allegiance are acquired'.[21] These traditional conservative ideas gradually came on to the wider political agenda in the 1970s. In 1974, for example, Sir Keith Joseph, writing in *The Times*, said, of working-class lone mothers: 'They are producing problem children, the future unmarried mothers, denizens of our borstals, subnormal educational establishments, prisons and hostels for drifters.' In similar vein, Patrick Jenkin said of working mothers: 'Quite frankly I don't think mothers have the same right to work as fathers . . . If the good Lord had intended us to have equal rights to go out to work he wouldn't have created men and women.'[22] For Mrs Thatcher, '[t]he ties of the family . . . are at the heart of our society and are the very nursery of our civic virtue', and, as Dr Rhoydes Boyson put it, '[t]he family was under attack from extreme feminists, the youth cults and the homosexual lobbies'.[23]

It was against this background of social change in the 1970s that schooling began to acquire a dual significance for the political right. Although it was regarded as a contributory factor in the cause of Britain's decline, it was also seen as the means to providing a solution to the 'problems' that it was felt had to be addressed. These included respect for authority, discipline and morality; the defence of traditional academic values and qualities; and a general deference to the notions of nation, family and race. The key areas of educational debate therefore became informed by ideas about the nation and the defence of the national consciousness (in particular, what makes a particular people 'different' from other nations, and the notion of 'Englishness'); the family (in particular, the defence of patriarchy and authority); and finally race. By defining the issues in this way, it becomes possible to define Englishness negatively via an 'internal enemy' who is the 'foreign body in our own streets'.[24]

The final focus of attention was the weakness of the political left when it had to defend and justify the post-war social democratic settlement. In the area of education there were a number of reasons for this. The left had not really developed or extended the egalitarian educational ideas of the post-war period: equality of opportunity, comprehensive schooling and progressive education. As a result it lacked a new set of ideals and aspirations to carry the debate and agenda forward when the right began to re-establish its dominance. Ironically it was at this time, also, that the right was becoming more ideological, and beginning to develop a more coherent, structured and thoughtful case built around the old ideas of choice and freedom, excellence and quality, tradition and stability, authority and respect. It took over, as it were, the utopian, blueprint, ideologically based radical approach from the left. To do this it acclaimed 'the known, the tried, the proven' and 'placed the past in a modern setting'.[25]

This was a reassuring view in a complex and changing world. The English educational system, while it produced a high-quality education for an élite minority, still did little for the majority. This meant that the political popularity of, and political support for, the system was always fragile and limited. Another critical factor was that it was a *Labour* prime minister, in his Ruskin speech, who put the issues on the political agenda. This confirmed what many people had suspected – that the educational changes introduced since 1944 had promised more than they had delivered. Finally, the media played a crucial part in the educational debate by constructing a view of the 'crisis' in education and how it could be 'solved' which the left failed to influence or counteract. Indeed, in the late 1970s the educational agenda and political proposals of the left were perceived as being inadequate for dealing with these wide-ranging changes in the *Zeitgeist*. During this period, too, there developed a suspicion of the traditional 'grand narratives' of communism, socialism and community. It was the New Right coalition which was to bring the idea of a grand narrative back into fashion with the metaphysics of 'the hidden hand of the market'. In the fluid and flexible world of the 1970s and 1980s 'the market', as a mechanism, looked perfect, especially as the old liberal and conservative ideological baggage which went with it took some time to identify.[26]

These, then, were the dramatic economic, ideological, political and social changes that were taking place in the 1970s and 1980s, and they were putting a severe strain on the post-war social democratic consensus. It is at times such as these that people are inclined anxiously to summon up the spirits of the past to their aid, 'borrowing from them names, rallying-cries and costumes, in order to stage the new world-historical drama in . . . borrowed speech'. And into this world marched the New Right with explanations, solutions to the problems, and a political agenda for education, which did indeed 'summon up the spirits of the past' in new guises.[27]

Ideas, intellectuals, and the rise of the New Right coalition

Ideas count. In politics, they are a material force, organizing people and providing the terrain on which the political struggle takes place. In education they are part of the process whereby people imagine alternatives, or defend the status quo; they are often built around the 'grand rhetoric' of notions such as 'democracy', 'equality', 'citizenship', 'excellence', 'selection' and 'choice'. Ideas provide dreams and hopes as well as justifications and legitimizations. Society, and political parties, use them to reflect about educational aims and processes; institutions require them to generate statements about their purposes, values and 'missions'; and individual teachers use them to explain, guide and make sense of their practical actions. Often the most potent and powerful ideas are implicit – embedded in unexamined social practices, vocabularies and perspectives. Sometimes they are explicit and critical of established traditions. A society in transition from pre-democratic structures to modern democratic ones has a particular need of them to re-construct the traditions on which it has been erected.

Historically, those whose business is to formulate and critically evaluate ideas – the intellectuals – have been seen as marginal with respect to the rest of society, and this gave them claims to be 'socially detached' and, therefore, more 'objective'. Gouldner saw intellectuals as committed to a critical dis-course and as the most likely focus for pursuing the Enlightenment ideals of emancipation.[28] A more accurate, if prosaic, view is that intellectuals should be seen as a mixed group some of whom produce ideas, while others trans-late and modify ideas, and still others disseminate and popularize them. Intellectuals can be 'radical' in the sense that they invent and imagine dif-ferent ways of organizing and legitimizing social activities. But they can also be politically subservient, helping with the complex process of turning ideas into ideologies, rhetoric, slogans and myths.

Edward Said takes a different perspective and suggests that intellectuals ought to be characterized as individuals who represent and embody a 'view, an attitude, philosophy or opinion to, as well as for, a public'.[29] He sees *professionalism* as the enemy of the intellectual, and he takes this to be the process of seeing work simply as something which one does for a living, with one eye on the clock, and which encourages 'proper behaviour', 'not stray-ing outside the accepted paradigms or limits, making yourself marketable . . . Hence uncontroversial and unpolitical and "objective"'. He contrasts this with *amateurism*:

> the desire to be moved not by profit or reward but by love for and unquenchable interest in the larger picture, in making connections across lines and barriers, in refusing to be tied down to a speciality, in caring for ideas and values despite the restrictions of a profession.

Said suggests that there are social pressures which challenge the intellectual's ability to live by these ideals. Specialization is the first of these – knowing more and more about a smaller and smaller area and sacrificing 'one's gen-eral culture to a set of authorities and canonical ideas'. Expertise and the 'cult of the certified expert' are another pressure. To become an expert you have to be 'certified' (by the proper authorities), and 'they instruct you in speaking the right language, citing the right authorities, holding down the right territory'. The drift towards 'power and authority' is the third pressure brought about by professionalism. Intellectuals can resist these pressures by celebrating amateurism because an amateur is 'someone who considers that to be a thinking and concerned member of a society one is entitled to raise moral issues at the heart of even the most technical and professionalized activity'. The habits of mind which induce a turning away from controver-sial and difficult political issues, and from the attempt to develop a reputa-tion for 'being balanced, objective, and moderate', are for the intellectual 'corrupting *par excellence*'. Said argues that 'unquestioning subservience to authority in today's world is one of the greatest threats to an active, a moral, intellectual life'.[30]

Ideas and intellectuals have, therefore, a number of different functions in different social contexts, and any serious political party wishing to influence education has to be able to challenge the dominant system of ideas. Its ability to influence power and policy 'is directly proportional to the intellectual resources at its command'. It will have to develop the ideas within its organization and structure, translate and explain the policies for different audiences and interest groups, and maintain the momentum of ideas when it is in office.[31] In education the role of non-decision-making and agenda setting – controlling and limiting what is talked about – is critical. Likewise the taken-for-granted historical tradition and characteristics of English education set the framework within which educational policies have to be constructed, evaluated and imagined.

The particular intellectual origins of the ideas of the New Right coalition emanate from two sources – conservative thought and nineteenth-century liberalism. It has often been noted that liberalism and conservatism 'contradict each other on a number of important issues including the role allocated to the state; the role of the individual; the nature and scope of freedom; and the importance of religious and familial values in society'. While the central belief of liberalism is the freedom of the individual achieved by emancipating people from 'religion and traditional bonds of the social order', conservatism stresses 'the values of community, kinship, hierarchy, authority and religion' and abhors the 'social chaos' that ensues 'once individuals ha[ve] become wrenched' from their traditional social contexts. The 'conservatives began with the absolute reality of the institutional order as they found it, the order bequeathed by history'.[32]

Modern conservatism 'came into existence as a reaction to the French Revolution and it began in disapproval, shock, fear and resistance'.[33] Its key text remains Edmund Burke's *Reflections on the Revolution in France* (1790), which 'attacked the revolution and extolled the virtues of the English political tradition'.[34] The conservative perspective in politics includes a general scepticism towards change, and an opposition to the views of human progress which have flourished in liberal and socialist thinking since the Enlightenment. Following Plato, it emphasizes the danger of chaos following change, and it proposes that 'existing social and political forms have a special virtue because they are refined and sanctified by *tradition*.' As Chesterton put it, 'tradition means giving votes to the most obscure of all classes: our ancestors. It is a democracy of the dead.'[35]

Another characteristic of conservative thought, which is especially important for education, is that of human imperfection. It generally endorses the Christian account of the 'fall of man' and Hobbes's view of human life as 'solitary, poor, nasty, brutish and short'.[36] The main purpose of the state is to keep all this potential depravity in check, and a government is 'primarily a device for keeping order'. Fortunately, there is a natural inequality whereby superior groups can be identified and are able to form an élite group which can provide political leadership. As with Plato, the philosopher kings rule, and the artisans labour. Burke referred to the 'natural aristocracy' as the 'repository of virtues', and Carlyle claimed that the 'few wise will have . . . to take command of the innumerable foolish'. It follows from this that it is important for all members of a society to know their place and to act out the duties that that place requires. As Burke put it, society has to operate 'according to a fixed compact sanctioned by the inviolable oath which holds all physical and all moral natures each in their appointed place'. This requires 'the permanent necessity for hierarchical and inegalitarian social and political institutions', and *'authoritative leadership*, carried on by an élite, often without the participation . . . of the mass'.

Mannheim, in his well-known critique, suggests that conservatism 'only becomes an ideology *after the event*, justifying a way of life which has already been established'.[37] Honderich proposes that conservatism is about selfishness and self-interest:

> selfishness is the rationale of [conservatives'] politics, and they have no other rationale. They stand without the support, the legitimisation, of any recognisably moral principle . . . [T]hat they are opposed to all change is false. The particular change to which they are opposed is change which is against their interests . . . [T]he resistance of conservatives to decent lives for others has no other rationale but their selfishness.

When conservatives evaluate policies they always have 'an eye on the main chance'.[38]

What was the relevance of conservative ideas to Britain in the 1970s? After the Second World War there was an official consensus about the general direction of social, economic and political policies and broad agreement that the social rights of democratic citizenship should be extended to the entire population. One important reason for this consensus was the self-evident failure of capitalism between 1918 and 1939, which was seen as a direct cause of the rise of fascism in Germany, Italy and Spain. It was therefore seen to be vital to attempt to manage capitalism so as to avoid the social conditions which, it was believed, had resulted in totalitarianism. It was hoped that economic growth, full employment and a measure of social justice would avoid a recurrence of these mass movements. The New Right coalition arose out of the breakdown of this social democratic consensus and the economic and social conditions, especially full employment, which made it possible.

Green suggests that the term 'New Right' was first applied to the ideas and policies put forward by Ronald Reagan when he contested the governorship of California in 1966. David Collard, in a Fabian Society pamphlet published in 1968, was among the first 'to label the new liberals the New Right.[39] Probably the most famous individuals associated with this movement were Ronald Reagan, who was President of the USA from 1980 to 1988, and Mrs Thatcher (later Baroness Thatcher), who was Prime Minister of the UK from 1979 until she was removed from power by a *coup de théâtre* in November 1990.

Like all political movements, the New Right coalition is highly contradictory. It is best regarded as a 'phenomenon for investigation' rather than a set of fixed and coherent doctrinal beliefs and policies.[40] Green argues that the label includes those who wish to roll back the power of the state and allow voluntarism and self-help to flourish; those who are against an egalitarian redistribution of resources and in favour of an environment that allows enterprise to develop; those who think that professionals in public sector organizations are just as likely to pursue self-interest and sectional advantages as any other group; those who favour sound money over all other economic objectives and who prefer monetarist theory to Keynesian demand management; those who have doubts about how social democracy has turned into 'elective' dictatorships that enabled sectional interests to hijack the state and subvert the public interest; and finally, those who eulogize the enormous power of the 'hidden hand' of the market to provide consumers with what they need and believe they want.[41]

Perhaps the most important division within the New Right 'is between a "liberal tendency" which . . . argues the case for a freer, more open, and more competitive economy, and a "conservative tendency" which is more interested in restoring social and political authority throughout society'. The liberal tendency gives central importance to the 'market' and regards it 'as axiomatic that markets are inherently superior to any other way of organising human societies'.[42] This necessitates creating optimum economic and social conditions for markets to function which include: 'sound money' and keeping inflation down through strict monetary controls; reducing taxation and public expenditure; and, wherever possible, removing state influence in industry through a programme of privatization. For liberals, the political imperative to control, and if possible reduce, public expenditure is extremely important. It means that the search is continually on for policies which offer, through carefully constructed rhetorics, quality, excellence and value but which actually cost less money.

The conservative tendency within the New Right has given central importance to the conditions which are required for 'the establishment and maintenance of social order'. 'These . . . include the need for authority, hierarchy and balance'. Like the liberal tendency, the conservative tendency places 'great emphasis upon property as one of the foundations of authority and order'; but unlike them, it also stresses the need for a strong and legitimate state.[43] A strong state is required for a number of purposes: to free society and the economy from all the special pleading and interest groups which are covered by the labels 'social democracy' and 'welfarism'; to police the market so that it becomes more efficient in allocating resources, thus providing incentives and stimulating growth; and to uphold and legitimate all forms of social and political authority in the family, in schools and in institutions generally.

The conservative tendency also agrees with New Right liberals about the 'pernicious' growth of public sector professionals who have a vested interest in the continued growth of that sector. Their general writings are often in the form of a ' "moral" discourse . . . about the good society and the enemies that [threaten] it'. These enemies include 'the enemy without' – particularly communists and socialists – who require moral, ideological and political resistance as well as military action. There are also 'the enemies within' – due to the 'decadence of democracy' which have allowed 'subversives and militants the space ... to attack the soft underbelly of western society'. Authority has to be re-established at all levels in society. This involves changing the climate of ideas which has created a new class of public sector professionals whose tentacles reach into every corner of the modern state to exert enormous influence on the way that 'political correctness' was defined. The conservative tendency within the New Right, therefore, places

> great stress on the problems of the family and erosion of patriarchy; on the schools and the standards and content of education; on the multiplying threats to public order; on the problems of racial and sectarian division; on the churches and the threat to public and personal morality; and on the limits of democracy.[44]

They are, therefore, preoccupied with the whole issue of civil society and the characteristics of political culture and authority.

Bosanquet characterizes New Right thought as a relationship between a 'thesis and an antithesis'. The thesis is that 'society has a natural tendency to order and the economy an inherent tendency to growth'. Inequality is both inevitable and beneficial because it is a spur to greater achievement. The antithesis is the process of politicization, whereby the mechanisms of the market are inhibited. The main culprit here is democracy, under which efficiency will be checked by decisions organized by 'producer group, unions and intellectual agitators'. It will also lead to a 'subsidy morass' where the mechanism of the market will be protected by state funding, welfare payments and related activities.[45] The claim 'markets good, government bad' is both an empirical and a metaphysical claim.[46]

Another approach to the problem of understanding the meaning of the label 'New Right coalition' is to see it as a shorthand term for all the tendencies (conservative and liberal), elements and interest groups, which came to be associated with the movement. As Welsh shows, it is a label probably invented by opponents (the New Left) to make the political landscape clearer, simpler and more stereotyped, and is best regarded as a 'label of convenience' applied to a heterogeneous collection of individuals and organizations of people whose purposes vary considerably. It is an ideology and, like ideologies in general, its characteristics include simplification, vagueness and vacuity about content and detail, combined with moral dogmatism and empirical looseness. There is, of course, no necessary connection between 'the truth content of a set of ideas and their political effectiveness'.[47]

An important reason for the style and variety of the New Right coalition is that it has 'no unified central apparatus, paid bureaucracy, established hierarchy'. Rather, like some of the left-wing movements that it criticizes, it works by permeating and capturing 'larger parties and movements by propaganda and slow colonisation'. This meant that 'think-tanks' and related pressure groups are particularly important in understanding the coalition. The common political education of these conservative functionaries was often a highly theoretical business and is acquired from books studied in the comfortable world of public schools and élite universities. It involves the assimilation of 'abstract ideas' not, as Oakeshott recommends, qualified 'by a genuine, concrete knowledge of the permanent interests and direction of movement in a society'.[48]

The final characteristic of the coalition was just that: it was a *coalition*. Different interest groups, with quite distinct ideological and political views, were prepared to work together for the greater good of helping to sustain Conservative governments in power. The opposition to consensus, combined with political pragmatism, had the potential for making the coalition an effective operation when it came to influencing opinion, and later policy and practice. In this sense, the term 'New Right coalition' is a shorthand label to cover all this intellectual and ideological baggage and biographical variety. The label and its use, do not imply a deterministic view of events or, least of all, the view that what took place was part of some inevitable 'movement' in history.

It is also important to recognize that the New Right did not simply 'raid' traditional conservatism and nineteenth-century liberalism and reapply them in the 1980s. What it did was to develop and extend these ideas to the apparent predicaments, problems and issues of the world as they defined it in the 1970s. As Gamble puts it:

> the New Right ... is an expression of the new politics of the 1970s ...
> Their doctrines are not intended to create some lost golden age but to
> make the free economy the new Utopia which can guide the develop-
> ment of contemporary industrial societies.[49]

The success of the New Right coalition was based on a 'complex interaction of theory, biography and public opinion' in the area of practical politics. The coalition bypassed the experts and professionals and developed a 'populist strategy' which was designed to 'appeal directly to the common-sense of the masses'. At the heart of this appeal was the idea that the 'little man' could be set free from the dulling paralysis of the bureaucratic regulation of the modern state, from the demoralizing dependence of welfare protectionism and 'from the moral relativism of left liberalism'. It portrayed a good society as one characterized by a minimal non-interventionist state, strong government, free markets, low taxation, a strong military defence, and an ethic of responsible individualism. For Mrs Thatcher this was derived from the 'fantasised past' of mid-Victorian England, 'with its thrusting industries, its nonconformist chapels and its entrepreneurial drive'. It offered to ordinary people a journey to a new utopia but one which was 'safe and familiar from school history books'. The New Right coalition resurrected the myths of the past not to replicate them

> but to provide the content of a political programme, based on the in-
> terests of the 'individual' which were constructed in such a way that
> they appeared to respond to the experience and aspirations of concrete
> individuals located in rather different parts of the social body.[50]

Much of the intellectual groundwork for this view of the good society was done by F.A. von Hayek, who was awarded the Nobel Prize for economics in 1974. Hayek was an exponent of 'the cause of liberalism, the modern

successor to the political liberalism of the nineteenth century' who concentrated on the problem of how individual freedom could be maintained in a
world of increased economic controls.[51] For him, what people 'think about
different institutions' is 'largely determined by what we believe to have been
their effects in the past'.[52] His most famous work, *The Road to Serfdom* (1944),
argued for an 'economic system based on free markets and a political system
granting individual freedom within the law' and 'warned that the unquestioning faith of intellectuals in central planning and central direction was
preparing the way for totalitarian rule'.[53] For Hayek liberty was essentially
'negative' – the absence of coercion – and he believed that the increasing
demand for 'social justice' has meant that the coercive power of the state has
been used to alter economic and social relationships and to interfere in the
free market. He felt that the expression 'social justice' should be 'wholly
extinguished from the language'.[54] He regarded change through education as
a rationalist illusion, and he valued 'prejudice over reason, instinct over
knowing, in an anti-educational logic'.[55] For Hayek ideas were central to
politics, and, in his view, the dominance of socialism had been due to its
grip among intellectuals – 'the second hand dealers in ideas'. He took the
view that once the more 'active part of the intellectuals has been connected
to a set of beliefs, the process by which these become generally accepted is
almost automatic and irresistible because they form the opinions of the
ordinary person'.[56]

Another intellectual who was important to the New Right was Milton
Friedman, who was awarded the Nobel Prize for economics two years after
Hayek.[57] Friedman became the leading exponent of monetarism which claimed
to be able, through economic policy, to recreate 'sound money' and low
inflation. His reputation is 'bound up with his unswerving ideological commitment to *laissez-faire* liberalism rather than any pioneering advances in
theory'.[58] He gave the intellectual and theoretical backing to the political
imperatives to reduce public expenditure and to balance the state's books; to
reduce taxes to the lowest possible levels; and to leave levels of demand and
employment to the market – to pretend, as it were, that Keynes had never
existed. His most influential works included *Capitalism and Freedom* (1962),
Free to Choose (1979) and the *Tyranny of the Status Quo* (1983).[59] Like Hayek,
Friedman regarded political freedom as dependent upon economic freedom
which was guaranteed by a capitalist market economy. He was especially
concerned about concentrations of political (rather than economic) power
and felt that the over-zealous pursuit of equality (particularly the attempt to
seek equality of outcome) had led to excessive concentrations of political
power and had resulted in the subversion of the US Constitution.

Friedman saw the greatest threat to be what he called the 'iron triangle':
an alliance of bureaucrats, politicians and special interests.[60] He also argued
that government involvement in education had caused standards to decline
and that professional educators ran the educational system rather than parents. He supported the theory of bureaucratic displacement (formulated by
Dr M. Gammon) which claimed that 'in a bureaucratic system . . . *increase in
expenditure* will be matched by a *fall in production* . . . Such systems will act

rather like "black holes" in the economic universe, simultaneously sucking in resources, and shrinking in terms of "emitted production"'.[61] Friedman provided a number of useful resources for the battles to come: the undermining of social democracy as a political system; the significance of the market; the close links between capitalism and freedom, with the implication that capitalism is a *sine qua non* of individual freedom; the critique of alliances between special interests, politicians and bureaucracies; the arguments for a minimum role for the state; and the pointlessness of additional resources for public sector activities.

What Murray Rothbard and Robert Nozick contributed to the New Right agenda were ideas about taxation and the minimal state. Rothbard believed in the absolute right of property, defining taxation as 'forcible theft', and he looked forward to the abolition of all taxation.[62] He also favoured the abolition of the welfare state and of compulsory schooling. Robert Nozick regarded individual rights as absolute and argued that a

> minimal state, limited to the narrow functions of protection against force, theft, fraud, enforcement of contracts, and so on, is justified; that any more extensive state will violate persons' rights not to be forced to do certain things, and is unjustified; and that the minimal state is inspiring as well as right.[63]

He proposed an 'entitlement' theory of justice and generally supported a free market economy.[64] He ruled out the use of state taxation to help the poor, preferring to leave that to the 'vast array of voluntary methods'. He took the view that the minimal state provides a framework within which each individual can pursue his or her own vision of utopia. From these thinkers there is, again, a strong case against the state and a belief that the good life, for individuals, is most likely to be found when the role of the state is reduced to the absolute minimum.

The Public Choice School of thinkers has its centre at the George Mason University in Virginia, USA, and its main theorists were Gordon Tullock and James Bucanan. For them, public servants and professionals were not to be seen as dispassionate people but as 'self-interested persons' whose own private preferences and interests are separate from the interests of the clients that they claim to serve. The lack of competition for many public services means that public servants are protected from the pressures of the market. They see motivation largely as self-interest. If the state has considerable power and influence, professionals organize it 'to protect and advance their own interests' and then use it to 'reallocate' other people's money.[65] So the state turns out to be just like the market, but without the controls of the market provided by competition. Probably the most valuable theoretical weapon that this group provides is the useful one of undermining the status and motivations of public sector workers and professionals. The image moves from the dedicated, caring and self-sacrificing Florence Nightingale figure, to the self-seeking, empire-building, feather-bedded operator, out for what s/he can get. Public institutions, on this model, are not places that help clients and customers but places run in the interests of the employees: organizations captured by the producers.

Roger Scruton, another important New Right theorist, was famously described by Ted Honderich 'as the unthinking man's thinking man'.[66] He is a follower of the conservative tendency of the New Right coalition and, as for all conservatives, he assumes that the central task of politics is to 'uphold the authority of the state'.[67] For him, the emphasis is always on allegiance, patriotism and tradition. Democracy has limited significance in his intellectual firmament,[68] and he suggests that conservatives 'esteem democracy only in so far as it contributes to conciliation, and are wary of abuses which democracy makes possible in the hands of demagogues, activists and doctrinal fanatics'.[69] He also suggests that 'no conservative . . . is likely to think that democracy is the central axiom of his politics' and wonders 'whether unenfranchised citizens are happier or unhappier than their fellows'. He claims that it is 'hard to know whether the right to vote would be missed by the populace were it now to be removed from them'. For Scruton the 'constitutional essence' of Britain 'would remain unaffected were the franchise to be confined to people of position, education, wealth or power – to those, in other words, with a self-conscious interest in the fortunes of the nation'. For many institutions – schools, Church and university – where there '*must* be a principle of authority (as legitimate power) and where there *cannot* be democratic procedure without the immediate collapse of the institution'.[70] The 'contagion of democracy', like that of egalitarianism and equality of opportunity, has 'wrought havoc' in institutions such as universities and pushed them 'towards the brink of destruction'.[71]

Putting ideas to work: intellectuals in the Conservative and Labour parties

In the 1960s a few individuals came to the view that since 1944 the right had been losing the battle of ideas in British politics. Conservative governments had been in power, but they had had to work within the agenda and policies set by the post-war settlement. After the Second World War the Conservative Party had been keen to distance itself from its pre-war record in economic and foreign policy. The desire of the electorate, in 1945, to try to build a land fit for heroes (and heroines) was very real and the 'big' political ideas of the post-war consensus – democracy, equality, citizenship, full employment, better health care, housing and education – had to be worked with rather than opposed. Outright opposition to these ideas might have meant permanent electoral annihilation.

But some on the right of the party were beginning to see that this pragmatic, anti-ideological, consensual politics, characterized by people such as Sir Edward Boyle and Edward Heath, had to be changed to a more intellectual and more ideological stance. As Mrs Thatcher told the Conservative Philosophy Group: 'we must have an ideology. The other side has got an ideology they can test their policies against. We must have one as well.'[72]

Cowling put the same point in a more historically informed way when he said (in 1978) that 'in the last thirty-five years the intelligentsia has been united in constructing a Labour platform, in validating it once it had been constructed and in making Conservative criticism seem morally or intellectually disreputable'. In 1967, Angus Maude had proposed that 'the lack of philosophy was at the root of current Conservative malaise'.[73]

The Conservative Party regards itself as the natural party of government, and takes periods of opposition to be exceptions that require immediate action. It is acutely aware that ideas are of no use unless they can be put to work to influence opinion and win elections. There was a suspicion among those on the right that in some areas – law and order, trade union reform, education – 'the public' (that is, potential or actual Conservative voters) might be impressed if the party raised the ideological and political temperature by taking on issues, institutions and practices that were not traditionally seen as part of the political agenda.

A central part of this process was an acute sensitivity to the importance of publishing and the media in the promulgation of ideas and in the process of influencing opinion. The right was aware of the importance of *institutions* as opinion formers and that, to change the dominant beliefs and the *Zeitgeist*, institutions would have to be changed. In education those targeted for treatment included the Department of Education and Science itself, universities, the inspectorate, teacher trainers, and, of course, the unions. Scruton made the general clarion call when he said that:

> It is necessary to establish a conservative dominance in intellectual life
> ... because ... it is the only way to create a climate of opinion favourable to the conservative cause. The importance of regaining the commanding heights of the moral and intellectual economy has got to be clearly perceived by the partisans of conservatism.[74]

These hopes and aspirations had to be developed in the context of the policy-making structures and traditions of the Conservative Party. It is not a party which believes in democratic traditions for itself. The 'leader directly controls the entire central office party organisation with its research and policy forming committees, its educational and propaganda functions, and the spending of party money'. The party's structure is 'thus effectively the personal machine of the leader who appoints all its senior officials'. When Heath was leader, and in opposition between 1965 and 1970, he established around 30 policy groups. These were made up of Members of Parliament and outside experts all appointed directly by him. When he won the 1970 general election the demands of government distanced the government from this source of support and ideas.[75]

When Mrs Thatcher became leader (in 1975) she inherited these arrangements but was unsympathetic to the ideas and proposals they were producing. She appointed Angus Maude as Chairman of the Research Department (replacing Sir Ian Gilmour) and made Sir Keith Joseph Chairman of the Advisory Committee on Policy. In 1974, she and Keith Joseph had founded the Centre for Policy Studies. The aim of this 'think-tank' was to move the party away from the old Heath agenda and towards a more thought-out, historically and philosophically informed, radical right agenda. Mrs Thatcher, therefore, had to construct a new identity, invent a new language and rhetoric, and move away from past policies which had failed either to deliver the new Jerusalem or to win elections.

'Think-tanks' became an important element in constructing the new political reality. Between 1975 and 1979 Alfred Sherman, Director of the Centre for Policy Studies, brought together right-wing intellectuals who wanted to influence the direction of Conservative policy. Sir Keith Joseph was a central figure in this whole network. He was an important member of the Conservative hierarchy and able to combine the roles of both intellectual and politician. He sensed that the 'middle ground' did not deliver intellectual coherence or electoral victory. As he said, 'we had ceased to fight the battle of ideas', and because '[we] told the public instead what we thought they wanted to hear, we tended to hear what we were saying, rather than what they were saying'. As part of his moral and political crusade Sir Keith, between 1975 and 1976, made 60 speeches in universities and polytechnics, advancing the moral case for capitalism.[76]

The Institute of Economic Affairs (IEA), founded in 1958, also played a crucial part in the development of these new ideas and policies. It saw itself as 'a clearing house for ideas' and it 'sponsored, produced, refined and timed the ideas through an assiduous and prolific publication policy'. It gave central importance to the market as a mechanism for distributing measures and rewards. In 1975, Roger Scruton and John Casey, of the 'Conservative tendency' of the New Right coalition, established the Conservative Philosophy Group. They worked through the *Cambridge Review* and the *Salisbury Review*, and emphasized a Conservatism 'based on a respect for order, authority, Nation and traditional institutions'.

In the area of education the New Right saw the 'need for intellectual entrepreneurs, brokers and popularisers to promote and disseminate its ideological themes to mass and élite audiences alike'. It appreciated that one characteristic of intellectual dominance is that there are social processes and institutional arrangements which actively discourage debate. The first thing to do, therefore, was to show that something had to be done about the dominant liberal-progressive consensus. This entailed taking on the entire educational 'establishment', from the Department of Education and Science to the teacher unions. The New Right could argue that whereas the left was in control of centres of power *it* was in touch with the aspirations of ordinary people, especially parents.

The *Black Papers* were the first weapon in the long ideological fight which was to come. These were published between 1969 and 1977, and the first three sold 80,000 copies. One pressure group which identified its interests with those of the New Right immediately were the independent schools. Headmasters who contributed to the *Black Papers* included those of Eton, Harrow and St Pauls. The idea for an 'independent' university (established at Buckingham) was supported by the heads of Harrow, Tunbridge and Manchester Grammar, and the provost of Eton.[77]

The rise of the New Right coalition partly depended upon the networks and alliances developed between intellectuals, politicians, academics, journalists, media people, publishers and pressure groups. In the early years of power the influence of the serious theologians and ideologues was probably limited, controlled and specific. As more elections were won the ideological and intellectual momentum provided by intellectuals and ideas was critical to extending the scope for what was politically possible and ideologically desirable.

If the party machine of the Conservative Party is at the service of the leader, the situation in the Labour Party is more complex. Traditionally, policy-making within the Labour Party is shared between the annual party conference, the National Executive Committee, and the Parliamentary party. When the party is in government, power (and policy-making) shifts to the prime minister and the Cabinet. The peculiar British political tradition is evident whereby, until recently, trade union leaders could, through the 'block vote', cast millions of votes 'on behalf of' their members. They could do this through votes at the annual conference, through their representatives on the National Executive Committee and through Members of Parliament whom they support financially. The 'modernizers' within the party have, since the mid-1980s, been engaged in an attempt to move the party towards the somewhat modern idea of 'one member, one vote'.

This complex institutional arena makes the role of intellectuals within the policy-making process quite difficult to plot. There is a tradition, on the left, whereby intellectuals, 'while claiming to operate within the working class movement, really address each other, often in terms which are incomprehensible to anyone outside'. Beatrice Webb articulated this élitist tradition when she described the constituency parties as made up of 'unrepresentable groups of nonentities dominated by fanatics and cranks and extremists'.[78]

An interesting case study, which echoes more closely the relationship between the New Right intellectuals and the Conservative Party, is provided by Kogan's personal account of Labour policy· formation in the late 1950s and 1960s. The old policy agenda of the eleven-plus and tripartite secondary education had been undermined by a series of factors: a succession of official reports which cast doubt on current institutional arrangements; the work of psychologists which was highly sceptical about the reliability and validity of the eleven-plus examination; sociologists who showed that class was still more important than opportunity; and, crucially, the Labour politician, Tony Crossland, who had an informal consultative group of advisers meeting regularly at his home in London and who brought in academics when he was Secretary of State.[79] These intellectuals did not work in a social vacuum, and, besides the important brokering work done by Crossland, journalists took the ideas to a wider audience. Within local education authorities people like Margaret Miles and Alex Clegg did the same. These networks and structures helped to establish, and also reflect, a political landscape which celebrated a move towards equality of opportunity, at least at the level of rhetoric, and at the level of modest policy changes.[80]

The situation from the mid-1970s, for the left, was very different from that in the 1950s and 1960s, and it involved failure in a number of areas: political, intellectual, institutional, and in the media. In a two-party political system, the political terrain is altered fundamentally if there is no effective opposition. If it looks as if the governing party will go on winning elections, the normal controls on policy are eliminated. The lack of a serious opposition during the 1980s reduced the power of the Conservative moderates and increased that of the Thatcherite ideologues, allowing them to 'use the economy as a laboratory for experimenting with their nostrums' and also enabling the New Right coalition to have a clear run at restructuring the entire state educational system in their image. In addition, the changes within the Labour Party in the early 1980s 'precipitated the foundation of the SDP', so the opposition 'was divided as well as impotent'.[81]

The intellectual failure, particularly in education, meant that the left had to try to defend and justify the old settlement built around large comprehensive schools, progressive methods in primary schools, local education authorities, teacher unions, and teacher education. The old rhetorics found it difficult to compete with the new built around choice, standards, parent power, excellence and quality. The requirement to shift the social democratic agenda on to new and more relevant issues and policies seemed to stall.

The intellectual failure followed the other failures. The New Right appealed over the heads of the 'educational establishment' to voters and parents and then, as power permitted, restructured the institutional arrangements. The old educational institutions – local authorities, HMI, teacher education, teacher unions, universities, and schools – did not generally form effective alliances and coalitions. The networks were not formed and the pace of change was such that by the time the networks were in embryo the action had moved on. Individuals made out cases, and put forward arguments, but educational *institutions* did little that was effective. For example, the opposition to the more lunatic aspects of the early 'National' Curriculum was left to the teacher unions to mount, which they did successfully, albeit with little help from other institutions. Finally, the failure was one of communication and an inability to take the debate into the media and publishing. The left did not find equivalents to Rhodes Boyson, and for that they paid a high price.

Putting ideas to work: techniques of persuasion and the New Right coalition

'Think-tanks' were a speciality of the New Right. Some were registered charities, some limited companies, and most received financial support from industry. Think-tanks helped those on the right to look at issues which had 'not been looked at very critically and [to do] something on them ... We have pushed back the boundaries of what is sayable, and now there are a number of things which are sayable which weren't sayable ten years ago'.[82] Such institutions 'sprouted like mushrooms throughout the 1970s and 1980s' and, particularly in education, they were 'incestuous, feeding off each other'.[83]

The Economic League (founded in 1919) was among the oldest of these think-tanks whose aims included discouraging 'political interference in industry' and refuting 'unsound economic doctrines based on sentiment and false assertions'. Likewise, Aims of Industry (founded in 1942) campaigns for 'freedom and free enterprise and against the extension of nationalisation and state control'. On the liberal wing of the New Right can be found the IEA, which promotes 'learning by research into economic and political science by educating the public therein'; the Centre for Policy Studies which aims to improve the 'standard of living, quality of life and freedom of choice for the British people, with particular attention to social market forces'; and the Adam Smith Institute (founded in 1978 in Virginia, USA, and in 1981 in the UK) which is about the 'advancement of learning by research into public policy options'.

The Conservative tendency of the New Right coalition has its own groupings: Common Cause (founded in 1952) whose aim is to 'preserve parliamentary democracy' by opposing 'dictatorship either of the right or left'; the Freedom Association (founded in 1975) whose aims include campaigning for the 'preservation, maintenance and extension of freedom and free enterprise', and whose educational priorities cover 'greater freedom of choice in education,' and 'the rights of parents to have their children educated according to their religious or philosophical convictions'; the Salisbury Group founded (in 1979) for the purpose of 'promoting discussion of current issues on the basis of the traditional Conservative principles associated with the third Marquis of Salisbury'. The Salisbury Group's co-founder, Diana Spearman, took the view that Conservative governments had faced political problems in areas such as education, and law and order, because their policies were not based on firm theoretical foundations.[84]

In the more specialized area of social policy, and in particular education, a whole raft of think-tanks sprung up. In 1972, Cox, Dyson and Maude founded the Council for the Preservation of Educational Standards (which was renamed the National Council for Educational Standards). This was 'concerned with the maintenance of standards and values in all branches of education', and believed that schools should pass on what Dr Boyson called 'traditions' which were 'the memory of the race'.[85] The first statement that the Council published said that it was 'organized by men and women actively engaged in education, and is wholly non-political'. Associate members were to be 'encouraged to form local groups, write to newspapers, MPs etc., to undertake local initiatives, and help in every way to further the aims which they share with the council'.[86] It was supported by élite schools and their headteachers.

The Social Affairs Unit was founded in 1980 (as an offshoot of the IEA) to publish studies of 'controversial social issues in order to encourage informed public debate'. The Hillgate Group was formed in 1986 and the Parental Alliance for Choice in Education (PACE) was set up in 1985 as an offshoot of the Freedom Association. Nick Seaton (an Executive Member of PACE) went on to form, in 1987, the Campaign for Real Education which is 'opposed to the teaching of sociology, peace studies and world studies and believes that British culture and Christian religion should predominate in state schools'.

The collective work of these think-tanks helped the New Right in several ways. By constant repetition, and by quoting each other like academics in citation clubs, they created a counterveiling reality to what they called the 'educational establishment's view'. To take one example, the Hillgate Group publication *Whose Schools?* contains 20 notes and seven appendices. The majority of these notes are to New Right supporters and publications and the 'research findings' are those of the National Council for Educational Standards. Footnote 12 (on p. 21) claims that findings about standards have been agreed 'between the NCES and senior statisticians at the DES', but the statisticians remained unnamed. The overall impression of the notes and publications is that the views presented in the paper are supported by well-founded research – a view which would be difficult to substantiate.[87]

The continuous output of these think-tanks, and the cross-referencing between them, gave a coherence to the policies of the New Right which was lacking in those of its opponents. Further, after each general election victory, when the question was raised concerning what should be done to sort out education, the reports and papers of the think-tanks were at hand. They looked, to the inexperienced eye, like well-developed and consistent programmes of policy. Further, as Bills were going through Parliament additional 'New Right ideas' could be bolted on at almost any stage so that the statutes became amalgams of unexamined sectional interests and partisan prejudices, often speaking to different traditions within the Conservative Party.

The New Right also produced a range of plausible characters and moral entrepreneurs, people who appeared to have some legitimacy and status in education and who could tell a good story. Some of them were academics who could switch from an esoteric mode of communication to more popular ones. These included the down-to-earth, experienced headmaster from the North of England (Rhodes Boyson) who had actually come to public notice in London; learned and cultivated professors (Cox, Scruton and O'Hear); and the sensitive liberals who had been damaged by the militant left (Baroness Cox and Ray Honeyford). There was, as it were, a cultural clash between the characters of the old educational establishment (HMI, teacher unions, local education authorities, teacher educators, teachers) and the New Right's characters (effective communicators, common-sense people, parents and heads).

Rhodes Boyson had the advantage over many on the right in that he had been a headmaster and claimed to 'know' the state system. He had been a member of the Labour Party, but had left it in 1964. He moved from being an intellectual of the New Right to Under-secretary of State at the Department of Education and Science from 1979 to 1983. He was white, male and Christian and, in the mainly southern-based Conservative Party, his northern English accent added an element of 'reality' to what he said. His audience was not other educationalists or headteachers, but voters and parents.

He helped formulate a view of the crisis in education and came up with solutions, and he brought together various interest groups under the New Right rhetoric. He had many media contacts and he used them well. Some commentators see him as the 'main figure-head of the Conservative counter-revolution in education'.[88] It is a sobering thought that the detailed critiques of key texts, such as Nigel Wright's *Progress in Education* (a detailed analysis of the *Black Papers*) and the serious academic criticisms made of Bennett's book, *Teaching Styles and Pupil Progress*, made little impact on the course of the political debate. Hopkins, for example, points out that Wright spent 18 months assessing the evidence on the topics covered by the Black Papers. His conclusion was that there are 'an enormous number of errors, inaccuracies, misrepresentations, contradictions and confusions' in the papers. As a 'contribution to serious educational debate' they are of 'limited value' but as 'a political battle-cry they are extremely stirring'. Unfortunately it was the battle cry that was to be important. Statistics, facts and evidence do not adequately deal with a political debate primarily about values, rhetorics and ideologies. Boyson was part of a long tradition in the Conservative Party of redefining its appeal to new interest groupings. He brought people together in a common rhetoric and made disparate interests feel similar. Boyson was a populist, with parents and voters as his audience. His media skills were first-class, and he could be relied on to produce a succinct 'ten-second sound-bite'. He had a close relationship to the Conservative Party and intended that his work would influence policy.[89]

In education this propaganda offensive was particularly important. While television and radio can provide space for serious argument, the mass circulation newspapers and prime-time television deal in stereotypes, simplifications, sound-bites, and vivid and emotional language. A good educational example of this simplification process is provided by the way the inquiry by Robin Auld QC into the William Tyndale School in Islington (London) was handled by BBC TV. The report was 280,000 words long, and was complex and detailed. Within the space of two and a half hours it was 'translated' into a three-minute television slot. The report had been 'embargoed' (that is, was not to be released by the press) until the following Monday, after it had been published on a Friday. The London *Evening Standard* broke the embargo on a Friday, and then all the media had to follow suit. All the information used for the television slot had come from newspaper cuttings. A 'magic quote' was used in the BBC's 9 p.m. news bulletin, where a mother said her child could play chess but could not read or write. (This had come from the film library.) The whole story was dead, in news terms, by the end of Friday evening. BBC TV had hoped to have the entire weekend to get the story together. In reality it had two and a half hours. It was the story as it actually appeared on television that made the political points.[90]

The New Right was better at turning complex educational issues into this type of media event which was both easy to understand and politically rewarding. Right from the beginning, with the first *Black Paper*, the New Right took the media seriously and realized the media had to be involved if the fight was to be won. It developed good relationships with the educational correspondents of key newspapers, but the background noise was the 'discourse of derision' that the 'educational establishment' had to endure in the press. As the authors of *Unpopular Education* show in their analysis of the *Daily Mail* and the *Daily Mirror*, between 1975 and 1977 there was 'a monologue concentrating on items concerning teachers' lack of professional competence and on the negative aspects of pupil behaviour'. Images were of 'incompetence, slovenly, subversive, or just trendy teachers who failed to teach or control the pupils in their charge'. The background actors were 'wild-eyed theorists, out of touch bureaucrats and the complacent self-interested leaders of some unions'. These were compared with figures such as Rhodes Boyson and *Black Paper* authors who 'care passionately about standards' and are 'the real radicals'. [91]

Another technique developed by the New Right coalition in education was 'the black paper style' (of which Dr Boyson was a brilliant exponent) which constructed a 'language in which change could be evaluated, and fragmentary dissatisfactions brought together'. The papers were 'humorous, critical, nostalgic . . . [and] evoked enduring but presently neglected values'. They also brought together a range of voices from academics to primary teachers and probation officers. They used a vivid, strong language and 'established a pamphleteering tradition which was to serve the right well'.[92]

The popular style was developed in the vast range of texts and pamphlets which the New Right coalition produced. Jones, in an analysis of Honeyford's article 'Education and Race', shows how Honeyford, by the subtle use of words, is able to reassert the standard stereotyped images of ethnic groups. He talks about 'brown parents', the West Indian's right to create an ear-splitting 'cacophony', Muslim parents 'imposing a purdah mentality' and 'Asian immigrants' who 'have a habit of sending their children to the Indian sub-continent during term-time, with obvious deleterious educational consequences'. The style and approach of this article 'triggers with great facility a familiar variety of hostilities toward ethnic minority parents'. Honeyford must know that he establishes a 'relationship with a whole discourse of racism . . . most fundamentally . . . the claim that the presence of blacks is a factor that holds back the achievement of white children'.[93]

Similar facility and skill can be found in two of the key texts in New Right educational thinking: the *Omega File* published in 1985 by the Centre for Policy Studies, and the Hillgate Group's *Whose Schools? A Radical Manifesto* of 1986.[94] The *Omega File* was a review of government policy of a neo-liberal kind, and, can be regarded as a utopian proposal, derived from the systematic application of the idea of free economic competition to education.[95] *Whose Schools?* reflected the neo-conservative tendency of the New Right. The *Omega File* and *Whose Schools?* have much in common. Both wished to see consumer power restored; both wanted to reduce radically the power of local authorities in education; both wanted to move some of the funding of schools away from the state; and both wanted to see teaching deprofessionalized. They differ, to some extent, in the degree of power that consumers would have over the curriculum and over the extent to which the curriculum should be directly vocational. What is remarkable is how much of the Conservative education legislation of the 1980s and 1990s is to be found in these two documents, even down to the way in which they express the tensions between the two wings of the New Right.

Conclusion: intellectual and political dominance and the New Right coalition

A key characteristic of any ideology is the way it unifies, promotes and legitimates the ideas, values and interests of socially significant groups by securing the 'complicity of subordinate classes'.[96] What is noticeable about the rise of the New Right coalition is the manner in which its sectional ideas, values and interests became generalized, so that an increasing number of people tolerated them as part of their own perspectives on social and political life. This was especially important in education where, for example, the interests and values of élite educational institutions (choice, selection, specialist curriculum, traditional values and pedagogy) seemed to be being made available to new groups. This was similar to the sale of council houses where, it was hoped, this process would give the apparent advantages of home ownership to a wider constituency which would then be more likely to support the 'market' in home ownership and the idea of home ownership itself.

If, as Gramsci (1891–1937) insists, ideology is best seen as providing the 'cement' out of which hegemony is built then the one way of understanding the New Right coalition is as a 'hegemonic project'. For Gramsci, hegemony refers to the 'ways in which a governing power wins consent to its rule from those it subjugates'.[97] To achieve hegemony 'is to establish moral, political and intellectual leadership in society as a whole, thus equating one's own partisan interests with the interest of society as a whole'.[98] Its creation requires moral and intellectual reforms which actually alter people's consciousness and how they see the world. In this process 'common sense' (for Gramsci the 'uncritical and partly unconscious way in which people perceive the world') has a vital role to play. It is both the 'site on which the dominant ideology is constructed' and 'the site for the resistance to that ideology'.[99]

The New Right clearly understood that the processes and institutions of schooling and education are central to any hegemonic project. As Green points out, the 'process of winning consent and transforming the consciousness of the people to conform to modern conditions of production is precisely a process of education and the schools are therefore a crucial instalment in the process of state formation'. Schools are 'always at odds with the culture of the children', and their social role is to detach children from their 'localised and folkloric' culture and to 'remake them anew after the image of the dominant culture'. It is in schools, and other educational institutions, that the battles of ideas take place, and such institutions are 'strategic battlegrounds' and a particularly important 'site of struggle'.[100]

The New Right understood this and therefore grasped that if it was to discredit the previous dominant hegemony – social democracy – and replace it with a quite different social, economic and political agenda, it had to reconstruct, and in some cases destroy, social and educational institutions and policies which had been 'buttresses of the old' social order. In this sense, the New Right educational project can be seen as an attempt both to undermine and destroy the post-war social democratic consensus and to replace it with the new hegemony of the market.[101]

Because education is an area where it is commonplace to find ideas being used to defend sectional and partisan interests, it is always necessary to discount superficial explanations and examine the wider historical, political, economic and ideological context in which educational ideas and policies are formulated. The danger of failing to do this is to revert to base and vulgar writing, to mistake rhetoric and apologia for serious analysis, and to run the risk of becoming merely a 'hired prize fighter' or 'bought advocate'. The task is to explore the bias and implicit assumptions of social values; to see ideology as thought 'constructed from a narrow social point of view'; and to expose thought which is 'systematically biased towards a particular social group'. It is this task that is undertaken in the next chapter, where the role of New Right ideas and ideologies in the development of educational policy-making is discussed.[102]

6 THE NEW RIGHT OFFENSIVE AND THE DEMISE OF DEMOCRATIC EDUCATION IN ENGLAND

> The trick is to keep doing outrageous things. There's no point in passing some scandalous piece of legislation and then giving everyone time to get worked up about it. You have to go right in there and top it up with something even worse, before the public have had a chance to work out what's hit them.
>
> (Jonathan Coe)[1]

Introduction: ideology and politics in the Conservative Party

This chapter has four general aims. The first is to consider how and why the New Right coalition emerged as a major political force and to what extent its ideas were translated into the educational policies of successive British governments between 1979 and 1993. The second is to link this to the political question of how the Conservative Party, after a series of electoral defeats in the 1960s and 1970s, became so successful in national politics that it was able to win four consecutive general elections.[2] The third is to examine the historical relationship between the Conservative Party and education, and to reveal how Conservative governments set about reconstructing the educational system, either explicitly or implicitly, in ways which were sympathetic with New Right educational ideas and ideologies. The final aim is to consider the extent to which the educational changes achieved by the New Right are consistent with the aims and values of a democratic society. This aim is pursued by examining the National Curriculum as a case study and by assessing the extent to which the main characteristics of the English educational system have been adapted or confirmed by the policies of the New Right coalition.

Although educational policy-making during this period was more explicitly ideologically driven than had traditionally been the case, it has to be remembered that the process of policy construction and implementation is always, in part, messy, uncontrollable and unpremeditated. Governments are 'not monolithic' and events often shape policies and practices more than ideologies and plans.[3] As Harold Macmillan replied when asked what was the biggest problem in politics, 'events, dear boy, events'. This is why

> the policy and administrative trajectories of different fields and government departments may differ widely from each other. Cabinet government, and a unified civil service, may strive to keep discrepancies within tolerable limits, but they cannot eliminate them ... [T]he networks or policy communities through which action is negotiated may have few points of tangency.

Governments, particularly those of a New Right tendency, may dislike teachers, local authorities, teacher trainers, inspectors and advisers, academics, teacher unions and researchers, but it is impossible to implement most education policies without working with at least some of these groups. As even Chairman Mao found, agricultural change required partial co-operation from the peasants.[4]

What has to be remembered is that New Right thinking was only one strand of thought in the wider Conservative Party, and its dominance within Conservative governments had to be maintained under pressure from those holding quite different positions. Sometimes what emerged as policy was a compromise which pleased hardly anyone, least of all the New Right. Jones makes a distinction between 'traditional' and 'modernizing' tendencies within the party. The former 'is nostalgic for traditional culture and continuity, and seeks to restore selection and privilege'. The latter 'is entrepreneurial, technological and oriented to the national economy, but also favours selection'.[5] But since, as we saw in Chapter 5, the New Right is essentially a coalition, these contradictions are to be expected. The policy process at all stages – ideas, proposals, legislation, amendments and implementation – is contested.

Probably the most productive way of looking at New Right influence in educational policy-making under the Conservatives is to see it both as an ideological project (putting ideas to work) and as a political programme concerned with getting support and winning elections. There is always a close connection between these twin imperatives – the ideological and the political. It may be that an important part of the appeal of the New Right agenda for education was that it represented a coherent attack on the post-war ideological consensus *and* offered what seemed to be a developing, well-thought-out and alternative political programme.[6]

It is also unwise to assume, because the Conservatives won four successive elections, and because the New Right was an important force within government, that either the government or the policies they pursued were popular in the sense that the majority of people supported them. Understanding the attitudes and views of the people raises complex issues, and 'populist' does not necessarily mean 'popular'. Some evidence supports the view that while people voted for Mrs Thatcher's party they had serious reservations about the policies that she pursued.[7]

The Conservative Party is adept at winning elections and staying in power. To do this it has to ditch policies and leaders likely to lose elections, and support policies and leaders which look like winning them. This political pragmatism is often more important than ideological purity. The poll tax, fees for students, low taxation, and closing down coalmines can all be dropped (permanently or temporarily) if electoral survival seems to depend upon it. Even the ideologue-in-chief would have to go if it became clear that she had become a serious electoral liability.

Education provided a valuable experimental setting to try out some of the agendas and ideologies of the New Right. These included: re-establishing traditional authority at the level of the state and within educational institutions; re-establishing a more traditional curriculum, pedagogy and assessment for the whole educational system, and removing clutter, subversion and indoctrination; making the market the allocating mechanism for resources; curtailing the power of professionals and providers; reducing the significance of social democracy; and, through choice, variety and differentiation, allowing some parents to have more influence over their children's education. The advantages of using education as an experimental laboratory for New Right ideology are obvious. Apart from occasional political problems, education did not seem to present serious electoral dangers. Most of the consequences of the changes are difficult to evaluate, and the government's elaborate public relations machine could always provide parents with acceptable rhetoric and reassurance. Finally, apart from widespread resistance by teachers to testing under the National Curriculum (during 1993), there has been little serious political opposition. Some would argue that the teachers' strikes (during the 1980s) were used to increase political support for the Conservative Party in key constituencies and areas. Because the English educational system has always produced more losers than winners it is fairly easy for determined and ruthless politicians to plug into this reservoir of discontent and unfulfilled ambition among voters.

Statecraft, power and the Conservative Party

The precondition for the success of any new educational or political agenda is power. The Conservative Party, like all serious political parties, is opportunist, but, unlike most other parties, it is ruthlessly and successfully opportunist.

Since 1885 the Conservatives have won 17 out of 30 general elections and been in power, either alone or in coalition, for 74 out of the 108 years between 1885 and 1993.[8] The Conservative Party is the political juggernaut of British politics: easy to get on board but quite difficult to stop. The purpose of the party is to govern, and to do that it has to be united, flexible and quick to get politically important groups to identify with it and to vote for it. It is an efficient machine for winning elections. As Ian Gilmour puts it: 'while every party wants to win the next general election, the Conservative party's will to win is especially strong. Nothing makes it more open-minded than the prospect of being beaten at the polls.'[9]

Given the pre-eminent political role of the Conservative Party, it is reasonable to assume that it both reflects and helps to construct and maintain British political culture. As Johnson argues, that culture is essentially a Tory culture, stressing the identity of Britons as subjects rather than as citizens. In this political culture, conservatism 'swims like a fish in the sea', and the party's own internal structure is so undemocratic that 'the only real analogies are to be found in fascist parties'.[10] The core assumptions of this national culture include: racial and national superiority; a deferential attitude towards authority; the preference for secrecy in the practice of high politics; an anti-egalitarian ethos; and the awarding of status and respect to hierarchies. The Conservative Party has been adept at reflecting and manipulating this 'national' culture. In Churchill's words, it is a

> party of great vested interests, banded together in a formidable confederation: corruption at home, aggression to cover it up abroad; the trickery of tariff juggles, the tyranny of a party machine; sentiment by the bucketful, patriotism by the imperial pint; the open hand at the public exchequer, the open room at the public house; dear food for the millions, cheap labour for the millionaire.[11]

The party has historically drawn support from the economically advancing geographical areas, and from classes and groups who see themselves as growing more prosperous. Indeed, in England, voting Conservative is almost a sign of having arrived socially. Since the late nineteenth century, it has been the 'normal party of the Establishment, the wealthy, and the middle classes' and has always favoured 'London-based financial and commercial capitalism at the expense of manufacturing industry in the North'.[12] This world of 'semi-detached South East England' is an important constituency in the educational debates and policies of the 1980s and 1990s.

Given the Conservative Party's historic role as the natural party of government, one of its central political tasks has been to win, and retain, the support of newly enfranchised groups – particularly the working class and women. The process of enfranchisement was slow in Britain, and the main pieces of electoral reform legislation, between 1832 and 1928, enfranchised landowners and tenants, householders and leaseholders first in towns and then in the country, and finally female voters. In 1869 the electorate was about one in three of the adult *male* population, and in 1886 two in three.[13] However, even in 1911, only about 30 per cent of the adult population were on the electoral register, and about 63 per cent of the adult *male* population.[14] Female voters (over 30 years of age) obtained the vote in 1918, and in 1928 this was lowered to 21 (the same age as for men).[15] Multiple voting was only finally abolished by the Representation of the People Act in 1948. This covered additional votes for those who owned businesses in constituencies other than the one in which they resided, and the provision under which graduates could 'cast a second vote for one of the twelve university seats'.[16] The first general election in Britain run on formally democratic lines was that of 1950.

Despite its long history of electoral success, when Mrs Thatcher became leader of the Conservative Party (in February 1975) it 'had lost four out of the last five general elections and, in addition, had suffered embarrassing defeats by the National Union of Mineworkers in 1972 and 1974'. Mrs Thatcher turned this around. If President Reagan was the great communicator, she is probably best regarded as the great opportunist. Her 'statecraft' was unsurpassed and covered managing the party, developing a winning electoral strategy, constructing a winning rhetoric and hegemony, and making the electorate believe that the party is competent.[17] Education had its part to play in these processes. The political issue was not empirical questions about the actual outcome of educational policies, but how much political capital could be culled in key constituencies and areas from educational changes. Put crudely, this might mean that it would be worthwhile attacking teachers if this created or sustained political support in the core parts of the electorate. From this perspective, educational policy becomes partly a by-product of political decisions about how to keep a party in power.

A further element in the opportunism and statecraft of the leadership of the Conservative Party was its clear grasp of the characteristics of the electorate in British society. Given the history of the English educational system, it is likely to produce a largely politically illiterate electorate with little serious interest in or knowledge of politics. This will be reflected in how the popular press deals with political issues and it has implications for the successful management of news, electoral campaigns and political advertising, and the general use of the mass media in elections.

The success of the New Right crucially depended on this political dimension. Winning one election makes some things possible. Winning four almost makes it seem that anything is possible. As a result, the party developed what Lord Donoghue called a 'majority mentality' that put it, so it thought, beyond criticism and made it politically unassailable. This meant that interest groups and institutions which previously had seemed to be fireproof (such as HMI) could come within political range. As Gilmour shows, there was little effective opposition to the Thatcherite programme within the Conservative Party, and the Labour Party 'seemed in fast terminal decline and could only win if the government committed suicide (to which it often seemed prone)'.[18]

There are three aspects of the New Right's statecraft which are important for educational policy: the promotion of a governing class; high politics; and re-establishing the authority of the state. Historically, the Conservative Party's view of statecraft required a 'stable governing class' that has a strong resemblance to Plato's philosopher kings. The élite system of public schools and ancient universities provided a system of education which was ideally suited to producing, for each generation, a slightly modernized governing class. The idea of a governing class links in with the notion of 'high politics' which was developed when Lord Salisbury led the Conservatives in the period after the franchise was enlarged in 1884–5. Under high politics a 'tightly knit governing class . . . chooses to reserve certain matters for itself and attempts to exclude the participation of others'. The 'matters' which were to count as 'high politics' included foreign and imperial matters, while areas of 'low politics' were left to local authorities.[19] Under Mrs Thatcher, education moved from 'low politics' to 'high politics' and the same anti-democratic tradition of limiting democratic control and openness, which applied to foreign and imperial affairs, was applied to education. The quangos, set up during the 1980s and 1990s, contained people who were appointed by and answerable to the Secretary of State, and the institutional frameworks made absolutely no concessions to democracy even at a formal level. One obvious but important consequence of moving education from low politics to high politics was to eliminate any effective democratic mechanisms for resisting change.

The third aspect of the New Right's statecraft – re-establishing the authority of the state – involves reasserting Roger Scruton's view that authority comes from 'established power'.[20] For the New Right the power and authority of the state are threatened by enemies without and by enemies within. Given that the national culture both reflects the values of the Conservative Party and, in turn, is reflected in the values and myths promulgated by the Conservative Party, then statecraft which reasserts authority was likely to be popular. Such authority covers that of employers and managers over unions and workers; of vice-chancellors over students and academics; of headteachers and governors over teachers; of teachers over children and young people; of parents over children; of the police over yobs, louts and muggers; of traditional married couples over lone parents and others; of the indigenous 'English' (if you can identify them) over foreigners; and of 'the state' over interest groups and special pleaders of all sorts. Mrs Thatcher's success in this area was 'due to her ability to combine passion and vulgarity'. Her ultimate appeal is 'not to classes or interests but to widespread, secular, individualist, conservative moralising opinion . . . [A]s a result . . . she . . . tapped a layer of Toryism running through the whole nation'.[21]

These old aristocratic and pre-democratic techniques of statecraft – an established governing class, high politics and reasserting the power and authority of the state – are important for an understanding of the educational agenda and policies of the New Right. Schools are a crucial arena in which to reassert the traditional values of authority, hierarchy, established power, status and deference, against the dangerous modernisms of democracy, contestability, variety and respect for differences. The democratic counter-position to this tradition, precisely because it requires openness, deliberation, and 'a willingness to admit the existence of better options, to be aware that one's knowledge is always open to refutation or modification', represents the very opposite of the values, rhetoric and policies of Thatcherism.[22]

It is quite easy to exaggerate the success of the New Right's statecraft and the extent to which it actually reflected public opinion. Certainly, there was, in the New Right movement, an understanding of the peculiarities and complexities of the British electoral system which was conscious and explicit. Given that the New Right signalled the end of the old consensus politics, the new politics was to be about using conflict, confrontation and division to sustain enough electoral support in key areas of the country (mainly in the South of England) to support a Parliamentary majority. From 1979 to 1992 the Conservative Party never had majority electoral support. All that had to be done was to keep support running at around 43 per cent of the electorate in the key geographical areas.[23]

The 1992 election marked a significant change in the political support for the Conservative Party. Its majority fell from 102 to 21 and its share of the popular vote from 42.3 per cent to 41.9 per cent. The party had to get used to a much smaller Parliamentary majority after years of large majorities. Traditionally it is said that the party consists of two camps, 'the Christian Union and the Forty Thieves'; during the leadership campaign of November 1990 it was claimed that 'the Christian Union wanted its power back'.[24] The code words and phrases for this section of the party are 'caring', 'one nation' and, among the historically knowledgeable, 'Disraeli'. These changes, and new rhetorics, have had little discernible effect on educational policies in the 1990s.

Education and the Conservative Party

Educational policy after the Second World War was, as we have seen, formally non-partisan and consensual. The 1944 Act and the tripartite system were implemented with all-party agreement, and the universities were expanded in the 1960s, and polytechnics in the 1970s, with cross-party agreement. Conservative politicians such as Butler and Boyle were concerned about state education, and Boyle was even in favour of comprehensive schools.[25] Traditionally the party saw education as belonging to the area of low politics. Most mainstream Conservative politicians came from and identified with élite schools and universities, and were not knowledgeable about state schools and schooling. They generally used independent schools for their own children, and universities were seen as independent institutions which ought, for political reasons, to be kept at arm's length from government.

But some central figures in the New Right coalition did not come from this exclusive background and many of them had had nasty experiences while their children were at school. Baroness Cox, for example, had three children attending comprehensive schools in the early 1970s, and 'in English literature, the only work which was set for one of her sons for a whole year and a half a term was two essays on rock music with no reference whatsoever to English literary heritage'.[26] Professor Cox and Tony Dyson had both been students of F.R. Leavis at Cambridge and had dedicated their lives to 'presenting, teaching and celebrating great art'. Cox had witnessed the student revolt at the University of California at Berkeley in 1964 and came to see this breakdown of order as a threat to high culture and civilization. When he returned to Manchester his children went to a new purpose-built state school where there seemed to be no formal teaching and where they 'chose their own activities all day'. There was even an apocryphal story that the school had a piano which no one taught the children to play.[27]

Labour governments in the 1960s gave education a fairly low priority. As Donoghue puts it, 'no educational matter was on the agenda of Harold Wilson's Cabinet throughout our first year in government and in the following years it was still a rare occurrence'. As the 1970s developed, Labour became identified with the teacher unions (especially the NUT) as 'educational policy was conducted by the local authorities and the ... unions, with the DES, as Harold Wilson once commented to me, being little more than a post-box between the two'.[28] The political danger of these factors was that if a New Right offensive took off, the left, and the Labour Party in particular, might be identified with the sectional interests of the teachers and forced into defending an educational system which reflected the inequalities of the society which produced it, rather than extending and developing appropriate rhetoric, agenda and policies for the end of the twentieth century. Defending comprehensive schools, given their structural location within the system of education, was a politically risky thing to do if it was not combined with new radical ideas and policies. This would be especially difficult if it was believed that some teachers were using methods of teaching and organization which did not have the support of the parents and were apparently looking after their own interests rather than those of the children they taught.

One central aim of the New Right was to break down this consensus about educational policies. A symbolic target was Sir Edward Boyle, who had been Minister (and then Shadow Minister) in the 1960s. He was pragmatic and sceptical of ideology. According to the New Right, it was people like Boyle who had enabled the Labour Party to capture the 'ideological middle ground of politics by default'.[29] He resigned as Shadow Minister in 1969, and in 1970 Mrs Thatcher became Secretary of State for Education, after the general election in that year.

But the real change came when Mrs Thatcher was elected leader of the party in 1975: that event allowed the educational counter-revolution to be staged. It was during the years of opposition (1974–9) that the Conservative Party 'finally came to fashion a *Conservative* educational policy', and this meant 'taking a long, close look at what was actually happening in the nation's schools as opposed to placing trust in the version of events supplied by so-called 'education experts'.[30] As Robert Dunn (Parliamentary Undersecretary of State, 1983–8) said:

> For nearly forty years from the time of Butler the party had no real educational policy ... [U]p until about 1974 the Conservative Party in parliament did not have in it men with any real experience of the state education system. Boyson's arrival changed all that. From 1975 the Party

was at last able to begin to devise a positive educational policy of its own.

In matters of education the Conservatives tagged along behind the Liberals and Labour, and they appeared 'primarily as the party of the transient *status quo* and as the party of the public schools and older universities – in a word – privilege'.[31] It was the achievement of the New Right coalition to make the Conservative Party the champion of the intelligent and motivated child, and at the same time the apparent supporter of the non-academic 40 per cent of children who were a constant cause of *Angst* to Sir Keith Joseph. As he said, there were children 'unsuited to an academic curriculum' for whom education would be 'effective only if it directly prepared for life and for the world as the pupils themselves could be enabled to see it'. Such children were, for Keith Joseph, 'a very large minority'.[32]

With consummate political, media and rhetorical skills the New Right coalition began to 'restate and re-invent in the modern context in politically acceptable ways the ideas of selection, privilege and excellence. It is not just a return to old values but re-constructing the old values.' Selection

> in the past privileged relatively small groups ... Conservative policy now proposes several different types of selection ... [P]ositive selection will not now be limited to those near the apex of an educational pyramid, but will also involve a large middle sector ... [I]ts newness corresponds to other developing features of the economy, and of class and political relations, in Mrs Thatcher's Britain.[33]

This was a good example of statecraft and policy reinforcing each other because this new selection (or specialization) would, it was thought, appeal to potential Conservative voters.

The detailed story of how the New Right coalition moved from the periphery of educational policy-making to its centre is complex, and involves those whom Knight calls the 'preservationists' (who defend excellence, standards, quality and the grammar school ethos) gradually coming to occupy central positions in the main institutions of the Conservative Party.[34] These institutions included Central Office, the Research Department, Political Centre, Education Committee, and National Advisory Committee on Education. The key individuals included Dr Boyson, Professor Cox, Baroness Cox, Lord Griffiths, Anthony Dyson and Dr J. Marks. As a result of their increasing influence within the Conservative Party, the New Right was in a good position to influence policy when the party started to win general elections. Their work achieved a number of important results. They captured and annexed an educational vocabulary of 'best words'. These included excellence, quality, core subjects, traditional, discipline, standards, examinations, parents, freedom, market, choice, and local autonomy. These could be contrasted with 'bad' words such as equality, experts, expertise, educationalists, militant teachers, loony left councils, ill discipline, falling standards, progressive education, clutter on the curriculum, anti-racism, anti-sexism, local bureaucrats, political indoctrination and many more. The 'discourse of derision' often uses these 'best' and 'bad' words in a repetitive but politically effective manner.[35]

The New Right helped to construct a view that education, at all levels (but especially in schools and in teacher education), was in severe crisis. It did this by a careful selection of research findings and by continual reference to *cause célèbre* schools and cases. These included the Bennett study, William Tyndale School, the McGoldrich case and the Alexander Report. By a 'filleting' of evidence and careful use of unrepresentative schools, it followed the common characteristics and traditions of ideological thought.[36] Further, by means of rhetoric, evidence and story-telling it reconstructed a 'golden age' view of the past. In that golden age opportunities existed for the working classes (via grammar schools and especially the sixth form); educational standards were high because nearly everyone could read, write and do their sums; schools were centres of discipline and order; and teachers knew how to teach and keep order through whole-class formal pedagogy. Teachers declaimed from the front of the class and led the children forward to real learning. Headteachers (usually headmasters) were in charge and knew what was going on in the school. Subjects were proper subjects (such as Latin and physics) and assessment was done in the only way that really tests children – two- or three-hour examinations with pencil and paper. Selection, differentiation and streaming ensured that children were taught in a way which reflected their abilities: there was no nonsense about mixed-ability teaching. The New Right established the view that all new developments had to be judged and evaluated against this traditional golden age. If they did not measure up they were to be discounted. Through these techniques and processes it constructed an alternative view of the past to that presented by the 'educational establishment'.[37]

The New Right, through its techniques of persuasion and, by hard work and the imaginative use of language and the media, created a new, populist form of discourse based on pamphlets and the 'findings' of its think-tanks. This discourse was directed not at educational experts or teachers but at parents and voters. It also developed and exploited close links with the media, especially newspapers and television. This gave far greater coverage to its claims, assertions, fictions, myths and proposed policies.

During the 1980s and 1990s the Conservatives won power four times and faced the awkward question of what was to be done about education. The New Right was ready with ideas and proposals which could become policy almost overnight. What in the 1960s had seemed to be bizarre, poorly thought-out ideas, could suddenly be translated into policy. The tradition of major reports on aspects of education, followed by serious Parliamentary and public debate, and consultation with professionals, was about to be replaced by the instant 'solution' and the 'quick fix'.

Educational policy-making and the Conservative Party, 1979–93

The period from 1979 to 1993 was one which left consensus behind and was intentionally antagonistic towards the 'educational establishment'. Underlying the policies pursued, from the Education Act of 1979 to those of 1993, there is a clear vision of the good life and the good society that includes: the celebration of the free market against the domination of institutions by producers and professionals; a stress on traditional authority and values; opposition to teacher education and training; a dislike of any serious public debate about education; and a sophisticated, and not entirely unintentional, removal of centres of dissent and opposition and their replacement by quangos, appointees, *apparatchiks* and place-people responsible solely to the Secretary of State. Taken in isolation, a particular policy might look less than radical, but the overall momentum and collective consequences of the policy decisions of the period are a substantial, significant, and largely calculated attempt to shift education towards the ideology, beliefs and values of the New Right coalition and to reconstruct the traditional characteristics of the English educational system in their likeness.

According to Bowe and Ball, there are at least three arenas in educational policy formation. There is the 'context of influence' where 'public policy is normally initiated'. Particularly important here are the various think-tanks; official and unofficial advisers to politicians; and the individual civil servants in the Department for Education who work closely with ministers – the modern equivalents, as it were, of Kay-Shuttleworth and Morant. Then there is the 'context of policy text production'. This relates to the ideological and other commitments of the party in power. Examples would be Acts of Parliament (the 1988 Education Act) and official commentaries on these texts in print and the media. Finally, there is the context of practice. Here there is a further area for conflict, contestation and compromise in particular schools, educational institutions and local authorities.[38]

These characteristics of the policy process mean that it cannot be 'summed up by a "top-down" approach that takes central government's legislation and declarations of intent as *faits accomplis* on the ground'.[39] In practice, elaborate, complex policy changes in education will be redefined and amended as they are implemented in particular schools. Government agencies are not monolithic but contested terrains where networks and policy communities modify what the centre intended.[40] Government institutions themselves (such as the Department for Education) have their own agenda and 'bureaucratic dynamics'.[41] In the 1970s the Department of Education and Science had its own particular problems. It had no real role within education and had been heavily criticized by both the House of Commons Select Committee and the OECD, so the 'centralizing instincts' of the Department fitted in quite well with some of the aims and agenda of the New Right coalition. The desire for more control, order, efficiency, testing, planning, standards and centralized syllabus all dovetailed neatly with the Department's natural bureaucratic concern with national planning, administrative control, and empire building.[42] By infiltrating the Department of Education and Science and other state institutions, the New Right coalition was able to make radical and substantive changes to the environment in which education policy-making is conducted; to the allocation and distribution of resources; and to the discourses, rhetorics and agenda setting within which official and semi-official debate takes place.

The Conservatives' manifesto for the 1979 election had been modest, and

Peregrine Worsthorne said that the Tories must see themselves as 'the true conservers of social democracy'.[43] In the Conservatives' first term of office, there was 'little Cabinet discussion of general educational policy'.[44] But in the area of legislation there were two important Education Acts – one in 1979 and one in 1980. The 1979 Act repealed the 1976 Act which had attempted to abolish selection for secondary education and to make comprehensive secondary education national policy. This meant that those local authorities which had not reorganized on comprehensive lines could withdraw plans, and it opened up the option of 'a massive *reversion* to selective systems if and when this is thought to be politically (and socially) desirable'. During 1979 the government also decided against a common examination at 16, and implemented regulations which allowed local authorities to finance pupils to attend independent schools.[45]

The 1980 Act largely abolished the requirement on local authorities to provide free school milk and meals, and confirmed that education for the under-fives was discretionary. It gave parents more choice about the school they wanted their children to attend, and they were allowed to be represented on school governing bodies. The most important provision of the Act was to establish the assisted places scheme under which pupils from state primary schools could transfer to the independent sector and have all or part of their fees paid by the state. By 1987, when the scheme was fully operational, '26,897 pupils were holding assisted places, at a cost to the government of over £48 million'. As Dr Boyson put it, under the scheme 'able children from our poorest homes will once again have the opportunity of attending academically excellent schools'. The *Daily Telegraph*, in similar vein, had said in 1979 (when the scheme was under consideration) that it would establish 'a secure basis of academic excellence' against which state schools could be compared. The key justifications for the scheme included: a belief in the special qualities of grammar schools; that it would be a mechanism for widening parental choice; and that it would offer a meritocratic ladder for the able children of the poor. Edwards *et al.* take the view that the 'ideological roots' of the policy go back to the 'traditionally meritocratic arguments for a ladder of opportunity'. But, as they also point out, the scheme did embrace parental choice, and it emphasized the importance of academic selection, high academic standards, the traditional curriculum and pedagogy as bulwarks 'against any dilution of national culture and identity'.[46] The scheme, like the Acts that followed, derives its importance partly from its particular antecedents and characteristics and partly from the total context of social, economic and educational policy of which it was a small part. As Jones argues, although the numbers were small, the assisted places scheme was an important symbolic statement about where 'real' schools could be found. The scheme 'inaugurated a search for new forms of selection that could develop alternatives to the comprehensive system, without facing it in open and uncertain battle for the restoration of the grammar school'.[47] Alan Howarth, of the Conservative Research Department, took the view that the 1980 Act was 'one step along the road down which he wanted the government to travel to further strengthen parental rights'.[48]

In the early 1980s the debate about national testing of basics went to the

Assessment of Performance Unit where it ran into technical problems, and got lost in the 'core curriculum labyrinth' of professional manoeuvres.[49] The wider debate about the curriculum took place as a form of institutional conflict between the Department of Education and Science, HMI, the Schools Council and the Manpower Services Commission. The Secretary of State (Mark Carlisle) kept the 'rash promises to reform the schools curriculum' under control.[50] But from this time the Department of Education and Science began to 'use its central influence to co-ordinate local curriculum development'.[51]

In the autumn of 1981 Carlisle was replaced by Sir Keith Joseph. Joseph had been to Harrow School and Magdalen College, Oxford. Stuart Sexton became his special adviser. Dr Boyson was appointed Parliamentary Under-secretary of State (Schools). Oliver Letwin was responsible for education at the Conservative Research Department and was political adviser to Keith Joseph from 1982 to 1983.[52] Joseph had a deep commitment to, and interest in, education, and appreciated its moral, intellectual and political importance. His educational philosophy centred around notions of 'excellence', and he took the view that excellence depended on 'effective' education and the teaching of 'sound' knowledge. Such knowledge included the traditional basic subjects (English, mathematics and science) plus technology and business studies. It specifically excluded peace studies, sociology and politics, which were best left to élite universities. Such subjects, like *Lady Chatterley's Lover*, could do a lot of harm in the wrong hands.[53] In general he saw 'Britain as a country let down by its intelligentsia, which had shunned the disciplines of productivity and competition to cultivate softer areas of interest. Education was implicated in this long process of betrayal.'[54]

The key educational processes for Keith Joseph were differentiation and rigour in the school curriculum. He appreciated that the Conservatives must move away from the defence of narrow élite educational privilege and find new forms of selection, differentiation, quality and excellence which would appeal to their supporters. Between 1981 and 1983 Joseph launched a series of initiatives to achieve his objectives. These included: greatly increased centralized control over initial teacher training; discussions about an agreed national curriculum; reform of public examinations; and preparations to introduce pupil records of achievement.[55] In November 1982 the Technical and Vocational Educational Initiative (TVEI) was launched as a 'salutary shock to the established educational culture'.[56] This initiative, for the first time, gave resources to schools if they followed a centralist line. It also contained reformist and progressive elements, particularly with regard to pedagogy.

A key dimension on the political agenda was the removal of institutions and groups that acted as centres of dissent and critique, particularly those that were formally, at least, independent. In April 1982 Sir Keith moved against one of these – the Schools Council – when he announced that it would be disbanded. The Council had been established in 1964 and had become independent of the DES in 1970. It was 'conceived as a hopeful act of reconciliation between central and local government and teachers'. Mrs

Thatcher had described it as 'a lousy organisation', and in 1973, as Secretary of State for Education, when she was shown material from the Schools Council Humanities Project, her comment was: 'When I was a girl, I was taught to know the difference between right and wrong.'[57]

In 1981 an independent inquiry was set up into the work of the Council under Mrs Trenaman. Her report recommended that the Council continue in existence. But, as Dr Boyson commented, 'we must have some ritual blood-letting' and the Council was abolished. To fill the vacuum Sir Keith established the Secondary Examinations Council and the School Curriculum Development Committee (1983). Both were under far greater centralist control. The end of the Council was, also, the end of an important experiment in co-operation and pluralism.[58]

In the 1983 general election the Conservatives increased their majority from 43 to 144, and Labour's share of the popular vote fell from 37.0 per cent to 27.6 per cent. This landslide victory meant that both the government and the New Right coalition were able to advance on all fronts. The 1984 Education Act enabled the government to give limited funds to local authorities for 'specific innovations and improvements' which they wished to encourage. It was another sign that centralist control was moving from rhetoric to reality.[59] In teacher training more obvious signs of centralism could be detected. On 13 April 1984 Sir Keith Joseph established the Council for the Accreditation of Teacher Education (CATE) to 'advise the Secretaries of State for Education and Science . . . on the approval of initial training courses'. This meant that every initial training course had to have the indirect approval of a politician. In a government White Paper on *Teaching Quality* (1983), Sir Keith had sketched out the content such a course should have and the criteria that should be used to accredit it. One of them concerned 'ways in which pupils can be helped to acquire an understanding of the values of a free society and its economic and other foundations'. CATE itself laid down how students on initial teacher training courses were to be selected; what expertise and experience the staff should have who were to teach them; how the areas of educational and professional studies were to be related to each other; and how students were to be assessed.

The statutory apogee of Keith Joseph's reign were the two 1986 Education Acts. The first of these made important changes to the governing bodies of schools and increased parental representation. Governors had to make annual reports to parents; they had to decide about how 'sex education' was to be taught; and they had to prevent 'political indoctrination' in schools by forbidding 'the promotion of partisan political views in the teaching of any subject'. Jones describes this act as 'a carnival of reaction' and argues that it was 'the creation of the Tory backbenchers rather than the leadership; its accent was upon restraining at local level the work of progressive schools'.[60] The second Act introduced new forms of in-service training for teachers under the direct control of the secretary of state. Thus, the curriculum of teacher education for serving teachers, its style and organization, was beginning to be set in a way that a politician thinks best. This was a radical change from the old devolved and decentralized system.

A further important political event during this period was the teachers' dispute of 1984–6. In March 1984 the second dispute with the miners had started. The first, in 1981, had resulted in government defeat and compromise. This time preparations had been made, cost was not an issue, and the dispute ended in February 1985 in almost total defeat for the miners.[61] As one parents' leader said, having sorted out the miners the government would have the teachers for breakfast.[62] In reality, the teachers turned out to be quite a difficult problem. The action began in the summer term of 1984 with a work to rule and strikes in selected areas. The dispute continued throughout 1985 and into 1986, when the unions more or less reached an agreement with their local authority employers which conceded management control of conditions for quite substantial increases in pay.[63] It was, however, generally agreed that Sir Keith Joseph had 'lost the propaganda battle on the teacher dispute', and on 20 May 1986 he was replaced by Kenneth Baker. Baker moved quickly to gain the political advantage, announcing 'that he would not fund the deal and instead would introduce a Bill . . . allowing him to impose his own deal, removing from teachers the right, in future, to negotiate their salaries'.[64] The General Secretary of the National Union of Teachers called the action 'the longest dispute in the history of public education over salaries'. The dispute had all the 'usual after-effects of failure' on teacher morale and resulted in a loss of resilience to resist further government attacks. Teachers had done what they could and they had been defeated. They had seen the headteacher unions, and the non-TUC unions, who had not taken action, experiencing the 'sweetness of unchallenged power' and the 'salaried rewards of industrial inactivity'.[65]

In October 1986 Baker launched the City Technology Initiative. This was to be a new form of technical school for inner-city areas, largely funded by money from private industry. It was to provide a novel form of institutional segregation and differentiation. Such schools were to be independent of all local authority control, and their curriculum was to have a strong technological bias. In the first period of development there were to be 20 such schools. Baker also made moves towards a 'national curriculum' and suggested that if the Conservatives won the next election there would have to be major reform legislation to 'cure the malaise that had crept into the system'.[66]

The Conservatives did, indeed, win the 1987 election but their majority was reduced to 102 and their share of the popular vote fell from 42.4 per cent to 42.3 per cent. Johnson suggests that education was more significant in this election than it had been in 1979 or 1983.[67] The manifesto promised action on teachers' negotiating rights, and more educational reforms. The first significant educational Act of this period was The Teachers' Pay and Conditions Act of 1987. This abolished teachers' negotiating rights, established an 'Interim Advisory Committee' on pay and conditions, and gave the secretary of state power to impose pay and conditions on teachers. The professionals had been taught a significant lesson: that the government was in charge and that their agreement to policy and other changes was expected and required. The Act was the political quid pro quo from the Conservative government for the teachers' disruption and strikes.

As well as moves towards greater centralization and state control, the impact of the neo-liberal wing of the New Right – and particularly its belief in the virtues of the free market – was increasingly being felt, and various measures were introduced to 'deregulate' the educational system and increase parental choice. Chief among these were the various experiments to create an 'internal market' in education by introducing a 'voucher' scheme which would enable parents to act as 'consumers', shopping around in search of the 'best buy' for their children's education. Eventually the scheme was abandoned, not because it was regarded as flagrant violation of social justice, but because of the practical problems surrounding its implementation and because the legislation of the 1980s had introduced market principles into education in a less overt, and more politically acceptable, way.[68]

The central legislative development of this period was, undoubtedly, the 1988 Education Reform Act. It contained a vast range of proposals and was 'a major political success' that effectively brought together in a set of compromises the common ground that existed between the various factions and groupings in the New Right coalition. It represented the pinnacle of New Right thinking and revealed all the familiar tensions between its neo-liberal commitment to the free market and the privatization of public services.[69] The Act introduced 'local management of schools' (LMS) whereby a school's income would depend on the number of pupils it attracted and hence on the degree to which it satisfied its clients. It also devolved control of school budgets to governors and headteachers, so encouraging schools to operate as small businesses that had to be 'managed' and made 'effective' and 'efficient' in order to survive.

The Act also sought to increase 'choice' by encouraging the emergence of an 'alternative network' of schools.[70] These would attempt to create a quasi-independent system of state schools which would be in competition with ordinary comprehensive schools. This 'network' would consist of city technology colleges and the new category of grant-maintained schools which would be financed directly by central government and be free from local authority control. Once a school had achieved grant-maintained status the premises, land and contracts of employment of staff would pass to the governing body. The 'foundation' governors of such schools had to include 'members of the local business community' and representatives of the parents of children attending the school. Teachers appointed to such schools did not have to have a teaching qualification nor did the statutory probation arrangements for new teachers apply to them. The secretary of state has considerable discretion about the level and amount of grant awarded to such schools.[71]

The neo-liberal view of creating a 'market' in schooling was also followed in the Act's provisions for 'open enrolment', allowing parents a lot more choice about which schools their children attend. The view underpinning these proposals was that the skills, power, status, wealth and knowledge of those responsible for children should have a decisive influence on the schools that their children attend. Markets are about social and power relationships.[72] Children benefit from the market in housing in the same manner –

they live in dwellings that can be afforded by those responsible for them. In the same way, they can expect the sort of education that their parents can afford. The sub-text is that 'good' parents are those who send their children to 'good' schools, and that children should choose their parents with care. The assisted places scheme was also part of this process of creating an alternative vision and network of schools. Along with city technology colleges and grant-maintained schools they would become the 'gold standard' by which comprehensive schools could, should and would be judged. Markets reproduce the inequalities which consumers bring to them, and markets actively confirm and reinforce 'the pre-existing social order of wealth and privilege'. They are a 'crude mechanism of social selection'.[73] The Act intended and achieved the biggest 'redistribution of power and responsibility in education since 1944'. It aimed at placing the provision of education within a framework of 'market and consumer choice' and restricted 'professional and bureaucratic control over schooling by transferring much of it to parents and business interests whilst also emphasising a newly asserted control by government ministers'.[74]

If part of the 1988 Act was about deregulating the educational system in accordance with neo-liberal principles, another part of it was about giving expression to the neo-conservative allegiance to the restoration of state authority and the reassertion of traditional culture values. This was to be accomplished by introducing a statutory, complex, and highly bureaucratic 'national curriculum' which was to impose a system of testing and assessment, and under which detailed specifications would be laid down for the syllabuses to be followed. This national curriculum was not to be applied to independent schools, and this had the clear implication that, as such schools had been created by the 'market', they did not require detailed regulation.

The principle of a 'common' curriculum, which provided a shared educational experience for all pupils and so avoided the divisiveness and academicism of the traditional subject curriculum, had always been part of the democratic vision. But the purpose of the subject-dominated National Curriculum and national assessment system introduced by the Education Reform Act, was to signal a return to traditional educational values in pursuit of conservative political, cultural and economic goals. As conceived in the 1988 Act, the National Curriculum was to apply to all children between the ages of 5 and 16 in state-funded schools in England and Wales. It was to consist of three core subjects (English, mathematics and science) plus seven foundation subjects (technology, a modern foreign language, history, geography, art, music and physical education). The three core subjects were to take up most of the curricular time in primary schools, and a modern language was not to be taught in primary schools. Programmes of study and associated age-related attainment targets were to be set nationally for most of the ten subjects, although art, music and physical education would have to make do with guidelines. Pupils were to be tested nationally according to standard attainment targets at 7, 11, 14 and 16. The results of the tests were to be moderated externally, made public, and used as a basis for comparison between schools. Decisions about the National Curriculum, and its evolution, were firmly in the hands of the secretary of state.

The 1988 Act established a National Curriculum Council (NCC) with oversight of the curriculum as a whole, and the School Examinations and Assessment Council (SEAC). The elaborate mix of political and ideological control, bureaucratic structures, subject groups, assessment groups and special interest groups led to an overloaded, contradictory and test-led curriculum. The period of 'implementation' was characterized by a culture of almost permanent revision and amendment while the government and its advisers struggled to control the monster that they had created.[75] The original curriculum was quickly superseded by new, improved versions.

In terms of the continuing theme of the removal of centres of dissent and counterveiling power, the main achievement of the 1988 Act was to reduce substantially the power and influence of local education authorities and to put their future existence in doubt. The provisions which were intended to create a market in education for schooling made planning impossible and the intention of the new arrangements about governors moved power away from local education authorities. As Johnson suggests the consequences of the 'erosion of Local Education Authority competence is to reduce local power overall, especially as a counterbalance to the centre'.[76] In addition to the changes at school level, the Act removed polytechnics and other higher education colleges from local control, making them 'free-standing statutory corporations' whose governors were to consist of people experienced in industry, business, commerce and the professions.[77] The power of local authorities was further reduced by the 1991 Further and Higher Education Act, which removed all sixth-form colleges and colleges of further education, from local authority control. They were placed under the control of the Further Education Funding Council.

The Conservatives won the 1992 election, but their majority was reduced from 102 to 21. In education, a new secretary of state, John Patten was appointed, and a new name created for the Department of Education and Science – the Department for Education. The Prime Minister at the 1992 Conservative Party conference said that the government wanted 'high standards, sound learning, diversity and choice in all our schools'. He said that if local authorities could not provide good schools in inner cities then 'we will give the job to others'. He went on:

> Yes, it will mean another colossal row with the educational establishment. I look forward to that. It's a row worth having. A row where we will have the vast majority of parents and the vast majority of good, committed teachers squarely on our side.[78]

In 1992 a White Paper called *Choice and Diversity: A New Framework for Schools* was published. It was said that most of it was written by the Secretary of State personally. Under its main provisions NCC and SEAC were to merge into the School Curriculum and Assessment Authority (SCAA), which was to have 15 members, a chairman and a chief executive. All would, either directly or indirectly, be appointed by the Secretary of State. Its role would be to keep 'the curriculum under review', and ensure that 'it maintains its relevance and vitality as a force for raising expectations and standards, with the closely related task of seeing rigour, simplicity and clarity in National Curriculum testing and examination arrangements'.[79] As the Secretary of State said, 'selection will not be an issue for the 1990s, 'the "s" word for socialists to come to terms with is, rather, specialisation'.[80] Schools would be able to specialize in one or more subjects, and there would be a new network of 'technology schools' which would have specialist facilities. There would, in addition, be 'technology colleges' which would involve business sponsorship and public funding. Voluntary-aided schools, via grant-maintained status, would be able to evolve into these new institutions.[81]

The White Paper also proposed a Funding Agency for Schools (FAS). This government quango will take over responsibility for funding grant-maintained schools, and for deciding (with local authorities) the availability of school places. When 10 per cent of school places in an area are provided by grant-maintained schools, FAS will share responsibility with the local authority. When more than 75 per cent of places are provided by grant-maintained schools, the local authority loses its responsibility to provide places. The agency, therefore, takes over from the Department for Education for funding recurrent and capital grants to grant-maintained schools. As Chitty and Mitchell put it, the government is looking forward 'eagerly to the abolition of all LEAs and is willing to legislate for costly and cumbersome administrative arrangement to fill the resulting vacuum'. The aim seems to be 'to destabilise, to disrupt and finally to abolish local education authorities'.[82]

The 'agency' concept raises a whole series of constitutional issues about who is responsible for schooling in a democratic society. Since 1988 around 300 new powers have been taken over by the secretary of state, but it is unclear to what extent the government will be willing to answer Parliamentary questions about schools. The question arises who, in other words, now runs the nation's schools.[83] Where schools are, in the government's opinion, 'failing' they will be taken over by an 'educational association' which will provide new management. This will be a 'small and cohesive body consisting of a chairman and typically some five other part-time members appointed by the Secretary of State'. It will be expected to provide the 'essential leadership and management that has previously been lacking at the school'.[84] The White Paper considers that the role and importance of LEAs are likely to decline, and that some local authorities 'may soon be in sight of no longer needing education committees'. The transition to grant-maintained status will be 'eased' by simplifying the tasks governing bodies have to undertake when deciding whether or not to ballot parents.

The White Paper stresses the importance of 'the nation's Christian heritage and traditions in the context of both the religious education and collective worship provided in schools'. It says that '[e]ducation cannot and must not be value-free' and that at

> the heart of every school's educational and pastoral policy and practice should lie a set of shared values which are promoted through the

curriculum, through expectations governing the behaviour of pupils and staff . . . Every attempt should be made to ensure that these values are endorsed by parents and the local community.

Finally, the White Paper suggests that 'it is sometimes hard to pin down what exactly makes people point at a place and say "that's a good school" '. But the paper asserts that the following are critical: parental involvement in the school; freedom from 'excessive control and regulation'; and finally, 'teachers of high quality under the strong leadership of the head teacher'. A key factor in all this is 'good management'. It is not made explicit how these aims are to be achieved or how successful the government's own policies have been in 'avoiding excessive control and regulation' in the day-to-day running of schools.

The White Paper, therefore, promises more specialization, differentiation and selection, and will ensure that educational provision and resources 'mirror' the power and resources of parents. These changes, far from adding new resources to the education budget,

> should yield significant increases in value for money over the years ahead . . . Overall, once the implementation of the Government's pro- posals is complete, the government looks to secure significantly greater value for money and improvements in quality from the substantial re- sources already devoted to schools.[85]

As in the nineteenth century, these reforms promise a cheap and efficient state system of schooling, under centralized surveillance, which will deliver new generations of what Baroness Blatch (Minister of State) called 'compe- tent, wholesome young people'[86] who will be able to make the transition to whatever work is available (or, for an increasing minority, to no work) with- out difficulty or trauma, who know 'right' from 'wrong', who have a healthy respect for authority, and who are able to speak and write 'proper' English.

In 1992 a further change was introduced by the Education (Schools) Act which created a new Office for Standards in Education (OFSTED) and sub- stantially reduced the role of Her Majesty's Inspectorate. The Inspectorate had been established in 1839 and had built up a reputation for knowledge and independence. In recent years it had published reports and papers which drew attention to a whole series of difficult questions about education and its resourcing. It was part of the state, but not under the complete control of the secretary of state. In *Whose Schools?*, the Hillgate Group stated that 'the time has come to define the procedures, criterion and accountability of the Inspectors, who are as likely as any other section of the educational establishment to be subverted by bureaucratic self-interest and fashionable ideology'.[87]

In 1985 there were 500 HMIs, and the 1992 Act reduced this figure to 175. Under the Act every school has to be inspected every four years by an OFSTED 'team', one member of which has to have business or financial experience and one has to have no specific experience of education.[88] The ori- ginal idea was that individual schools would 'choose' their own inspection team. But this proposal was defeated in the House of Lords, and it was agreed that teams for specific schools would be selected by the chief inspector. This represented a further reduction in the status and influence of LEAs and a move towards shorter, quicker and simpler views about inspection which could play a part in the 'marketing' of schools, enabling the 'winners' (with good reports) to increase market share and the 'losers' (with bad reports) to decline and possibly close.

In teacher education the next major development was *The Government's Proposals for the Reform of Initial Teacher Training*. This document proposed a Teacher Training Agency to fund teacher training and research 'relevant to the other funding activities' of the agency. The agency is to determine the distribution of places between courses and, between school-based and higher education-based routes, to teacher training. It will administer grants for licensed teacher and related schemes. The aim of the agency is to 'ensure high quality without unnecessary bureaucracy'. The press release announcing the establishment of the new agency stated that Professor O'Hear and Baroness Cox would both be members of it, and, that the chairman would be Geoffrey Parker, a retired high master of Manchester Grammar School.[89] Further, the paper asserts that teacher training, like all training, has to 'be closely linked to . . . practical application' and that 'the best way to learn classroom skills . . . is by observing and working with teachers'. It stresses that 'teachers must have the key classroom skills necessary to maintain discipline' and that courses have to develop competence to enable new teachers 'to manage, maintain order and teach effectively in their classrooms'.[90] A previous secretary of state (Kenneth Clarke) had put the same point clearly at the North of England Education Conference in 1992:

> The college based parts of training must be fully relevant to classroom practice. The acid test must be whether or not the models they offer can actually be made to work effectively by the average teacher in the real classroom. That is the way to break the hold of the dogmas about teaching method and classroom organisation which are now being challenged not only by me but by very many other people.[91]

These views and policy imperatives echo those of Professor O'Hear in his 1988 pamphlet, *Who Teaches the Teachers?*, in which he suggests that the best way to learn about teaching is through an apprenticeship model and that the 'induction and assessment of trainee teachers . . . [is] better left in the hands of teachers who are actually practising as teachers'. This is to be preferred to leaving training to 'outsiders whose primary concerns may be theoretical and even ideological rather than the practical running of a particular school'. O'Hear suggests that if this does not happen there is a danger of educational studies laying

> a disproportionate emphasis on questions of race and inequality, an emphasis which is surely unhealthy in its implicit assumption that education is to be seen in terms of its potential for social engineering, rather than as the initiation of pupils into proven and worthwhile forms of knowledge.[92]

An aim which is, presumably, neither theoretical nor ideological.

Democracy and the New Right: the National Curriculum as a case study in non-democratic politics

Democracy has no great appeal to many New Right thinkers. As Scruton argues, 'it should not be thought that the cost of a system which makes an idol of ignorance and a prophet of the crowd is small'.[93] Where democracy does appeal to the New Right, it is likely to be in the élitist form. Sir Keith Joseph is said, on his arrival at the DES, to have given his civil servants a copy of Schumpeter's *Capitalism, Socialism, and Democracy* to read.[94] In this, Schumpeter outlines the conception of democracy most consonant with capitalist economies: a conception that gives little importance to sustained public discussion or serious consultation; to the development of a democratic culture, institutions or processes; or to the emergence of a democratic system of schooling appropriate for a society which celebrates variety and diversity and places emphasis on respect rather than deference.

The National Curriculum provides a useful case study of the élitist conception of democracy. Like the 1988 Act of which it was a part, it was introduced without serious public consultation and implemented with the political muscle provided by a large Parliamentary majority. There was no public inquiry or Royal Commission, no cross-party agreement, no discussions with teachers or professionals, no time for deliberation or debate. The press release issued with the initial consultation document stated that 'this historic reform represents the culmination of over 10 years of debate which has resulted in general agreement about the aims of school education and widespread support for the idea of a National Curriculum'. The implication of this was that further debate was not required, and it is unsurprising that the period for consultation (from July to September 1987) coincided with the school holidays. Nor is it surprising that when the Education Reform Act was published on 20 November 1987, the 20,000 responses to the various consolation papers had virtually no effect on the original proposals.[95] The National Curriculum was an effective operation in statecraft and political manipulation rather than a serious attempt to develop a well-founded view about a curriculum appropriate for a modern democratic society.

The National Curriculum has all the characteristics of a utopian blueprint where openness, flexibility, variety and consensus are replaced by directions from the centre and a lack of explicit discussion of rationale and practice. Questions which should have been discussed – questions, for example, about why a compulsory curriculum was necessary and why this particular curriculum should be adopted – were largely ignored and the 1988 Act remains the only major education Act which offers no statement of its philosophy or its underlying ideals. Although the 'consultation' document that preceded the National Curriculum promised 'a curriculum which will develop the potential of all pupils and equip them for the responsibilities of citizenship and for the challenges of employment in tomorrow's world', it conspicuously failed to give any indication of what the responsibilities of citizenship are, or how the challenges of employment are to be understood.[96] Similarly, the official aims of the National Curriculum are: 'to promote the spiritual, moral, cultural, mental and physical development of pupils at school and of society; and to prepare such pupils for the opportunities, responsibilities and experiences of adult life'.[97] But neither in the Act nor in the supporting documents from the Department of Education and Science is there a coherent statement about how these principles are to be translated into practice or how this particular curriculum furthers these principles. There are no indications of the kind of society for which pupils are to be prepared, or of the 'social responsibilities' they need to acquire. Nothing is said about why these statutory and binding provisions should not apply to children in independent schools.

The 1988 Act also fails to provide any explanation of why the specific subjects included in the National Curriculum, and the system of assessment it introduced, will achieve these educational aims, and there is more than a suspicion that its content and organization were determined by a selective pillaging of the past. For a start, the central place given to testing reflects concerns seen in the Revised Code of 1862 and its system of payment by results. There is, too, a strong similarity between the subjects listed in the 1904 Board of Education Regulations and those of the National Curriculum, and an even closer similarity to a list of subjects from 1935. In general, the shape and content of the National Curriculum amount to a restoration of the old grammar school subject curriculum; as such, it is a distinctively secondary school curriculum which has no regard to the very different curriculum and pedagogic traditions of primary schools.[98] This curriculum, with its origins in the nineteenth-century public school system, was only intended for a small minority of the population. It was extended to the middle classes in order to license their entry into a decreasingly oligarchic system of government and so enable them, in addition to the aristocracy, to be fitted for leadership in that élite Platonic form of democracy where representatives exercise best judgement.[99]

In the National Curriculum the tension between the political and economic role of education is resolved on the side of the economy. In its dual aim of preparation for life in a democratic society and preparation for work, the National Curriculum clearly privileges the roles of producer, consumer and worker over that of democratic citizen. 'Citizenship' is reduced to the status of a 'cross-curricular theme' and the National Curriculum Council's 'guidance' on how it is to be taught largely reflects the New Right's depoliticized and individualist view of citizenship as referring to the rights and responsibilities of persons acting in a private rather than a public capacity. How little weight the notion of democratic citizenship carries in the National Curriculum can be readily seen by contrasting it with that kind of 'education for citizenship' which a more participatory democracy would require.[100]

The institution established to 'deliver' the National Curriculum, SCAA, which resulted from the forced merger of the NCC and SEAC, is self-evidently non-democratic. It is directly under the control of the secretary of state, and it brings together bureaucrats (who carry out broad orders of the government), technicians (who construct and reconstruct the tests and related instruments) and public relations people (who ensure that the story is told as well as possible). This lethal cocktail of technicians, bureaucrats, politicians and public relations personnel ensures that serious issues about education remain off the political agenda. The traditional view of policy-making whereby a major change is debated, questioned and discussed both in Parliament and outside, is replaced by an attempt to portray all educational issues as technical issues and to reduce consultation to a public relations exercise.

Another crucial feature of the National Curriculum which betrays its anti-democratic origins and characteristics is that its rhetorical claim to offer all children a similar curriculum – 'entitlement' and 'empowerment' in the official language – does not take seriously the fragmented and diverse nature of English society and culture. Class, gender, ethnicity, religion, geography and many other factors create a society where interests, attitudes, values and aspirations are diverse. To select a subject-based traditional curriculum and to argue that it is appropriate to everyone is bound to disadvantage those children and young people who do not share its explicit and implicit cultural assumptions. Such a curriculum makes it more difficult for teachers to take seriously the cultural and other differences of those they teach. The complex process of both understanding and valuing the educational significance of students' culture, and the advantages of wider cultural repertoires, is unlikely to be achieved by a 'National' Curriculum which, while claiming relevance to all, 'neglects the specific conditions' of students' lives 'and the interests which motivate or impede their learning.[101] Furthermore, while the rhetoric of the National Curriculum speaks about a 'common curriculum for all children', the curriculum, in practice, contains lots of separate routes, and special papers, in the classical English tradition. What, to the superficial observer, looks like communality turns out to be subtle differentiation.

There is ample evidence that the government took the view that teachers, far from being part of the solution to educational problems, were rather part of the problem. The top-down, utopian nature of the early forms of the National Curriculum is full of examples of this. It was an educational experiment but the politicians responsible for creating it were not open-minded about the serious problems which emerged from it for children, teachers and parents. Teachers

> found in the case of assessment and testing guidance from SEAC . . . that what was proposed could not be made to work in . . . normal classroom settings. Yet it took four years before the full extent of the difficulties facing teachers . . . was formally acknowledged.[102]

The final characteristic of the National Curriculum which demonstrates the impoverished view of democracy it represents, relates to issues of ownership and control. These are important issues because once educational institutions are controlled by a particular group, that group can decide whose narratives and stories (curriculum content) are told in them, how they are told (pedagogy), and what processes should be used to see how well they have been told (assessment). Control of narratives, pedagogy and assessment is crucial because they have a central role in the reproduction of knowledge, skills and consciousness. They embody views about what knowledge is worth passing on, and about how such knowledge should be distributed among citizens. They have, accordingly, a function in legitimating views of the good life, of individuals' interests, and of individual differences.

The official government rhetoric about ownership and control is one of moving power from the centre to the periphery (to parents, governing bodies, and so on) but in reality, power has flowed away from children, professionals and LEAs to bureaucrats, technicians and politicians. This is reflected in the framework in which schools are increasingly seen. For example, the consultative document on the National Curriculum talks of the 'customers' of education and of 'consumers'.[103] The general discourse is in terms of input/output, targets and products. What are taken to be prevalent modes of industrial and bureaucratic organization are taken, uncontentiously, to set the tone for all educational institutions as well.

In any adequately institutionalized democracy there would be a public arena, with institutional space and resources, for discussion about the purposes, content and organization of education. In the 1970s the debate about education was largely between professionals, and in the 1980s it was between politicians, bureaucrats and employers. By the 1990s, professionals had been marginalized. This is also true of parents, in spite of the government's rhetoric for 'moving to the rim of the wheel'. The role of parents is to ensure that schools adhere to the requirement of the National Curriculum. Unless they can send their children to a private school of their choice, they have no say in the curriculum to which their children are taught and they have no way of placing their children in schools unencumbered by a test-laden competitive ethos. The conceptions of education parents might wish to inform the practices of the schools their children attend are given no weight.[104] As Ranson argues, the task is to 'rediscover local democracy' and re-establish education as a 'public good' in which all citizens have a legitimate interest. This requires 'wide public agreement' which 'will legitimate authority because it is grounded in the consent of the public'. It presupposes 'public participation and mutual accountability'.[105]

If democracy is to be taken seriously, then schools need to be subject to the local democratic control of all those who have an interest in them. As J.S. Mill put it:

> A democratic constitution, not supported by democratic institutions in detail but confined to central government, not only is not political freedom, but often creates a spirit precisely the reverse, carrying down to the lowest grade in society the desire and ambition of political domination.[106]

Such local democracy focused on schools, and the open democratic debate about schooling that goes with it, would have important implications for curricular aims and content, for styles of pedagogy, for school organization, and for modes of teacher accountability and professionalization.

Conclusion: the English educational system after the New Right offensive

By the mid-1990s the New Right coalition has had a decisive influence on the agenda, rhetoric, policy and practice of education. Central government has taken over control of the curriculum, teacher education and resource allocation. The secretary of state has unrivalled powers to appoint place-people and sympathizers to a vast range of quangos, non-democratic organizations and structures. Local authorities, and the embryonic local democracy which went with them, seem to be in terminal decline. Independent and semi-independent bodies such as the School Council, HMI, researchers, advisers and teacher educators had either been abolished or emasculated. Class teachers, and their unions, have been defeated and have been warned that they are no longer to be regarded as a major influence on policy formation.

The New Right coalition has established moral, political and intellectual leadership, and it has been able to get sufficient support for its sectional interests for them to be seen as the interests of society as a whole. But such settlements are always fragile, and continually being challenged by the realities of social, economic, political, moral and intellectual change. Settlements can never be taken for granted, which is why there is always a 'struggle' both at the national level and within institutions. But, equally importantly, the New Right's political project has undoubtedly been successful. Through state-craft it has won and maintained power. But, like its intellectual pre-eminence, its political dominance could suddenly evaporate if the Conservative Party lost its ability to retain the support of key constituencies within the wider electorate.

One of the main reasons why the New Right has been able to establish overall dominance in education is that it has been able to reconfirm, and subtly redefine, characteristics that are the essential core of the 'peculiar and special' traditions, practices, structures and institutions which make up the English education system.[107] In some areas the traditional rhetoric has changed but, overall, the nineteenth-century values and exclusion techniques have been resurrected and resuscitated. The old ghosts and gremlins of the exclusive and excluding aristocratic tradition have come back to haunt the embryonic democratic vision and modernizing aspirations.

The first of these characteristics – the lack of a coherent education system – has been reconfirmed. There is no developed education *system* but simply more 'add-on tracks', many of which echo the old mechanisms of exclusion. There is still underdeveloped provision for nursery and pre-school education which remains largely in the private sector. Voluntarism, along with a minimal role for the state, is still celebrated, particularly in the new élite tracks created by grant-maintained schools which have 'opted out' of local control and responsibility; in the City technology colleges which, for a small minority, offer a new 'ladder' out of the inner city; in the assisted places scheme; and in the considerable changes in higher and further education which give control to non-elected governors and worthies rather than local communities. As in the nineteenth century, the emphasis is on voluntarism, diversity and *laissez-faire*, all of which enable educational institutions to continue to magnify, legitimate and confirm cultural and economic inequalities. An apparently modernizing development, such as the National Curriculum, which put issues about what children should be taught on the wider agenda, is being implemented in such a way as to limit its democratic potential. Thus, the National Curriculum was enforced and imposed rather than agreed, and it made non-controversial the perennial and highly contested political and moral questions about what children should be taught, how they should be taught, and how they should be assessed. It excluded from its control the entire non-state system of education and established within its huge elaborateness all sorts of subtle and novel tracks and routes which effectively excluded some children from the full range of provision. In addition, the entire issue of how local communities and particular schools can relate to and develop dialogue with each other was not even on the agenda.

The second characteristic – a centralist surveillance of standards – has received a significant boost from the elaborate system of testing introduced by the National Curriculum. Even though the early bureaucratic nightmare has been modified, testing remains an important mechanism for allowing comparisons between schools and for 'league tables' to be constructed that reflect economic, social and other privileges. Like the Revised Codes of the nineteenth century, and the eleven-plus examination of the mid-twentieth century, such a system will reduce 'education' to what can be measured and quantified in league tables. The 'product' of schools will quickly be seen to be that which league tables measure, and that will focus the activities of schools on these 'measurable' factors. The most exclusive, and excluding, schools will achieve the highest scores, and this will reinforce the view that they are the 'real' schools, the true inheritors of the English educational tradition.

The third characteristic of the system – an emphasis on the 'political' curriculum and community and religious values – has been confirmed at all levels. 'Core', 'basic' and 'traditional' values are now continually seen as central to education. As Woodard put it in 1871, '[e]ducation without religion is, in itself, a pure evil'; and as the government put it in 1992,

> proper regard should continue to be paid to the nation's Christian heritage . . . At the heart of every school's education and pastoral policy and practice should lie a set of shared values . . . religious education and collective worship play a major part in promoting the spiritual and moral dimension in schools.[108]

The White Paper does not, of course, say whose religious values should be celebrated nor how these aims relate to a complex, multicultural, secular, urban society undergoing massive change at the end of the twentieth century. Religious schools, particularly in the secondary area, allow subtle and complex forms of social selection to continue under the rhetoric both of parental choice and of religious freedom.

The English system retains its fourth characteristic by remaining a largely sponsored one. The new routes and institutions of secondary education are mirrored in higher education, where the linguistic device of transforming polytechnics into universities does not significantly alter the way in which privilege, status and power continue to be distributed in traditional ways. The modernizing moves towards 'research selectivity' in universities put on the public agenda criteria and evidence about quality, but mask historical and other issues concerning resources. They also establish league tables for universities. In the same way that grammar schools opened up access for some children, so do the changes to higher education. But the choice of institution, type of course, and other factors remain subtle mechanisms of sponsorship. Indeed, with high youth unemployment, some parts of higher education are now not dissimilar from the 'schemes' provided for those who leave school at 16. These mechanisms of exclusion in state schools begin to operate, under the National Curriculum, at 7 and continue through to 16. The definition of 'talent' and 'absolute standards', central to a sponsored system, will become identified with the test results of the National Curriculum. The 'gold standard' will remain the achievements of élite universities and élite schools. The new super-A grade (at GCSE) becomes a useful way of differentiating 'super talent'.

The fifth characteristic – grading, sorting, differentiating and classifying children – has been increased at all levels. The traditional concern of English educational institutions – not only what sort of children attend but also, and more importantly, who is excluded – apply to many of the new initiatives: the assisted places scheme, grant-maintained schools, and city technology colleges and schools. This issue was expressed starkly when administrators of the Conservative flagship local authority, Wandsworth (in London), were talking about 'magnet schools':

> Schools . . . could eventually fall into three groups. First, the élite high-performing schools: CTCs, opted-out schools and local authority magnet schools . . . ; then a larger group of 'run-of-the-mill' institutions delivering the standard National Curriculum; and finally, the deprived 'sink' schools, mostly in the inner cities, with large numbers of pupils who speak English as a second language.[109]

At all levels of education – pre-school, primary, secondary and university – institutional, curricular and assessment changes in policy have created novel ways to label and differentiate children and young people from each other, for example GNVQs and GCSEs. Opportunity and choice for an increasing minority of children, mean deprivation and exclusion for the rest. Like the eleven-plus selection procedure, the 'success' of the few is bought at the price of the 'failure' of the many. Education, on this model, becomes more like housing, under which the 'market' allows those with power, status and wealth to 'purchase' what they can afford. For the neo-conservative

element of the New Right coalition this characteristic has a particular resonance. This element would like an educational system which is controlled,
predictable, structured, hierarchical and ordered, rather than one based on
the 'Pandora's box of progressive education': a system that stands for openness, is uncertain and unpredictable, puts an emphasis on respect for difference and variety rather than deference, is difficult to control, and is sceptical
about notions of absolute standards.

Examinations, testing and differentiating are also essential for the New
Right because they 'are the cement which bind[s] educational structures
together giving them strength, cohesion and direction'. They can be easily
linked to classroom organization, pedagogy and discipline, so as to reinforce
'formal traditional teaching'.[110] A further advantage of examinations is that
they give individuals labels which indicate social worth, and they quantify
the educational 'value added' that individuals have acquired. This is seen
most clearly in the selection processes for universities, where A-level passes
are converted into points which can then be traded to 'buy' places in the
market. Such labels are, of course, 'hopelessly inadequate to convey the load
of meaning ... we ... believe we are putting into them and which other
people desperately try to get out from them again'.[111] But by simplifying
complex debates about educational standards into scores, grades and classi-
fications, it is possible to control, limit and define the parameters of the
debate.

The sixth characteristic – the central role of élite institutions, particularly
public schools and the ancient universities – has been reinforced and confirmed. Not only are the existence, consequence and implications of such
institutions for a developing democratic culture no longer on the public
agenda, but such institutions have, since 1979, been re-established as the
'gold standard' by which other institutions will be judged and to which they
should aspire. The National Curriculum does not apply to élite schools because they themselves both define and represent quality. As Salter and Tapper have shown in their study, independent schools

> have been given authority and legitimacy by an ideology which sees
> them as models to be followed both in terms of the quality of the
> education they provide and the way in which they provide it through
> their responsibilities to consumer, i.e. parental, demand.[112]

They have, throughout the twentieth century, fought a subtle, careful and
sophisticated campaign to align themselves with aspects of the forces of
modernization so as to be seen to have moved with the times. At the end
of the twentieth century they appear to be impenetrable to democratic demands, insulated from public debate and unwanted state interference, and
are still the ultimate model of what a school should be like. They are surrounded, on their pinnacle of quality, by a sea of legal, ideological and
economic protection which puts them, literally, in another land. Richard
Nixon used to say, when reviewing a policy initiative: 'That's OK, but will
it play in Peoria?.'[113] The litmus test for any proposed educational reform in

England is still how it will play in Oxford and Cambridge, Eton, Manchester Grammar School and Charterhouse.

The seventh characteristic – that of the great head – has likewise been celebrated and reconfirmed as central to the English tradition. In the nineteenth century the Arnolds had suggested that submission to the authority of the head was essential for pupils, and that heads had to establish obedience, authority and order. Echoing this tradition the government, *Choice and Diversity* said that 'central to a good school is strong leadership and deep parental involvement'.[114] The significance of headteachers, their salaries, status, training and power, can be seen in many official publications and policies since 1979, so confirming the traditional authority role of heads and their importance in the ideal school. This move towards autocratic, top-down leadership is to be found throughout further and higher education as power moves to senior management teams, with no elected representatives to control them. The political aim was to get the internal organization of educational institutions to mirror how the educational system itself ought to be run. A further important change, brought in by the legislation of the 1980s and 1990s, has been to move some power back to its nineteenth-century location: school governing bodies. These are to be made up of reliable, honest, hard-working people who will rescue schools from 'producer capture'. Headteachers have had to 'negotiate for themselves a new relationship with school governors as school leaders', rather than as 'curriculum or pedagogic' innovators. The head, under the new ideological dispensation, is seen as 'chief executive and managing director', and the aim is to 'achieve the maximum value-added product which keeps a school as near to the top of the league table of success as possible'. They are expected to 'market the school', to 'deliver the curriculum' and to 'satisfy the consumers'. The traditional democratic values of and commitments to community, collegiality, social justice and the public good (in so far as they existed) are being lost. These heads who can 'manage' their school governors will be able to 'retain a lot of operative leadership in their own hands'. This will also depend upon the social and political capabilities of the governing body. The 'imperatives of authoritative leadership, prescribed curriculum, [and] traditional moral values' contradict and remain in conflict with democratic aspirations and values.[115] Governors, of course, might also form alliances with teachers and become part of a political demand for more resources for education.

The ideology of 'managerialism' has had a considerable impact on the role of headteachers, governing bodies, and on the development of 'senior management teams'. A definite feature of such an ideology is to see others not as autonomous moral agents but as 'subjects' to be manipulated and 'managed'. The discourse of managerialism is 'an imperialist discourse . . . [which] marginalizes the problems, concerns, difficulties, and fears of "the subject" – the managed'. It is *'par excellence* what Foucault calls a "moral technology" or a "technology of power"' and, as such, 'is a modern, all-purpose equivalent of Bentham's panopticon'.[116] It works through surveillance, and 'the personal file and the personnel manager are key mechanisms in the moral technology of management'. Individuals are monitored via such processes as appraisal and promotion, and schools by 'school effectiveness research' and performance indicators. Managerialism attempts to take political and moral issues out of organizational discourses and to recast them in the neutral language of science, technology and bureaucracy. Managerialism, then, makes it difficult, if not impossible to raise moral and political issues about how schools should be run, and makes it almost impossible to provide a framework and an organizational structure *within* schools which will allow such questions to be pursued. Schools run on hierarchical and authoritarian lines with a 'great head' in charge are clearly not a social environment in which a democratic culture can flourish. If Britain is to move towards a fully democratic society then managerialism will have to join child labour, child prostitution and elementary schooling as a past way of living suitable only for the museums of nostalgia which are now increasingly to be found in the post-industrial areas of Britain.

The final characteristic of the English system – the low status accorded to teachers and their education – has also been confirmed by recent policy and practices. The 1987 Teachers' Pay and Conditions Act removed teachers' negotiating rights. Teachers are no longer consulted about educational policies, and 'teacher education' is once again called 'teacher training' and relocated from the mainstream of higher education into schools. The long march to improve the education, status, pay, conditions and social position of teachers has undergone a severe setback.

Thus, the traditional pre-democratic characteristics of the English education system have been redefined and re-established as a way of undermining the moves towards modernization and democratization. Conservative governments have altered the general discourse about education so that it reflects their vocabularies, concerns, claims and aspirations. Through Acts of Parliament they have changed the entire institutional framework within which education takes place and they have altered, in radical ways, the consensus about education which they inherited. They have ensured that the social and political role of education has been shifted towards creating the sort of society in which they believe. Through a combination of managerialism, centralization and bureaucracy they have asserted the neo-conservative view of society by strengthening the authority of the state. Through devolution, opting out and market forces they have also reasserted the neo-liberal view of the importance of the minimal state. Finally, they have moved the debate about education from its traditional, albeit rather weak democratic public forums, and replaced deliberation, evidence, argument and contestation with ideological assertion and unexamined political prejudice. Whatever their failings, the great nineteenth- and twentieth-century reports on education were explicit, public, supported by evidence and argument, and acknowledged that educational issues were complex and perennial. The decline in the quality and extent of democratic debate can be clearly seen from the 1992 White Paper, *Choice and Diversity*. It was published in July 1992, and comments on it had to arrive at the Department for Education by September 1992. The 1993 Act was announced almost immediately. Clearly, the government did not expect to learn a great deal from consultation. These educational policy changes were proposed and executed by people who felt no need to develop consensus, use arguments, or supply evidence. Presentation replaced debate, assertion replaced argument, and consultation became merely a cosmetic exercise. These developments not only represent a major decline in the quality of public debate. They also represent a break from a tradition, established in Victorian times, of regarding education as an intellectually, morally and politically important subject worthy of serious, open and public discussion.

Conceptions of education are always constituted by diverse intellectual and political traditions that speak to different visions of the good life and the good society. These traditions provide an intellectual and moral framework of understanding within which to address educational questions about what should be taught, how it should be taught and how it can be assessed. The New Right has looked back to nineteenth-century liberal and conservative traditions to find answers to these questions which were very different from those provided by the social democratic tradition. Under the guise of 'modernization', the New Right sought to reassert the liberal commitment to market forces, and, in this sense, the reforms of the 1980s represent

> a shift away from the state-initiated social integration within a . . . social-democratic consensus . . . [and the] revival of a nineteenth century 'contractual' model of social policy [according to which] the government [ceases] to provide social goods . . . and limits itself to defining and defending individual rights.[117]

Thus, behind the figures of Lord Joseph, Rhodes Boyson and Baroness Cox, can be perceived the ghostly figures of Kay-Shuttleworth, Lowe, Morant, Sadler and Norwood, reinterpreting the old aristocratic, exclusive, excluding, selective, pre-democratic system of education which speaks to a society which has adapted neither to democracy nor to its place in the modern world. One of the greatest political achievements of the New Right has been to leave the traditional élite system of education more secure, more confident and more significant than at any time since the late nineteenth century.

Thus the New Right's educational reforms were not only about the neo-liberal aim of 'rolling back the frontiers of the state'. They were also an attempt to reimpose on the educational system the neo-conservative cultural goal of reproducing a traditional, pre-democratic and hierarchical system of social roles and relationships. In this respect, the comment of Oliver Letwin that 'perfectly normal children had better learn from the earliest possible age to come to terms with their own capabilities' echoes Robert Lowe's famous nineteenth-century remark that 'the lower classes ought to be educated . . . so that they may defer to a higher cultivation when they meet it'. The same sentiments were to be found in colonial India under British rule. As one administrator put it in 1838:

> The Natives must either be kept down by a sense of our power, or they must willingly submit from a conviction that we are more wise, more just, more humane, or more anxious to improve their condition than any other rulers they could have.[118]

Applied to education, this view finds its apogee in Roger Scruton's insistence that 'it is not possible to provide universal education. Nor indeed is it desirable.'[119]

Because much of the immediate critical and political response to the New Right's educational policies appeared to be an attempt to preserve education in the hands of the 'professionals', it simply served to reinforce the New Right's allegations about 'producer capture' and to confirm the image of an educational establishment bent on protecting its own self-interest by preserving the status quo. This has not only strengthened the New Right's arguments for advancing the 'democratic freedom' of parents by allowing them increased involvement in and control over teachers and schools. It has also served to conceal the extent to which the educational policy agenda of the 1980s and early 1990s was an intrinsic part of the New Right's overall political, economic and social strategy for creating its own view of the good society. What it also concealed is the urgency of the need to reassert the case for a democratic conception of education that could expose the anti-democratic character of the New Right's educational policies, and provide a basis for developing alternative answers to educational questions to those it has prescribed. It is this task that is undertaken in the concluding chapter.

CONCLUSION: DEMOCRATIC

EDUCATION IN THE

TWENTY-FIRST CENTURY

When shall we realize that in every school-building in the land a
struggle is . . . being waged against all that hems in and distorts
human life? The struggle is not with arms and violence . . . But in its
slow and imperceptible processes, the real battles for human freedom
and for the pushing back of the boundaries that restrict human life are
ultimately won. We need to pledge ourselves to engage anew and
with renewed faith in the greatest of all battles and in the cause of
human liberation, to the end that all human beings may lead the life
that is alone worthy of being entitled wholly human.

(John Dewey)[1]

Introduction: education and democracy today

The previous four chapters have provided a historical account of the English
educational system which makes explicit the connections between decisive
periods of educational change and the broader political climate within which
it occurred. The main reason for doing this stems from a central argument
of this book: that the numerous educational reforms of the 1980s and 1990s
cannot be adequately understood unless they are placed within a much
longer history of educational change, and that this history cannot be adequately understood once it has been abstracted from the larger political and
cultural history through which our contemporary liberal democratic society
has evolved. Once contemporary educational reforms are considered from

this longer and broader historical perspective, they are revealed to be no more than the latest outcome of a continuous political struggle over how the internal tensions between the two political traditions of liberalism and democracy ought to be resolved. What also becomes clear is how New Right educational ideas, by successfully promoting the cause of liberalism against the progress of democracy, have managed to reverse the partial democratization of education which had been achieved through past intellectual debates and political struggles. The New Right has achieved this by reviving the central features of nineteenth-century liberalism in which the English educational tradition has its roots: an emphasis on enlightened self-interest and a general commitment to the view that, like everything else, education ought to operate in a free market in which private individuals can satisfy their own educational needs with minimal interference from the state. But as well as exposing its resonance with the political and educational traditions of the nineteenth century, a historical perspective also reveals the extent to which the New Right has ignored the advances that have been made in liberal political thought. By obliterating the lessons to be learned from its own history – by overlooking how the critical insights of Arnold, J.S. Mill, Green, Dewey and others transformed the central liberal concepts of freedom and equality – the impact of the New Right has been not so much radical as reactionary. If nothing else, this should serve as a timely reminder of the fact that democratic progress in education has been constantly resisted and always remains a fragile, partial and incomplete achievement.

Perhaps one of the most important lessons to be learned from this historical study is that the New Right's educational agenda cannot be effectively opposed through an educational debate that is confined to questions about 'choice', 'diversity' and 'standards' or by mounting a rearguard defence of the old educational status quo. Indeed, what this study makes clear is that the only way effectively to confront the New Right's educational policies is to re-engage in the 'battle of ideas' from which they emerged: a battle in which the New Right's interpretation of the core liberal values of freedom and equality can be challenged and fundamental questions about the role of education in a modern liberal democracy can, once again, be addressed. This does not mean that the political values and educational aims of liberalism have to be renounced. Rather, what has to be rejected is the bland assumption that these aims and values can be achieved in a society in which individuals pursue their own private interests with minimal political constraint. The correct starting point to the formulation of an alternative educational strategy is not a rejection of liberal democracy but an awareness of the continuing failure of liberal democratic societies to live up to their own self-avowed educational aims and ideals. As Lindley puts it:

> At least as far as children are concerned, it seems to be true that liberal democratic society is unable to deliver what its own principles declare to be essential ... The main failure of contemporary liberal democratic societies ... is that they seem incompatible with the development and maintenance of the capacity for autonomy in the majority of the

population . . . If autonomy is a vital interest and the autonomy of each person is to count equally then clearly liberal democratic societies are failing by the standards of their own values . . .[2]

If the failure of liberal democracy to 'deliver what its own principles declare to be essential' is to provide a starting point in the search for an alternative to the New Right's educational agenda, it will be important to recover those nineteenth- and early twentieth-century contributions to the liberal democratic tradition which insisted that this failure can only be rectified by critically reconstructing the meaning of the central concepts of liberal democracy. One concept which needs to be critically reconstructed is that of the individual as someone who exists prior to and apart from society. Another is the conception of freedom as a formal and abstract principle. As both Green and Dewey pointed out, individual freedom remains a meaningless concept unless individuals are able to control and change the conditions under which they live, and questions about the extent to which individuals are free are always political questions about the ways in which power is distributed and controlled through the institutions and agencies of the state. Understood in this way, freedom is advanced not simply by reducing the power of the state, but by the state distributing power democratically – that is, in ways that are conducive to developing the freedom of everyone in society. It is for this reason that both Dewey and Green interpreted the demand for 'equality' as nothing other than a demand for an egalitarian distribution of freedom, and regarded a liberal democracy as nothing other than a society which seeks to make the free development of each individual compatible with the free development of all.

Once the concepts of freedom and equality are reconstructed in this way, it readily becomes apparent why the New Right's separation of civil society from the state is seriously flawed. As T.H. Green noted, the state is so deeply implicated in sustaining the social relationships and practices of everyday life that to continue to regard it as a 'neutral' device for protecting the freedom of the individual is impossible. Since freedom refers to a particular form of power, and since politics is about how power is distributed and controlled, it is obvious that politics permeates the educational institutions through which the life of society is reproduced. It is also obvious that the educational systems of most liberal democracies are deeply implicated in the reproduction of inequalities of political and economic power that have a distorting influence on democratic life. From this perspective, the New Right's narrow conceptions of both 'politics' and the 'state' can be seen to be little more than a crude attempt to exclude from politics fundamental educational issues about how, in a liberal democracy, the state should intervene to create an educational system which does not simply ensure that the individual freedom of a privileged few is 'protected', but that the freedom of all can be progressively extended and enlarged.

By reformulating the core liberal values of freedom and equality in this way, liberal democrats as different as J.S. Mill and John Dewey were able to recast liberalism's concern with autonomy as a concern to specify the political

and educational arrangements which would give all individuals equal opportunity to determine the conditions under which they live. J.S. Mill believed
that the enactment of the principle of autonomy required an extension of
the sphere of democratic decision-making to more and more areas of social
life. For John Dewey, it required the revitalization of the 'public sphere'
which the liberal notion of the private individual had severely undermined
and which realist democratic theory had dismissed as an impossible ideal.
Throughout the twentieth century, Dewey's arguments for the revival of
democratically organized public life have been taken up by political theorists
as different as C.W. Mills,[3] Jürgen Habermas[4] and Alasdair MacIntyre.[5] Like
Dewey, each has argued for the urgent recovery of a vital 'public sphere'
which is

> conducive to the free ebb and flow of discussion . . . where people have
> an effective voice in the making of those decisions which vitally affect
> them, where the power to make such decisions is publicly legitimated
> and where those who exercise this power are publicly accountable.[6]

And like Dewey, each has argued that the task of recreating the public sphere
gives rise to some fundamental educational questions about the role that
education should play in a modern liberal democracy. How, in the closing
years of the twentieth century, is education to assist in the rebuilding of
democratically organized public life? How is a system of mass schooling to
be transformed into a system of public education concerned to foster the
growth of a democratic public and an educated democracy? What kind of
education will cultivate knowledgeable and enlightened citizens who can
participate in the collective formulation of common purposes and goals?
What is the role of the state in achieving these kinds of educational aims?

It would be a mistake to assume that these questions can be resolved by
resorting to answers derived from the past. Nor would it be fruitful to try and
answer them simply by reasserting the validity of the 'classical' conception
of democracy. What has to be conceded is that there is something to be
learned from 'contemporary' conceptions of democracy and that New Right
educational thinking has succeeded in raising many of the anxieties and
concerns to which the classical view of democracy gives rise.

What has to be learned from the 'contemporary' model of democracy is
that in modern industrial societies the major institutions of representative
democracy cannot simply be dismantled and that the classical ideal of continuous participation by *all* citizens in *all* the decision-making processes of
society is unrealistic. But to accept this is not to reject a commitment to the
extension of democratic participation. Nor is it inconsistent with the belief
that the conditions now exist for democratizing economic institutions and
cultural organizations – such as the workplace or the school – so as to enable
more people to participate directly in making decisions which immediately
affect their lives. Similarly, while it is necessary to concede to the New
Right that many of the strategies used to extend democracy have increased
the power of state bureaucracies in ways which curtail the freedom of the
individual, this does not mean that *any* attempt by the state to extend

democracy necessarily produces unwarranted limitations to individual liberty. Rather, it simply provides a timely reminder of the fact that democracy always remains vulnerable to those historical anxieties first voiced by Plato and from which the New Right has managed to derive so much political capital: anxieties about the extent to which any extension to democratic participation makes individual freedom vulnerable to either the 'tyranny of the masses' or the coercive dictates of the 'state'. In a more participatory democracy, what is to stop the majority from imposing some fixed version of the good life and good society on a minority? By reviving this question, the New Right has exposed some key educational issues that any democratic theory of education will need to confront. Who in a democracy should have the authority to determine the education of future citizens? How should educational policy be determined, and how should educational disagreements be resolved? What would constitute a specifically *democratic* response to these questions?

Towards a democratic theory of education

A distinctive feature of a democratic society is that it accepts that no single image of the good society can be theoretically justified to an extent that would allow it to be put beyond rational dispute, and that the arguments and disagreements to which such disputes give rise ought not to be concealed or repressed. The main purpose of any *democratic* theory, therefore, is not to offer a justification for a fixed image of the good society but to articulate the political principles, structures and practices that will ensure that the processes of contestation through which debates about the good society are conducted are those which are conducive to promoting the freedom of all its members. It follows from this that the main purpose of a democratic theory of *education* is not to stipulate the kind of education that would effectively serve to reproduce a fixed conception of the good society but to show how education can enable all future citizens to participate in the process of contestation through which their society – including its system of education – is reproduced and transformed. In other words, the purpose of a democratic theory of education is to articulate the educational conditions necessary to ensure that future citizens are able to engage in what Amy Gutmann calls 'conscious social reproduction':

> Although we are not collectively committed to any particular set of educational aims, we are committed to arriving at an agreement on our educational aims ... The substance of this core agreement is conscious social reproduction. As citizens we aspire to a set of educational practices and authorities of which the following can be said: these are the practices and the authorities to which we, acting collectively as a society, have consciously agreed. It follows that a society that supports conscious social reproduction must educate all educable children to be capable of participating in collectively shaping their society.[7]

To focus a democratic theory of education on the notion of 'conscious social reproduction' is simply to acknowledge that democracy is an ethical ideal rooted in a shared commitment to recreating society collectively by adopting principled ways of resolving the problems to which disagreements and differences over the nature of the good life and the good society give rise. But although the notion of 'conscious social reproduction' is relatively uncontroversial, it still raises, rather than resolves, age-old questions about who should have the political authority to determine educational policy and what the limits to this authority should be. For Plato, and many of his conservative heirs, the authority to determine the aims, content and organization of education should reside entirely in the hands of the state. More recently, the New Right have sought to curtail the power of the state by arguing – at least at the level of rhetoric – that educational authority should be exercised by parents acting as consumers in an educational market. Within the liberal political tradition, there has always been a commitment to the view that the values of freedom and autonomy can only be secured through a state educational system that is 'impartial' towards competing conceptions of the good life.

Any democratic theory of education will also be committed to the values of freedom and equality, but, unlike liberalism, it will insist that these values can only be enacted if the state actively seeks to promote educational aims that are derived from the values of a democratic society itself. Richard Peters has described these values in the following words:

> Democracy is a way of life in which matters of policy are resolved wherever possible by discussion . . . To decide things by discussion requires truth telling, respect for persons and the impartial consideration of interests as underlying moral principles . . . If these are to be more than a formal façade that can be manipulated by interest groups . . . a concern for the 'common good' is also required to encourage widespread participation in public life. This suggests a revival of the almost forgotten ideal of fraternity . . . to vitalize public projects as well as the ability to discuss and criticize public policy.[8]

By making 'demands on how social, political and public life ought to be conducted',[9] these democratic values provide the basis for determining what the aim of education in a democracy should be. In a democracy, the primary aim of education is to impart those democratic virtues such as tolerance, integrity, truth telling, impartiality, fraternity and the use of critical reason – virtues without which 'conscious social reproduction' would be impossible and 'which are fundamental principles of the democratic way of life'. A democratic society must therefore be committed to fostering a form of education that can enable individuals 'to acquire a general knowledge of how the political system works and be sensitive to the social and economic conditions that it has shaped and by which it is shaped'. It thus involves the kinds of knowledge and understanding 'that all members of a democracy should possess in order to participate in that form of life' and the skills 'necessary to participate in public affairs'.[10]

Although a democratic state is necessarily obliged to pursue this educational aim, it is also obliged to allow parents, employers, political representatives, professional educators and other social groups collectively and publicly to debate the specific educational policies through which this aim can be expressed. But what if democratically determined educational policies are incompatible with this aim? What if a democratically agreed educational policy is itself 'undemocratic'? Must it be assumed that those who participate in the democratic formation of educational policies always themselves possess the democratic virtues? Does this not imply that an enlightened and knowledgeable 'educated public' already exists and hence presuppose that a democratic culture – the kind of culture which democratic education seeks to promote – has already been created?

One response to this dilemma – made by both Rousseau and J.S. Mill – is that people will only acquire the moral and intellectual virtues required for democratic participation by actually participating in democratically organized public life. But this argument has to be treated with some caution. It is one thing to accept that people learn to participate by participating; it is quite another to accept that democratic participation will always produce democratically desirable decisions. As Held argues:

> While the evidence certainly indicates that . . . participation does help to foster . . . an active and knowledgeable citizenry . . . it is by no means conclusive that participation *per se* will trigger a new renaissance in human development. It would be unwise to count on people generally becoming more democratic, cooperative and dedicated to the 'common good' . . . It would probably be wiser to presuppose . . . that people will not . . . perform substantially better either morally or intellectually than they do at present.[11]

The implications of this for a democratic theory of education are twofold. The first is that a democratic theory of education must always be concerned to promote a process of 'double democratisation'[12] – a process aimed at the simultaneous democratic development of both education and society. Thus a key task for a democratic theory of education is to articulate a conception of education which recognizes that without a democratic development of society a more democratic system of education cannot be promoted, and that without a more democratic system of education the democratic development of society is unlikely to occur.

The second implication is that a democratic theory of education must show how democratic participation in educational decision-making is to be circumscribed by conditions designed to preserve and protect the democratic values and educational aims that such a theory is intended to foster and promote. What is required are principled restrictions to the process of democratic participation that can function to deny democratic legitimacy to educational decisions which would curtail the opportunities for future citizens to receive the kind of education that their own capacities to deliberate democratically presuppose and require. A democratic theory of education must, therefore, limit democratic decision-making in order to prevent educational decisions from being made which would prevent the next generation of citizens from acquiring the knowledge, virtues and dispositions that their participation in the process of conscious social reproduction requires.

Amy Gutmann has reformulated these principled limits to democratic educational authority in terms of the principles of *non-repression* and *non-discrimination*.[13] The principle of non-repression is intended to prevent 'the state, and any group in it, from using education to restrict rational deliberation of competing conceptions of the good life and the good society'. While it is, therefore, compatible with using education 'to inculcate those character traits such as honesty, religious toleration and mutual respect for persons that serve as foundations for rational deliberation of different ways of life', it clearly prevents adults using 'their . . . deliberative freedom to undermine the future deliberative freedom of children'.[14] In this sense, the principle of non-repression 'derives its defence from the primary value of democratic education, conscious social reproduction, which prevents adults from using education to stifle rational deliberation about competing conceptions of the good life and the good society'.[15] Gutmann's second limit to democratic educational authority – the principle of non-discrimination – is the principle that 'all educable children must be educated', and it applies to 'those forms of education necessary to prepare children for . . . participation in conscious social reproduction'. It requires that 'no educable child may be excluded from an education adequate to participating in the political processes that structure choice among good lives'.[16]

Together, the principles of non-repression and non-discrimination provide a distinctively democratic way of resolving those issues about the potentially dangerous consequences of unconstrained democratic authority that the New Right has so effectively exploited in order to gain political acceptance for its educational policies. They do so by effectively combining a commitment to the 'liberal' view that individual autonomy requires a 'negative freedom' from state-imposed versions of the good life and the good society with a commitment to the 'democratic' view that all individuals should have a 'positive freedom' to deliberate about and evaluate competing conceptions of the good life and the good society. To accept the principles of non-repression and non-discrimination is thus to accept that, in a democracy,

> all future citizens must have access to an education that is conducive to the development of their capacity for rational deliberation about competing conceptions of the good life and empowers them collectively to participate in shaping the future of their society.[17]

One of the obvious merits of Gutmann's democratic theory of education is that it recognizes how questions about the role of education in the process of social reproduction and transformation are always contested questions reflecting fundamental political and ideological disagreements. Another is that, by recognizing the need for education and society to be simultaneously democratized, it acknowledges the need for a democratic theory of education to confront the problem of 'double democratisation' and hence the matter of why, 'just as we need a more robust democratic system of politics to further democratic education so we need a more democratic system of education to further democratic politics'.[18] But perhaps the main attraction of Gutmann's theory is that it is a *democratic* theory offering us a way of thinking (and hence theorizing) about education *democratically*, rather than a 'logically tight system of axioms, principles and conclusions that flow from them'.[19] For Gutmann, as for Dewey, our allegiance to a *democratic* theory of education is never independent 'of its congruence with our deepest convictions'[20] and, as such, is nothing other than the expression of a faith in the capacity of ordinary people to resolve their differences in order to build and rebuild their communities on the basis of a shared understanding of the common good. As Gutmann puts it, 'the distinctive virtue of a democratic theory of education is that its principles and conclusions are compatible with our commitment to share the rights and obligations of citizenship with people who do not share our conception of the good life'.[21]

By erecting a democratic theory of education on the tradition of liberal democratic thought which this book has sought to reconstruct and revise, Gutmann's theory of education not only offers the theoretical resources for making a democratically principled response to the educational reforms of the New Right. It also provides the starting point for developing a vision for the educational future which takes seriously a commitment to democracy.

A democratic vision of education

Throughout this book it has been argued that the educational reforms of the 1980s and 1990s were part of a political offensive designed to reverse the democratization of liberalism that has gradually been achieved through the political and intellectual struggles of the nineteenth and twentieth centuries. What, in essence, is at issue, therefore, is the need to renew 'the struggle for democracy' by proposing a vision of education in which the tension between liberalism and democracy is no longer resolved by resurrecting nineteenth-century liberal ideas but by advancing a form of democratic social life in which the freedom and dignity of all can be secured. This democratic vision of education will be very different from that offered by the New Right and distinguishable from it in several crucial respects.

First, since a democracy is a society whose members collectively discuss issues which they themselves consciously recognize as having practical significance for the conduct and organization of their own shared social life, any democratic vision of education will be committed to fostering a wide public debate in which educational policies and proposals can be tested through critical dialogue and in which all can participate irrespective of occupational status or technical expertise. This kind of educational debate will be very different from the ideologically driven debate that has accompanied recent educational reforms: a debate in which public dialogue was reduced to a 'consultation' exercise, alternative educational views were marginalized, and the need to transcend and accommodate a diverse range of political interests and educational viewpoints was ignored.

Second, any vision of education that takes democracy seriously cannot but be at odds with educational reforms which espouse the language and values of market forces and treat education as a commodity to be purchased and consumed. Instead, it will regard it as self-evident that education is a public good rather than a private utility and acknowledge that, in a democracy, education has to be constantly 're-formed' as part of a broader process of social change aimed at empowering more and more people consciously to participate in the life of their society. Although, in this process, 'freedom of choice' will be a major principle in determining educational policy, the notion of 'choice' will not simply refer to the right of individuals to pursue their narrow self-interests in a competitive marketplace. Instead it will be recognized that, in a democracy, individuals do not only express personal preferences; they also make public and collective choices related to the common good of their society. A democratic vision of education is thus one that recognizes that education has a vital role to play in creating an informed and educated public who can exercise their collective choice about the future direction that their society should take.

Third, the large number of difficult and complex policy issues to which this vision of the role of education in a democratic society gives rise will, in general, be addressed and resolved in a way which takes account of the diverse values, needs and interests of the different social groups and communities that constitute a society. In this sense, educational policy would not be the outcome of a competitive struggle for superiority between conflicting political ideologies. Nor would policy-making be treated as a professional skill available only to unaccountable experts. Rather, educational policy would be the outcome of a consensual process of power sharing in which the conflicting educational views of a diverse range of social groups are translated into agreed educational policies on the basis of a shared commitment to democratic principles and beliefs. As such, it would be a way of formulating educational policy which, by seeking to take account of and reconcile disagreements and differences, seeks to transcend and accommodate diversity in a way which will itself enrich collective democratic life.

In formulating educational policy in this way, a democratic society will inevitably support a presumption that the need to educate all its future members to participate collectively in shaping the future of their society is a moral obligation quite independent of instrumental considerations or utilitarian concerns. It will thus sustain arguments in favour of the view that the primary aim of education is to ensure that all future citizens are equipped with the knowledge, values and skills of deliberative reasoning minimally necessary for their participation in the democratic life of their society. This will require some recognition of the extent to which an excessive emphasis on competition, in so far as it encourages a disposition to act on the basis of narrow self-interest, undermines the development of the co-operative social relationships that this educational aim implies and severely impedes the teaching and learning of those civic virtues – such as fairness, tolerance, empathy and respect for others – which democratic deliberation requires. Moreover, since, in a democracy, the opportunity to acquire this kind of education is a right of all educable pupils, irrespective of intelligence, wealth, or social class, it will not be distributed on the basis of meritocratic principles, but in a way that tries to ensure that all pupils are sufficiently educated to participate in the democratic process. In a democracy, 'equality of opportunity' means that any differences in educational provision are acceptable only if they do not deprive some pupils of an education that effectively guarantees their entitlement, as future citizens, to be members of an educated public.

One of the policy implications that follow from adopting this 'democratic standard' for the distribution of education is that diversity and choice in educational provision do not extend to tolerating the existence of schools that do not or (because of inadequate resources) cannot educate their pupils for future democratic citizenship. Another is that what is to be regarded as a minimally acceptable 'democratic curriculum' will constantly have to be revised to take account of the democratic developments that such a curriculum is itself designed to produce. What are regarded as the minimal requirements of a democratic curriculum at one time (for example, literacy and numeracy) may lead to democratic advances which will, in turn, require these minimal standards to be raised so as to ensure that an increasing proportion of citizens can participate in and contribute to democratic life and culture. In this sense, the development of a more democratic society and the development of a democratic curriculum are mutually reinforcing elements within a single process of democratic progress.

To adopt this kind of compulsory 'democratic threshold principle'[22] clearly implies adopting a principled position on some of the key contemporary issues concerning curriculum, content, pedagogy and school organization. It implies, for example, that issues about curriculum content always raise practical questions about the appropriateness of different subjects for developing democratic citizenship and about their effectiveness in teaching to all educable children the knowledge, virtues and skills required for democratic deliberation. It also implies a presumption in favour of pedagogies that will cultivate the social skills and commitments that democratic participation requires. In short, it implies that responses to curriculum and pedagogical issues will be informed by an appreciation of why, in a democracy,

> the most devastating criticism we can level at . . . schools . . . is not that
> they fail to give equally talented children an equal chance to earn the
> same income or pursue professional occupations but that they fail to
> give all educable children an education adequate to take advantage of
> their political status as citizens.[23]

In suggesting that any response to the New Right's educational reforms needs to be organized around a clear understanding of what constitutes a democratic education, the conventional view that a nationally imposed system of comprehensive schooling offers the most appropriate vehicle for achieving an educated democracy will have to be critically reassessed. Moreover, in making this reassessment it will have to be conceded that despite the strength of its initial commitment to the democratization of educational provision, comprehensive schooling has only had limited success in achieving the objectives of an educated democracy or in combating the élitism and divisiveness that are characteristic of the English educational tradition. Indeed, it could be argued that comprehensive schools, by adopting an explicitly democratic and egalitarian posture, have functioned to perpetuate the English educational tradition by reproducing inequalities and privileges in a way that is less transparently linked to social class than it was in the tripartite system, where the parallels between 'secondary modern', 'technical' and 'grammar' schools and the social origins of their respective pupils were blatantly obvious. This does not mean that comprehensive schools have not achieved impressive results, both in remedying some of the obvious injustices of the tripartite system and in providing educational opportunities to previously excluded groups, particularly working-class children and those from ethnic minorities. It is simply to make the general point that, despite its portrayal as an institution of democratic education, all the evidence suggests that the comprehensive school has reinforced rather than challenged those non-democratic aspects of the English educational tradition – exclusiveness, separation and segregation – that have always frustrated democratic educational advance.

One of the reasons why comprehensive schools have been unable effectively to resist the exclusiveness, divisiveness and élitism of the English educational tradition has been their reluctance critically to question the distinction between 'liberal' and 'vocational' education. Because of this, there has been a widespread failure to appreciate that, in a democracy, the main issue raised by 'vocational education' is not whether schools should prepare their pupils for future occupational roles but whether there can be any justification for an education system that, by continuing to preserve the antithesis between 'liberal' and 'vocational', merely preserves aristocratic educational assumptions and traditions. It thus deflects attention from the important task of developing a form of education that is both liberal and vocational: liberal in the sense that it 'liberates the capacities [of each member of the community] and thereby contributes to his own happiness and his social usefulness'; and vocational in the sense that 'it aims to prepare one for the more efficient and satisfactory performance of the activities of life'.[24] It is only by first dismantling the distinction between 'liberal' and 'vocational' education that the educational debate can begin to move beyond the unproductive conflicts between liberal and vocational ideologies and recognize that the democratic challenge is to move towards a form of 'liberal vocationalism'[25] which does not offer a narrowly conceived training designed to adapt future workers to the existing economic and industrial order, but enables individuals 'to act more autonomously and reflectively in the labour market because this is a precondition for an effective civil society'.[26]

Any serious attempt to move beyond the sterile divisions between liberal and vocational education will inevitably have to confront difficult questions about the role of élite schools in a democratic society. There can be no doubt that such schools, by continuing to pursue the Platonic educational ideal of a culturally superior élite, tend to exacerbate and magnify the divisions

between social classes in ways which are antithetical to democratic development. Nor can there be any doubt that by helping to preserve political
influence in the hands of a privileged minority, élite schools help to perpetuate pre-democratic educational traditions and structures and so make it extremely difficult for state schools to become 'public schools' themselves,
providing for a modern democratic society the kind of public education that
élite educational institutions so effectively provided for an aristocratic society. To raise questions about the future of élite schools in a democratic
society is, therefore, to raise questions about whether they obstruct the task
of transforming a state-provided system of mass schooling into a system of
genuine *public* education for which the gradual enlargement of an educated
public is a primary educational aim. It is also to raise questions about whether
this aim can be realistically pursued in schools that – despite the rhetoric –
continue to select pupils according to class, status and wealth, and about
whether private schools should, like any state school, be required to offer an
education which equips its pupils for membership of a democratic society
rather than for membership of an intellectual, political and economic élite.

In a society which takes democracy seriously, issues about the ways in
which teachers are themselves educated will always be central to the public
educational debate. Part of the New Right's educational strategy has been to
create widespread public concern about teacher education by employing a
rhetoric of 'teaching quality', 'professional competence' and 'good practice'
which serves to define the 'problems' of teacher education in a certain way
and justify particular recommendations about how they should be resolved.
With these recommendations largely implemented, teacher education is now
being driven by nationally imposed policies in which key questions about
the proper role of teachers in a democratic society are prejudged in a way
which simply endorses the ideology of the New Right. As a result, the educational values of teachers have been subjugated to the values of the 'system', teaching has been transformed into a value-neutral technical process,
and 'good practice' has been reduced to a bureaucratically framed specifica-
tion of competencies and skills. What is conspicuously absent from these
policies is any serious attempt to recognize – let alone answer – important
questions about the role of teachers in a democratic society and hence about
what the aims, content and organization of teacher education should be.

What, in particular, is absent is any appreciation of the extent to which
a democratic society is dependent on a teaching profession whose members
recognize their professional obligation to create an educational environment
which will sustain the development of democratic virtues and practices.
From the perspective of a democratic society, the professionalism of teachers
is based on a recognition of their right to make autonomous judgements
about how, in particular institutional and classroom contexts, to develop
their students' capacity for democratic deliberation, critical judgement and
rational understanding. Without this kind of professional autonomy teachers have no protection against external coercion and pressure, and they
quickly become neutral operatives implementing the 'directives' of their
political masters and mistresses. Indeed, in default of protecting this feature

of teacher professionalism, teachers' sense of themselves as professional *educators* committed to upholding the educational principles of a democratic society will evaporate, and one of the necessary preconditions for ensuring future generations of democratic citizens will disappear.

A strategy for teacher education which is informed by this understanding of the democratic role of teachers will have to confront difficult and complex questions about the nature of 'educational studies', the nature of 'teaching practice' and the relationship between the two. Moreover, the starting point for attempts to answer these questions will be an understanding of how the separation of 'educational studies' from 'teaching practice' is itself just one more manifestation of the deeper schism between 'liberal education' and 'vocational training' that has always frustrated genuine curriculum change and done so much to undermine the development of democratic educational reform. While this schism remains, 'educational studies' will continue to be understood as a body of disembodied theoretical knowledge that teachers can 'apply' to their everyday practice, and 'practical experience' will continue to be seen as a 'theory-free' source of the skills and competencies that 'good teaching' requires. While this understanding continues to inform debates about the content of teacher education programmes, these debates will continue to focus on meaningless questions about the relative weight and importance that should be given to either 'educational studies' or 'practical experience'.

Only when this dualism between 'educational studies' and 'practical experience' has been abandoned, will it become possible to envisage a programme of 'educational studies' which is simultaneously theoretical and practical: theoretical in the sense that teaching is understood to be a morally informed activity that requires a theoretical knowledge and understanding of the democratic educational values (such as individual autonomy and equality of opportunity) which teachers aspire to express; and practical in the sense that it recognizes that teachers' ability to translate this 'theoretical' knowledge and understanding into practice – to know, for example, when and how it ought to be invoked and to be able to judge its relevance to a particular educational situation – can only be acquired through practical experience. Interpreted in this way, neither 'educational studies' nor 'practical experience' would be pre-eminent: each would be informed and transformed by the other.

The need for an approach to educational studies which reinstates the notion of teaching as a theoretically based and morally informed profession has been made all the more urgent because of the way in which the New Right's reforms have reduced the professional autonomy of teachers to a limited technical discretion with a restrictive framework of bureaucratic inspection and technical control. This sense of urgency has been further reinforced by the way in which the New Right's educational reforms have systematically eliminated the educational values of teachers as the major guide to their educational practice. This has largely been achieved by eradicating from teacher education any reference to those shared traditions of educational thought which, by helping to expose the taken-for-granted

political assumptions and educational values governing contemporary practice, served to animate a critical debate within the educational professions
about what the values informing their work should be. It is thus unsurprising
that the canonical texts which largely constitute this tradition – such as
Plato's *Republic*, Rousseau's *Émile* and Dewey's *Democracy and Education* –
were once prescribed reading for future teachers but are now officially pro-
scribed. Nor is it surprising that instead of initiating future teachers into this
tradition, teacher education has now become a means of socializing them
into the unexamined values and taken-for-granted assumptions of 'the
system'.

Once the New Right reforms of teacher education are interpreted in this
way, it becomes readily apparent that the various procedures of inspection
and accreditation that now function to regulate and control virtually every
aspect of the content, organization and conduct of teacher education are
not only intended to produce more effective teachers who are able to raise
standards by improving test scores. They are also intended to prevent the
development of reflective teachers, constantly examining the extent to which
their teaching is governed by their educational values and ideals. As a result,
the prevailing view about the role that education should play in society is
now being determined by the interests and ideology of the New Right rather
than through an ongoing democratic debate within the educational professions and between the education professions and other social groups: a debate
which the shared traditions of educational thought served to nurture and
promote. The destruction of these traditions has meant that new generations
of teachers are being deprived of any moral and intellectual touchstone
against which the educational quality of their 'practical experience' can be
critically appraised and the educational value of their teaching can be judged.
In the present context, to propose the reinstatement of these intellectual
traditions would be to challenge the authority of the state.

But it would also be to propose the revitalization of teaching as a 'vocation' whose practitioners are committed to bringing general educational values
to bear on practical educational situations. It would be to propose a form of
'educational studies' designed to develop the kind of practical knowledge
that future teachers will need to acquire if they are to practise in ways which
will allow democratic educational values to be given practical expression.
Without this kind of 'educational studies', 'good practice' degenerate into
technical expertise and 'effective teaching' is reduced to achieving objectives, outcomes and attainment targets whose educational value is never
questioned. A programme of teacher education which does not include this
kind of 'educational studies' might produce teachers who are technically
accountable, but it will not produce teachers who are morally answerable.[27]

Conclusion: education and the struggle for democracy

Most discussions of the educational reforms of the 1980s and 1990s assume
that understanding these reforms is a purely mechanistic problem – a matter

of understanding the objectives they were designed to achieve, the policies that have been implemented in order to achieve these objectives, and the 'performance indicators' in terms of which the effectiveness of these policies can be measured. In this book it has been argued that what is required to understand these reforms is an understanding of the mode of educational discourse through which those objectives were expressed, the political and ideological context in which these policies were formulated, and the cultural and economic pressures prevalent at the time they were introduced. What also has to be understood is that these educational reforms were a central part of a much broader programme of political, cultural and economic change and thus part of the wider general process whereby a society reproduces and transforms itself over time. It is for this reason that these reforms have been deliberately located within the dynamic historical process of intellectual, political and social struggle that Raymond Williams called the 'long revolution': a process of contestation through which different conceptions of the good life and the good society have been – and continue to be – articulated, defended and opposed. It was through this process of contestation that the political ideas embedded in these reforms became dominant in the discourse of education, were translated into policy and are now being institutionalized in the organizational structures and practices of schools. And it is only by understanding the interests and values of the dominant participants in this process that their meaning and significance can be adequately analysed and understood.

One of the things that such an analysis reveals is that the protagonists who participated in this process started from different positions of power, so that what actually emerged represented the interests and values of some (particularly the New Right and employers) while those of others (particularly LEAs and the educational professions) were either neglected or ignored. This not only suggests that the process was distorted by an undemocratic exercise of power; it also explains why, in their efforts to make sense of and implement these reforms, many members of the educational professions have opposed the 'official' interpretation of what they mean and how they should be implemented. It is precisely because 'education' is an essentially contested concept that these reforms are not being 'delivered' on the basis of any prior agreement about what their aims and purposes should be. Rather, the ways in which they are being adopted, adapted and put into practice are always being conditioned by dialogues and discussions between teachers which are mediated through their educational values and conducted within those residual structures for rational deliberation and democratic decision-making that still remain intact.

It is these democratic decision-making structures that the recent educational reforms are now beginning to destroy. But it nevertheless remains the case that just as these reforms were the outcome of an undemocratic process of educational decision-making, so it is by seeking ways to create more democratic educational decision-making processes that their legitimacy can be challenged and more democratically informed educational policies can be advanced. This process can take many forms. It could, for example, involve examining the anti-democratic effects on the culture of a school of the ideology of managerialism which these reforms have introduced. It could involve exposing the contradictions between the official rhetoric of choice, diversity and individual freedom and the reality of a National Curriculum which has been defined and imposed by the state. It could also involve teachers, governors, parents, students and others resisting the effects of the bureaucratic modes of organization that these reforms require, by devising organizational structures that are more consistent with democratic values and practices. It is, in other words, only when the democratic inappropriateness of regarding parents, pupils and employers as 'consumers' and 'clients' is openly recognized that they can begin to be treated as active participants in the democratic processes through which educational decisions are made and educational policies are formed. And it is only by so reaffirming an allegiance to democratic practices that it will be possible to preserve the integrity of democratic educational values in the face of all those political and cultural tendencies which now undermine and degrade them.

The task of protecting and preserving democratic educational values and practices has been made all the more difficult by the introduction of educational policies which ignore the essential contestability of both education and democracy and assume that debates about what they should mean can be effectively closed. This book has argued that the meanings of 'education' and 'democracy' are always disputed and controversial and have emerged out of past struggles for individual freedom, self-fulfilment, social progress and political equality. What this book has also argued is that the story of these struggles is *both* a story of victories and achievements *and* a story of setbacks and defeats. When it is spelt out in all its concrete detail, the major landmarks in this story would include the Revised Code of 1862, the Haddow Report of 1926, the Black Papers of 1969–77 and the Educational Acts of 1870, 1902, 1944 and 1988. Its main antagonists and protagonists would include Jeremy Bentham, John Stuart Mill, Robert Lowe, James Kay-Shuttleworth, Matthew Arnold, Robert Morant, Richard Tawney and Cyril Norwood. And its last chapter would describe how, under the influence of a New Right coalition, successive Conservative governments introduced a series of educational reforms which have reversed the advance of democratic educational progress by returning to the pre-democratic educational traditions and structures of the past.

But this last chapter is not the final chapter, and the story of the struggle for democratic education remains unfinished. Although the New Right educational reforms may now be impeding and frustrating democratic progress, the commitment to democracy is so widespread and so pervasive that it is impossible – even in a modern market-dominated culture – to eradicate completely the idea that the primary aim of education is to prepare future citizens for membership of a democratic society. What, in effect, this book has tried to show is that since this aim can only be realized in a kind of society that does not yet exist, the outstanding educational task is not to *defend* democracy by *reproducing* society, but to *create* democracy by *transforming* society. As the historian, E.H. Carr, wrote:

To speak today of the defence of democracy as if we were defining something which we know and had possessed for many decades ... is self deception and sham. ... The criterion must be sought not in the survival of traditional institutions but in the question of where power resides and how it is exercised. ... We should be nearer the mark and should have a far more convincing slogan if we spoke of the need not to defend democracy but to create it.[28]

The purpose of this book has been to show that creating a democratic society is now largely a matter of opposing and transcending the contradictions, inadequacies and limitations inherent in the educational ideas, policies and practices prescribed by the New Right. Only if the present generation actively engages in this 'struggle for democracy' will future generations have any chance of receiving an education which does not just fit them into the culture and traditions of an aristocratic society that is dead and past, but empowers them to participate in and contribute to the kind of open, pluralistic and democratic society appropriate to the world of the twenty-first century.

NOTES

Introduction (pp. 1–16)

1 For a detailed philosophical critique of the role of common-sense thinking in education see Pring (1977). The inadequacies of common sense as a basis for theory have been exposed with great force by Popper (1972).
2 Eagleton (1990: 34–5).
3 See, for example, Bain (1879).
4 Bell (1962).
5 See O'Connor (1973).
6 The most influential rationale for this 'disciplines' approach to educational theory was provided by the contributors to Tibble (1966).
7 The classic statement of this approach to the sociology of education remains Bowles and Gintis (1976).
8 For an elaboration of this point, see Apple (1982) and Kemmis (1986).
9 Feinberg (1983: 153).
10 For a comprehensive philosophical justification for reconstructing educational theory in this way, see Carr (1995).
11 Throughout this book reference is made to 'the English educational system' and 'education in England'. This is not intended to conceal the important similarities between the English educational system and those of Wales and other parts of the United Kingdom. However, terms such as the 'United Kingdom' cover a diverse range of historical, cultural, political and educational phenomena. The intention behind using phrases such as the 'English educational system' is to recognize and acknowledge this diversity.
12 Williams (1965: 10).
13 Ibid.: 11.
14 Ibid.
15 Ibid.: 11–13.

1 Education, politics and society (pp. 17–38)

1 Hollis (1971: 153).
2 Quoted in Chitty (1990: 39).
3 Department of Education and Science (1985: 25).
4 Cited in Chitty (1990: 37).
5 Gallie (1955).
6 Aldrich (1988: 99).
7 Cox and Dyson (1969a; 1969b; 1970); Cox and Boyson (1975; 1977).
8 Conservative Research Department (1985) quoted in McKenzie (1993: 7).
9 Feinberg (1983).
10 Ibid.: 6.
11 Ibid.: 155.
12 Ibid.
13 Ibid.
14 Ibid.
15 Ibid.: 154.
16 Ibid.: 227.
17 Ibid.: 228.
18 Ibid.
19 Ibid.: 229.
20 Ibid.: 232.
21 Burke (1910: 94).
22 Popper (1947: 359).
23 Arblaster and Lukes (1971: 2).
24 Ibid.: 4–5.
25 Berlin (1969).
26 Ibid.: 22.
27 Marquand (1988: 163).
28 Plato (1974: 375).
29 Ibid.: 376.
30 Ibid.: 434.
31 Ibid.
32 Mill (1895: 319).
33 Rousseau (1968).
34 Rousseau (1974).
35 Quoted in Perkinson (1980: 138).
36 Ibid.
37 Rousseau (1974: Bk 2).
38 Quoted in Perkinson (1980: 140).
39 Ibid.: 141.
40 Ibid.: 143.
41 Ibid.: 143–4.
42 Rusk (1979: 100).
43 This contestational view of educational change has been developed in some detail
by Stephen Kemmis. See, in particular, Rizvi and Kemmis (1987) and Kemmis
(1990).

2 Democratic theory and democratic education (pp. 39–66)

1 Williams (1965: 171).
2 Held (1987: 3).
3 Pateman (1970).
4 Ibid.: 21.
5 Rousseau (1968).
6 Mill (1951).
7 Macpherson (1973).
8 Pateman (1970).
9 Schumpeter (1942).
10 Dahl (1985).
11 Lippmann (1922; 1925).
12 Hayek (1976).
13 Goodwin (1992: 231).
14 Jonathan (1986).
15 Held (1987: 261).
16 Arblaster (1994: 6).
17 Macpherson (1966: 1).
18 Macpherson (1977: 7).
19 Arblaster (1984: 56).
20 Quoted in ibid.: 15.
21 Ibid.: 56.
22 Lindley (1986: 6).
23 See, for example, Peters (1979); Bailey (1984); White (1989).
24 Quoted in Warnock (1962: 185–6).
25 Quoted in Arblaster (1984: 13).
26 Bentham (1843: 47).
27 Mill (1937).
28 Quoted in Macpherson (1977: 36).
29 Mill (1951).
30 Quoted in Arblaster (1984: 280).
31 Ibid.
32 Berlin (1969: 173).
33 Arnold (1932: 41).
34 Quoted in Bullock and Shock (1956: 123–5).
35 Green (1988: 370–2).
36 Ibid.
37 Ibid.: 373–4.
38 Lipmann (1922; 1925).
39 Shumpeter (1942: 295).
40 Ibid.: 284–5.
41 Arblaster (1984: 329).
42 Held (1987: 168).
43 Dewey (1922: 337).
44 The interpretation that follows of Dewey's political and social philosophy and of its importance to any understanding of his educational philosophy owes much to the highly influential intellectual biography of Dewey by Westbrook (1991).
45 Dewey (1917: 46).
46 Dewey (1920: 124).
47 Dewey (1927; 1935a).

48 Dewey (1927: 363).
49 Ibid.: 366.
50 Ibid.: 366–7.
51 Dewey (1935a: 38–9).
52 Dewey (1927: 319).
53 Ibid.: 327.
54 Dewey (1935a: 289).
55 Dewey (1935b: 291).
56 Dewey (1930a).
57 Dewey (1936: 370).
58 Dewey (1932: 341–2).
59 Dewey (1935a: 51).
60 Dewey (1937: 217–18).
61 Dewey (1899).
62 Dewey (1939: 400).
63 Dewey (1927: 371).
64 Dewey (1981b: 446).
65 Dewey (1916: 87).
66 Quoted in Westbrook (1991: 109).
67 Dewey (1916: iii).
68 Ibid.: 89.
69 Ibid.: 91.
70 Ibid.: 92.
71 Ibid.
72 Ibid.: 112.
73 Ibid.
74 Ibid.: 118.
75 Ibid.: 93.
76 Dewey (1981b: 446).
77 Dewey (1916: 50–1).
78 Quoted in Westbrook (1991: 173).
79 Dewey (1914: 4–6).
80 Dewey (1916: 328).
81 Dewey (1913: 99).
82 Quoted in Westbrook (1991: 176).
83 Dewey (1916: 328).
84 Quoted in Westbrook (1991: 177).
85 Ibid.: 509.

3 'Gentling the masses' (pp. 67–91)

 1 Clarke (1940: 31).
 2 Silver (1980: 15).
 3 Shannon (1974: 22). See also Stone (1969).
 4 See, as examples of a *comparative* approach, Archer (1979) and Green (1990).
 5 Green (1990: 33). See also Davie (1961; 1986).
 6 Simon (1976: 119).
 7 Richards and Hunt (1950: 175, 228). The population figures exclude Ireland.
 8 Inglis (1993: 206–7 and Chapter 9).
 9 MacIntyre (1981: 201).
10 Inglis (1993: 23, 214).

11 Silver (1980: 10, 82–4).
12 Ibid.: 8–9.
13 Hamilton (1989: 154).
14 See Gutmann (1987: 14–16).
15 Silver (1980: 116).
16 Connell (1950: 173–4, 182).
17 Shannon (1974: 33–4); and Silver (1980: 109–10).
18 Green (1990: 77).
19 Ibid.: 220–1.
20 Ibid.: 223.
21 Ibid.: 236, 243, 74, 237.
22 Gordon *et al.* (1991: 10–11). See also Hurt (1971: 229).
23 Green (1990: 75).
24 See, for example, Purvis (1992); Gordon *et al.* (1991: 123–40); and Purvis (1991).
25 Quoted in Johnson (1992).
26 MacIntyre (1981: 207).
27 Green (1990: 241).
28 Ibid.: 30–1. See also Johnson (1992) on the radicals.
29 See Chapter 1, pp. 33–6.
30 Hamilton (1989: Chapter 1).
31 Shannon (1974: 11).
32 Ibid.: 13.
33 Ibid.: 14–15; and Green (1990: 49). The population of Britain trebled between 1751 and 1851, and doubled between 1801 and 1851 (Green 1990: 49; Shannon 1974: 14).
34 Connell (1950: 2).
35 Ibid.: 3, quoting Knowles (1937: 139).
36 Rubinstein (1993: 7).
37 Green (1990: 209).
38 Wardle (1976: Chapter 1).
39 Ibid.: 7–8, 14 and 10. As Wardle (1976: 10) suggests, Edmund Gosse's book *Father and Son* (Chapter 5) 'remains the best brief account of the agony of a scientist who was also a fundamentalist Christian when faced with the necessity to stand emphatically in one army or the other'.
40 Green (1990: 272).
41 Mathieson and Bernbaum (1988). Quotation from p. 137. See also Knights (1978: Chapters 2 and 4).
42 Francis and Morrow (1994: 170–1).
43 Mathieson and Bernbaum (1988: 136, 139, 140–1, 150, 157).
44 Green (1990).
45 Ibid.: 80.
46 Wardle (1976: 20–1) and, generally, his Chapter 2 above.
47 Green (1990: 3).
48 Murphy (1972: Section 1, 9–34).
49 Green (1990: 261).
50 Green (1991a: 8).
51 Hurt (1979: 188).
52 Quoted in Donald (1992: 20).
53 Hurt (1979: 197).
54 Quoted in Wardle (1976: 25). On the views of Lowe generally, see Francis and Morrow (1994: Chapter 12).
55 Green (1990: 49–50).

56 Quoted in Donald (1992: 20–1).
57 Thompson (1968).
58 Gordon *et al.* (1991: 11–12).
59 Quoted by Green (1990: 259).
60 See Chapter 2, pp. 48–9.
61 Murphy (1972: 10).
62 Green (1990: 229–30).
63 Ibid.: 266.
64 Wardle (1976: 87).
65 Hurt (1971: 11).
66 Gordon *et al.* (1991: 3).
67 Green (1990: 279).
68 Morris (1973: vii).
69 Hurt (1971: 23–4).
70 Green (1990: 51).
71 Johnson (1970).
72 Ibid. Quotations from pp. 101, 104, 105 and 109.
73 Gardner (1984: 10, 85, 92, 84 and, generally Chapter 3).
74 Johnson (1970). Quotations from pp. 111–19.
75 Murphy (1972: 24–5) and Wardle (1976: 66). Accurate figures depend partly on definitions of what is covered. See Hurt (1971: 186–7) on this.
76 Green (1990: 7).
77 Hurt (1971: 186).
78 Ibid.: 199.
79 Maclure (1986: 72).
80 Hurt (1971: 48, 200–1).
81 Barnard (1947: 130).
82 Selleck (1968: 15).
83 In 1882 a 'seventh standard' was introduced. See Simon (1965: 116 fn. 1).
84 Selleck (1968: 33–4).
85 Maclure (1986: 79).
86 Green (1990: 282).
87 Simon (1965: 115) and Hurt (1971: 214).
88 Hurt (1971: 214).
89 Selleck (1968: 32–3).
90 Ibid.: 32, 40.
91 Quoted in Simon (1965: 118).
92 Hurt (1979: 22).
93 Selleck (1968: 13).
94 Lowe (1976). Quotation from p. 140.
95 Ibid.: 140.
96 Green (1990: 290–1).
97 Maclure (1986: 91).
98 Lowe (1976: 140–1).
99 Simon (1965: 107).
100 Green (1990: 304, 19).
101 Murphy (1972: 39).
102 Green (1990: 303–4, 7).
103 Simon (1965: 102, 113).
104 Green (1990: 10, 19).
105 Banks (1955: 15–16).

4 'Secondary education for all' (pp. 92–121)

1 Quoted in Plaskow (1985: 12).
2 Simon (1965: Chapter 1).
3 Lowe (1976: 139–48). Quotation from p. 141.
4 Allen (1934: 125–6).
5 Lowe (1976: 142).
6 Mathieson and Bernbaum (1988: 161–2).
7 Gordon *et al.* (1991: 279).
8 Gordon and White (1979: 152).
9 Lowe (1976: 142–3).
10 See also Gordon and White (1979: 151–2), who argue that Morant was very sympathetic towards movements aimed at widening the educational opportunities of working people.
11 Reid (1985). Quotations from pp. 296, 298, 299, 306 and 300.
12 Reid and Filby (1982: 23, 77–84).
13 Ibid.: 89–90, 91–3, 251–7. See also Newsome (1961).
14 Reid (1985: 306).
15 Quoted in Kazamias (1966: 171).
16 Ibid.: 175.
17 Ibid.
18 Gordon, *et al.* (1991: 295–8).
19 Quoted in Kazamias (1966: 233).
20 Lindsay (1926).
21 Barker (1972: 26–45).
22 Tawney (1922).
23 Ibid.: 71, 111.
24 Gordon and White (1979: 161).
25 Ibid.: 159–61. See also 158–64.
26 Inglis (1993: 15) and Gordon and Lawton (1978: 70, 86).
27 Maclure (1986: 179, 192).
28 Ibid.: 181.
29 Ibid.: 200; and McCulloch (1991: Chapter 4).
30 Reid and Filby (1982: 94, 244–5).
31 McCulloch (1993a). Quotation from pp. 174–5.
32 Maclure (1986: 201–2) and Reid and Filby (1982: 122–3).
33 McCulloch (1993a: 176). See also Banks (1955).
34 Maclure (1986: 210).
35 Tawney (1966: 72).
36 Silver (1980: 23).
37 Tawney (1922: 146).
38 Savage (1983).
39 Ibid.: 261–3, 272–7.
40 Ranson (1988). Quotations from pp. 3–4.
41 Ibid.: 4–5.
42 Gordon *et al.* (1991: 30–1).
43 Barker (1972: Chapter 5).
44 Gordon *et al.* (1991: 62–3).
45 Chitty (1988). Quotation from p. 324.
46 Barker (1972); see also Parkinson (1970).
47 Chitty (1988: 324).

48 Barker (1972: 90–1).
49 On the American tradition, see Kaestle (1983), especially Chapters 5 and 6.
50 Banks (1955: 206–7).
51 Gordon *et al.* (1991: 304–5). In 1954, 5,500 pupils entered for GCE, and, by 1958, 16,787.
52 See Vernon (1964).
53 Maclure (1986: 237).
54 Floud *et al.* (1957); Jackson and Marsden (1966); Hoggart (1957); Douglas (1964); Bernstein (1958).
55 Gordon *et al.* (1991: 114).
56 Crosland (1956). See also Kogan (1971).
57 Hopkins (1978: 25). See also McPherson and Raab (1988).
58 McCulloch (1991: 4) quoting Ball.
59 Cox and Dyson (1969a; 1969b; 1970); Cox and Boyson (1975; 1977).
60 Chitty (1988: 327, 329–30).
61 Callaghan (1989).
62 Chitty (1989: 331).
63 Lowe (1988: 202).
64 Johnson (1992: 267–98). Quotations from pp. 268–9 and 271.
65 Green (1990: 213).
66 Green (1991a: 11).
67 Ibid.: 23.
68 Green (1990: 142, 198).
69 McCulloch (1991: Chapter 2).
70 Green (1991b). Quotation from p. 61.
71 Green (1990: 109).
72 McCulloch (1991: 5, 17).
73 Gordon *et al.* (1991: 17).
74 Statham *et al.* (1989: 91).
75 Green (1991a: 23; 1991b: 68); and Gordon *et al.* (1991: 17–20).
76 McCulloch (1991: 15). McCulloch (1991: 2) refers to it as a 'moral' curriculum.
77 Stone (1969). Quotation from p. 83.
78 Bamford (1967: 30).
79 Reid and Filby (1982: 9, 20, 31, 205).
80 Johnson (1970). Quotations from pp. 113 and 110.
81 McCulloch (1988). Quotations from pp. 37–40.
82 Green (1991a: 14).
83 Stone (1969: 72).
84 Ibid.: 73.
85 Wilkinson (1964: 90–1); and Green (1991a: 15).
86 Green (1991a: 14–15).
87 Salter and Tapper (1985: 211).
88 McCulloch (1991: 16). See Salter and Tapper (1985) for ideas about how public schools achieved this political and ideological success. For a case study of Oxford and Cambridge universities, see Tapper and Salter (1992), especially Parts One and Four.
89 Turner (1961). Quotations from pp. 123, 124, 126 and 130.
90 Banks (1955: 51).
91 Reid and Filby (1982: 61, 97, 229–31).
92 McCulloch (1993b: 11–12).
93 Popper (1962: 7).

94 Torrington and Weightman (1985).
95 Grace (1993).
96 Ibid.: 355–6, 362.
97 Dent (1977: 13).
98 Gordon *et al.* (1991: 249).
99 Grace (1985: 8).
100 Ibid.: 3–16. Quotations from pp. 5–6 and 8.
101 Bergen (1988: 49, 55).
102 Gordon *et al.* (1991: 252–3).
103 Grace (1985: 10–11).
104 Gordon *et al.* (1991: 255–8).
105 Grace (1987). Quotations from p. 197.
106 Bamford (1967: 119–20).
107 Dent (1977: 36–7).
108 Green (1991a: 15–16).

5 The battle of ideas (pp. 122–49)

1 Horton (1967: 185–6).
2 Williams (1965: 57, 64, 69).
3 Rubinstein (1993: 7).
4 Jones (1989: 80).
5 Cairncross (1992: 230). See also Leys (1985); Roderick and Stephens (1982: Chapter 2).
6 Cairncross (1992: 22).
7 Rubinstein (1993: Chapters 1 and 2); Sampson (1962); Barnett (1972; 1986); Wiener (1981).
8 Cairncross (1992: 26–8).
9 *Education Statistics For The U.K.* (1986: 7). Despite this, UK expenditure on education, as a percentage of GDP, remains low by international standards. See OECD (1992: 41) where the UK comes fifth from last out of 20 countries. By 1988, the proportion of total GDP spent on education by the UK had fallen to 4.7 per cent.
10 Mathieson and Bernbaum (1988). Quotations from pp. 128–30.
11 Gamble (1988: 3).
12 Ibid.: 11–12.
13 Hall (1988: 96–7, 104, 108–9).
14 King (1987: 3).
15 Gamble (1986: 34).
16 Gamble (1988: 14–20).
17 Morgan (1986: 30–1); Harvey (1990: 125–7); Lipietz (1992: Chapter 1).
18 Harvey (1990: 147–56, 159–71).
19 Somerville (1992). Quotation from p. 94; Gamble (1988: 14).
20 Levitas (1985). Quotations from p. 7.
21 Scruton (1984: 32–3).
22 Somerville (1992: 99). Joseph's article (and related speeches) led to his being given the name 'Sir Sheath Joseph'. Some people took the view that this excluded him as a serious candidate for the leadership of the Conservative Party in 1974–5.
23 Johnson (1991b). Quotations from pp. 93 and 98.
24 Jones (1989: 53).
25 Somerville (1992: 104).

26 Inglis (1993: 14, 215).
27 Marx (1983). Quotation from pp. 287–8.
28 Salter and Tapper (1985: 31).
29 Said (1994: 3–10).
30 Ibid.: 55, 57–8, 60–1, 74, 82, 90.
31 Salter and Tapper (1985: 30–2, 34).
32 King (1987: 24), quoting Nisbet.
33 Honderich (1990: 1).
34 Goodwin (1992: 161).
35 Ibid.: 159, 161–2.
36 Ibid.: 163–6. See also Chapter 1 above, pp. 20–6.
37 Ibid.: 165–7, 170–1.
38 Honderich (1990: 238–9).
39 Green (1987: 2).
40 Gamble (1988: 22).
41 Green (1987: 1–5).
42 Gamble (1988: 27, 38).
43 Ibid.: 54.
44 Ibid.: 50–60.
45 Bosanquet (1983: 5–7).
46 Levitas (1986: 2).
47 Welsh (1993). Quotations from pp. 46, 57 and 53.
48 Ibid.: 50, 51 and 57.
49 Gamble (1988: 37).
50 Somerville (1992: 103–4).
51 Bullock and Woodings (1983: 311).
52 Johnson (1992). Quotation from pp. 269–70.
53 Bullock and Woodings (1983: 312).
54 Green (1987: 109, 127).
55 Johnson (1991b: 90).
56 Ashford (1993). Quotation from p. 41.
57 Green (1987: 56).
58 Bullock and Woodings (1983: 242).
59 See Green (1987: Chapter 3).
60 Johnson (1991b: 104).
61 Green (1987: 155).
62 Ibid.: 34–5.
63 Nozick (1974: Preface and Chapter 10).
64 Green (1987: 46–7).
65 Ibid.: 102–3, 107.
66 Honderich (1990: 22).
67 Gamble (1988: 170).
68 Scruton (1984: 33, 53).
69 Quoted in Johnson (1991b: 97).
70 Scruton (1984: 53, 56).
71 Ibid.: 56–9.
72 Gilmour (1992: 8).
73 Salter and Tapper (1985: 157–8).
74 Ibid.: 171.
75 Ibid.: 161–3, 165.
76 Ibid.: 165–6, 168–9.
77 Ibid.: 169–71, 180, 173–5.

78 Ibid.: 100–3, 106.
79 See Kogan (1971) especially pp. 24–5, 46–7 and 185. See also Salter and Tapper (1985: 237–43) on the methodology of this sort of work.
80 Kogan (1971: 44–8). See also Chapter 4 of this book pp. 104–5.
81 Gilmour (1992: 52–3).
82 Quoted in Ball (1990b: 32).
83 Gamble (1988: 147); and Hampson, quoted in Knight (1990: 62).
84 Knight (1990: 133 fn 110, 124). On pressure groups and think-tanks generally, see *Labour Research* (1984; 1987; 1990).
85 Knight (1990: 69–71).
86 Salter and Tapper (1985: 174–6).
87 Hillgate Group (1986).
88 Knight (1990: 50).
89 Hopkins (1978: 85–6); Jones (1989: 41).
90 Schlesinger (1988: 96–7).
91 Centre for Contemporary Cultural Studies, Education Group (1981: 210–15).
92 Jones (1989: 41).
93 Ibid.: 60–4.
94 Centre for Policy Studies (1985); Hillgate Group (1986).
95 Levitas (1985).
96 Eagleton (1991: 30).
97 Ibid.: 112; Kenway (1990). Quotation from Kenway (1990: 177).
98 Eagleton (1991: 116). See also Williams (1977: 112).
99 Simon (1991). Quotations from Chapter 2. On Hegemony generally, see also Anderson (1977).
100 Green (1990: 96, 99).
101 Gamble (1988: 26, 180, 237–8).
102 Parekh (1982: Chapters 2 and 3).

6 The New Right offensive (pp. 150–82)

1 Coe (1994: 313).
2 See, on this, Bulpitt (1986).
3 Raab (1993). Quotation from p. 239.
4 Chang (1993).
5 Raab (1993: 242).
6 Gamble (1988), especially Chapter 1.
7 For example, Jowell *et al.* (1989: 141, 63). See also the ICM poll reported in *The Guardian*, 21 September 1994, pp. 6–7, which showed that since 1990 the majority of those polled did *not* think that state schools were safe in the hands of Mrs Thatcher and Mr Major.
8 Adapted from Gamble (1988: 164).
9 Gilmour (1992: 52).
10 Johnson (1985: 224–55). Quotations from pp. 234–5.
11 Gamble (1988: 143, 170–1).
12 Rubinstein (1993: 73, 150–1).
13 Hanham (1971: 35).
14 Blewett (1965). Quotation from p. 30.
15 Butler (1963: 21–2, 29).
16 Ibid.: 148–9. See also Butler (1989: 55). Between 1918 and 1945, 113 university seats were filled: in 75 cases a Conservative was returned, in 18 a Liberal, and in

20 candidates with no application (Butler 1963: 149). On the franchise generally, see Jones (1966); Clarke (1972); and Dunbabin (1980).

17 Bulpitt (1986: 21, 29).

18 Gilmour (1992: 53).

19 Gamble (1988: 167–70).

20 See Chapter 5, pp. 128–9 and p. 139.

21 Gamble (1988: 173), quoting Grainger.

22 Ranson (1993). Quotation from p. 345.

23 The actual percentage of votes cast (with the Conservative majority in brackets) were: 1979, 43.9 per cent (43); 1983, 42.4 per cent (144); 1987, 42.3 per cent (102); 1992, 41.9 per cent (21). The percentage of votes cast for the Conservative Party in the following elections (all of which they lost) were: 1945, 39.8 per cent; 1950, 43.5 per cent; 1964, 43.4 per cent; 1966, 41.9 per cent. See, on this, Butler and Kavanagh (1988); and King *et al.* (1993: 249 [Appendix]).

24 Newson (1993: 133).

25 For a more detailed and critical account, see Centre for Contemporary Cultural Studies, Education Group (1981: Chapter 3).

26 Knight (1990: 115).

27 Hopkins (1978: 80–2).

28 Donoghue (1987: 109–10).

29 Salter and Tapper (1985: 178).

30 Knight (1990: 85, 89, 97–8).

31 Ibid.: 153, 168, 181.

32 Ibid.: 156.

33 Jones (1989: 4).

34 Knight (1990: 7–8).

35 Ibid.: 91; and Ball (1990b: Chapter 2).

36 Ball (1990b: Chapter 2).

37 See Dr Boyson's more realistic account in Chitty (1979: 157).

38 Bowe and Ball (1992: Chapter 1). See also Rizvi and Kemmis (1987).

39 Raab (1993: 234).

40 Ibid.: 239.

41 Salter and Tapper (1985: 228).

42 Ibid.: 229.

43 Johnson (1991a: 31–86). Quotation from p. 43.

44 Knight (1990: 138–9).

45 Simon (1985: 205).

46 Edwards *et al.* (1989: 1–3, 32, 58, 62–5).

47 Jones (1989: 14).

48 Knight (1990: 142).

49 Johnson (1991a: 46).

50 Ibid.: 46–7.

51 Jones (1989: 15).

52 Knight (1990: 164 fn. 6; 145).

53 Ibid.: 151, 164 fn. 3.

54 Jones (1989: 17).

55 Knight (1990: 156).

56 Jones (1989: 17).

57 Plaskow (1985). Quotations from pp. 1, 190 and 13. See also Lawton (1980: 76).

58 Plaskow (1985: 1, 190).

59 Chitty (1988: 332–3).

60 Jones (1989: 19).
61 Gamble (1988: 116).
62 Jones (1989: 133).
63 Ibid.: 26.
64 Pietrasik (1987). Quotations from pp. 186–7.
65 Jones (1989: 132–3).
66 Chitty (1989: 200–4).
67 Johnson (1991a: 62–3).
68 Chitty (1989: 180–9)
69 Johnson (1991a: 64–86).
70 Ibid.: 64.
71 Maclure (1988: Chapter 4).
72 Johnson (1991a: 81).
73 Ranson (1988). Quotation from p. 15.
74 Raab (1993: 232–3).
75 Hartnett and Naish (1990).
76 Johnson (1991a: 68).
77 Statham *et al.* (1989: 55).
78 Chitty and Mitchell (1993). Quotation from p. 22.
79 In April 1993, Sir Ron Dearing was appointed to bring the juggernaut of the National Curriculum under some sort of control. He reported in December 1993 and proposed a 'slimming down' of the 'statutory curriculum'. See School Curriculum and Assessment Authority (1993). The government accepted 'in full the main recommendations' of his final report. In the summer of 1994, Patten was sacked as Secretary of State and replaced by Mrs Shepherd. It was widely believed that his period in office had not been entirely successful.
80 Chitty and Mitchell (1993: 23).
81 Department for Education (1992: 44–7)
82 Chitty and Mitchell (1993: 23).
83 Simon and Chitty (1993: 65–7).
84 Department for Education (1992: 50–1).
85 Ibid.: 32–4, 36–7, 57.
86 Reported in *The Guardian*, 28 September 1993, p. 4.
87 Hillgate Group (1986: 14).
88 Statham *et al.* (1989: 97); and Simon and Chitty (1993: 67–70).
89 Department for Education (1993: 9, 12; 1994).
90 Department for Education (1993: 1, 4).
91 Quoted in Blake (1994). Quotation from p. 55.
92 O'Hear (1988). Quotations from pp. 18, 27 and 22.
93 Scruton (1984: 9).
94 See, on this, Bosanquet (1981).
95 Haviland (1988).
96 Department of Education and Science (1987).
97 Education Reform Act (1988), section 1.
98 Aldrich (1988).
99 Reid and Holt (1986: 94–9).
100 Carr and Hartnett (1996).
101 Chitty *et al.* (1991: 83–99). Quotation from p. 86.
102 Campbell and Neill (1994: 104).
103 Department of Education and Science (1987: paras 67, 95).
104 Hartnett and Naish (1986).

105 Ranson (1988: 17).
106 Mill (1965: 944).
107 See pp. 107–19 of this book.
108 Bamford (1967: 30); and Department for Education (1992: 37).
109 Simon and Chitty (1993: 105).
110 Salter and Tapper (1985: 176–7).
111 Rowntree (1989: 83).
112 Salter and Tapper (1985: 182).
113 Ibid.: 108.
114 Department for Education (1992: 7).
115 Grace (1993). Quotations from pp. 360, 361 and 363.
116 Ball (1990a). Quotations from pp. 157, 158, 162 and 164. See also Inglis (1989); Rizvi (1989).
117 Donald (1992: 128).
118 Ibid.: 155.
119 Scruton (1984: 157).

Conclusion (pp. 183–200)

1 Dewey (1930b: 297–8).
2 Lindley (1986: 139, 181, 182).
3 Mills (1963).
4 Habermas (1974).
5 MacIntyre (1987).
6 Hearn (1985: 168).
7 Gutmann (1987: 39).
8 Peters (1979: 463).
9 Ibid.: 463.
10 Ibid.
11 Held (1987: 280).
12 Ibid.: 283–9).
13 Gutmann (1987: 44).
14 Ibid.
15 Ibid.: 45.
16 Ibid.
17 Ibid.
18 Ibid.: 18.
19 Ibid.: 47.
20 Ibid.
21 Ibid.
22 Ibid.: 136.
23 Ibid.: 287–8.
24 Silver and Brennan (1988: 4).
25 The case for this kind of 'liberal vocationalism' is made in some detail in Silver and Brennan (1988).
26 Donald (1992: 133–44).
27 For a further discussion of this view of teaching and teacher education, see Hartnett and Naish (1986) and Carr (1989).
28 Carr (1951: 76), quoted in Arblaster (1994: 103).

REFERENCES AND

BIBLIOGRAPHY

Acton, H.B. (ed.) (1951) *Utilitarianism, Liberty and Representative Government*. London: Dent and Sons.

Aldrich, R. (1988) 'The National Curriculum: an historical perspective', in D. Lawton and C. Chitty (eds) *The National Curriculum*, Bedford Way Papers 33. London: Institute of Education, University of London, pp. 21–33.

Allen, B.M. (1934) *Sir Robert Morant A Great Public Servant*. London: Macmillan.

Anderson, P. (1977) 'The Antinomies of Antonio Gramsci', *New Left Review*, 100, 5–78.

Apple, M. (ed.) (1982) *Cultural and Economic Reproduction in Education*. London: Routledge & Kegan Paul.

Arblaster, A. (1984) *The Rise and Decline of Western Liberalism*. Oxford: Basil Blackwell.

Arblaster, A. (1994) *Democracy*. Milton Keynes: Open University Press.

Arblaster, A. and Lukes, S. (eds) (1971) *The Good Society*. London: Methuen.

Archer, M. (1979) *Social Origins of Educational Systems*. London: Sage Publications.

Aristotle (1981) *The Politics*. Harmondsworth: Penguin.

Arnold, M. (1932) *Culture and Anarchy* (ed. J. Dover Wilson). Cambridge: Cambridge University Press.

Ashford, M. (1993) 'The ideas of the New Right', in G. Jordan and M. Ashford (eds) *Public Policy and the Impact of the New Right*. London: Pinter, pp. 19–45.

Bailey, C. (1984) *Beyond the Present and the Particular: A Theory of Liberal Education*. London: Routledge & Kegan Paul.

Bain, A. (1879) *Education as Science*. London: Kegan Paul.

Ball, S.J. (1990a) 'Management as a moral technology', in S. Ball (ed.) *Foucault and Education: Disciplines and Knowledge*. London: Routledge, pp. 153–66.

Ball, S.J. (1990b) *Politics and Policy Making in Education: Explorations in Policy Sociology*. London: Routledge.

Bamford, T.W. (1967) *Rise of the Public Schools*. London: Nelson.

Banks, O. (1955) *Parity and Prestige in English Secondary Education: A Study in Educational Sociology*. London: Routledge & Kegan Paul.

Barker, R. (1972) *Education and Politics 1900–1951: A Study of the Labour Party.* Oxford: Oxford University Press.

Barnard, H.C. (1947) *A Short History of English Education 1760–1944.* London: University of London Press.

Barnett, C. (1972) *The Collapse of British Power.* New York: Morrow.

Barnett, C. (1986) *The Audit of War: The Illusion and Reality of Britain as a Great Power.* London: Macmillan.

Bell, D. (1962) *The End of Ideology: On the Exhaustion of Political Ideals in the Fifties.* London: Collier Macmillan.

Bentham, J. (1843) 'Constitutional Code', reprinted in J. Bowring (ed.) (1938) *The Works of Jeremy Bentham*, Vol. IX. Edinburgh: W. Tait.

Bergen, B.H. (1988) 'Only a schoolmaster: gender, class and the effort to professionalize elementary teaching in England, 1870–1910', in J. Ozga *Schoolwork: Approaches to the Labour Process of Teaching.* Milton Keynes: Open University Press, pp. 39–60.

Berlin, I. (1969) *Four Essays on Liberty.* Oxford: Oxford University Press.

Bernstein, B. (1958) 'Some sociological determinants of perception', *British Journal of Sociology*, IX, June, 159–74.

Bernstein, R.B. (1985) 'Dewey, democracy and the task ahead of us', in B. Rajchman and C. West (eds) *Post-Analytical Philosophy.* New York: Columbia University Press, pp. 48–59.

Blake, D. (1994) 'Teacher education reforms', *Forum*, 36, 2, 54–6.

Blewett, N. (1965) 'The franchise in the United Kingdom 1885–1918', *Past and Present*, 32, 27–56.

Bosanquet, N. (1981) 'Sir Keith's reading list', *Politics Quarterly*, 52, 324–41.

Bosanquet, N. (1983) *After the New Right.* London: Heinemann.

Bowe, R. and Ball, S.J. (1992) *Reforming Education and Changing Schools.* London: Routledge.

Bowles, S. and Gintis, H. (1976) *Schooling in Capitalist America.* New York: Basic Books.

Bowring, J. (ed.) (1938) *The Works of Jeremy Bentham.* Edinburgh: W. Tait.

Boydston, J.A. (ed.) (1969) *The Early Works of John Dewey (1882–1898).* Carbondale: South Illinois University Press.

Boydston, J.A. (ed.) (1980) *John Dewey: The Middle Works (1899–1924).* Carbondale: South Illinois University Press.

Boydston, J.A. (ed.) (1981a) *John Dewey: The Later Works (1925–1953).* Carbondale: South Illinois University Press.

Bullock, A. and Shock, M. (eds) (1956) *The Liberal Tradition: from Fox to Keynes.* London: Adam and Charles Black.

Bullock, A. and Woodings, R.B. (eds) (1983) *The Fontana Biographical Companion to Modern Thought.* London: Fontana.

Bulpitt, J. (1986) 'The discipline of the new democracy: Mrs. Thatcher's domestic statecraft', *Political Studies*, XXXIV, 19–39.

Burke, E. (1910) *Reflections on the Revolution in France* (Everyman edition). London: Dent.

Butler, D. (1963) *The Electoral System in Britain since 1918.* Oxford: Clarendon Press.

Butler, D. (1989) *British General Elections since 1945.* Oxford: Basil Blackwell.

Butler, D. and Kavanagh, D. (1988) *The British General Election of 1987.* London: Macmillan.

Cairncross, A. (1992) *The British Economy since 1945.* Oxford: Blackwell.

Callaghan, J. (1989) 'Ruskin College Speech' (1976) reprinted in 'Supplementary Readings for blocks 3 and 4', in *Exploring Educational Issues* (Open University course E208). Milton Keynes: Open University, pp. 2–5.

Campbell, J. and Neill, S. (1994) *Curriculum Reform at Key Stage I: Teacher Commitment and Policy Failure.* Harlow: Longman.

Carr, E.H. (1951) *The New Society*. London: Macmillan.

Carr, W. (ed.) (1989) *Quality in Teaching: Arguments for a Reflective Profession*. Lewes: Falmer Press.

Carr, W. (1995) *For Education: Towards Critical Educational Inquiry*. Buckingham: Open University Press.

Carr, W. and Hartnett, A. (1996) 'Civic education, democracy and the English political tradition', in J. Demaine and H. Entwistle (eds) *Beyond Communitarianism: Citizenship, Politics and Education*. Basingstoke: Macmillan Press.

Centre for Contemporary Cultural Studies, Education Group (1981) *Unpopular Education: Schooling and Social Democracy in England since 1944*. London: Hutchinson.

Centre for Policy Studies (1985) *Omega File*.

Chang, J. (1993) *Wild Swans*. London: HarperCollins.

Chitty, C. (1979) 'Inside the secondary school: problems and prospects', in D. Rubinstein (ed.) *Education and Equality*. Harmondsworth: Penguin Books.

Chitty, C. (1988) 'Central control of the school curriculum 1944–87', *History of Education*, 17, 4, 321–34.

Chitty, C. (1989) *Towards a New Education System: The Victory of the New Right?* London: Falmer Press.

Chitty, C. (1990) 'Education and training', in N. Entwistle (ed.) *Handbook of Educational Ideas and Practices*. London: Routledge, pp. 33–42.

Chitty, C. (ed.) (1991) *Changing the Future Redprint for Education*. London: Tufnell Press.

Chitty, C. and Mitchell, P. (1993) 'Attack on local democracy', *Forum*, 35, 1, 22–4.

Chitty, C., Jakubowska, T. and Jones, K. (1991) 'The National Curriculum and assessment: changing course', in C. Chitty (ed.) *Changing the Future: Redprint for Education*. London: Tufnell Press.

Clarke, F. (1940) *Education and Social Change*. London: Sheldon Press and Macmillan.

Clarke, P. (1972) 'Electoral sociology of modern Britain', *History*, 59, 31–55.

Coe, J. (1994) *What a Carve Up!* Harmondsworth: Viking.

Connell, W.F. (1950) *The Educational Thought and Influence of Matthew Arnold*. London: Routledge & Kegan Paul.

Conservative Research Department (1985) 'Education, Politics Today', No. 14.

Cosin, B., Flude, M. and Hales, M. (eds) (1989) *School Work and Equality*. London: Hodder & Stoughton.

Cox, C.B. and Boyson, R. (eds) (1975) *Black Paper 1975*. London: J.M. Dent.

Cox, C.B. and Boyson, R. (eds) (1977) *Black Paper 1977*. London: Temple Smith.

Cox, C.B. and Dyson, A.E. (eds) (1969a) *Fight for Education: A Black Paper*. London: Critical Quarterly Society.

Cox, C.B. and Dyson, A.E. (eds) (1969b) *Black Paper Two: The Crisis in Education*. London: Critical Quarterly Society.

Cox, C.B. and Dyson, A.E. (eds) (1970) *Black Paper Three*. London: Critical Quarterly Society.

Crosland, C.A.R. (1956) *The Future of Socialism*. London: Cape.

Dahl, R.A. (1985) *A Preface to Economic Democracy*. Cambridge: Polity Press.

Davie, G.E. (1961) *The Democratic Intellect: Scotland and Her Universities in the Nineteenth Century*. Edinburgh: Edinburgh University Press.

Davie, G.E. (1986) *The Crisis of the Democratic Intellect. The Problem of Generalism and Specialisation in Twentieth Century Scotland*. Edinburgh: Polygon.

Demaine, J. and Entwistle, H. (1996) *Beyond Communitarianism: Citizenship, Politics and Education*. Basingstoke: Macmillan Press.

Dent, H.C. (1977) *The Training of Teachers in England and Wales 1800–1975*. Sevenoakes: Hodder & Stoughton.

Department for Education (1992) *Choice and Diversity: A New Framework for Schools*, CM. 2021. London: HMSO.

Department for Education (1993) *Government Proposals for the Reform of Initial Teacher Training*. London.
Department for Education (1994) Press Release 240/94, 5 October.
Department of Education and Science (1985) *Better Schools*. London: HMSO.
Department of Education and Science (1987) *The National Curriculum 5–16: A Consultation Document*. London: HMSO.
Dewey, J. (1899) *The School and Society*. Chicago: The University of Chicago Press (revised edition 1915).
Dewey, J. (1913) 'Some dangers in the present movement for industrial education', reprinted in J.A. Boydston (ed.) (1980) *John Dewey: The Middle Works (1899–1924)*, Vol. 7. Carbondale: South Illinois University Press.
Dewey, J. (1914) 'Liberal education', in P. Monroe (ed.) *Encylopaedia of Education*, 4, New York: MacMillan.
Dewey, J. (1916) *Democracy and Education*. New York: The Free Press.
Dewey, J. (1917) 'The Need for a Recovery of Philosophy', reprinted in J.A. Boydston (ed.) (1980) *John Dewey: The Middle Works (1899–1924)*, Vol. 10. Carbondale: South Illinois University Press.
Dewey, J. (1920) *Reconstruction in Philosophy*. New York: Holt.
Dewey, J. (1922) 'Public Opinion', reprinted in J.A. Boydston (ed.) (1980) *John Dewey: The Middle Works (1899–1924)*, Vol. 13. Carbondale: South Illinois University Press.
Dewey, J. (1927) *The Public and Its Problems*. New York: Henny Holt and Co.
Dewey, J. (1930a) *Individualism, Old and New*. New York: Minton, Balch and Co.
Dewey, J. (1930b) 'Philosophy and Education', reprinted in J.A. Boydston (ed.) (1981a) *John Dewey: The Later Works (1925–1953)*, Vol. 5. Carbondale: South Illinois University Press.
Dewey, J. (1932) *Ethics*. New York: Henry Holt and Co.
Dewey, J. (1935a) *Liberalism and Social Action*. New York: Capricorn.
Dewey, J. (1935b) 'The Future of Liberalism', reprinted in J.A. Boydston (ed.) (1981a) *John Dewey: The Later Works (1925–1953)*, Vol. 1. Carbondale: South Illinois University Press.
Dewey, J. (1936) 'Liberalism and Equality', reprinted in J. A. Boydston (ed.) (1981a) *John Dewey: The Later Works (1925–1953)*, Vol. 1. Carbondale: South Illinois University Press.
Dewey, J. (1937) 'Democracy and Educational Administration', reprinted in J.A. Boydston (ed.) *John Dewey: The Later Works (1925–1953)*, Vol. 11. Carbondale: South Illinois University Press.
Dewey, J. (1939) 'The Modes of Societal Life', in J. Ratner (ed.) *Intelligence in the Modern World*. New York: Random House.
Dewey, J. (1981b) 'My Pedagogic Creed', reprinted in J. McDermott, *The Philosophy of John Dewey*. Chicago: University of Chicago Press.
Donald, J. (1992) *Sentimental Education: Schooling, Popular Culture and the Regulation of Liberty*. London: Verso.
Donoghue, B. (1987) *Prime Minister*. London: Jonathan Cape.
Douglas, J.W.B. (1964) *The Home and the School*. London: MacGibbon and Kee.
Dunbabin, J. (1980) 'British elections in the nineteenth and twentieth centuries, a regional approach', *English Historical Review*, XCV, 241–67.
Eagleton, T. (1990) *The Significance of Theory*. Oxford: Basil Blackwell.
Eagleton, T. (1991) *Ideology: An Introduction*. London: Verso.
Education Group II (1991) *Education Limited: Schooling, Training and the New Right in England since 1979*. London: Unwin Hyman.
Education Statistics for the U.K. (1986). London: HMSO.
Edwards, T., Fitz, J. and Whitty, G. (1989) *The State and Private Education: An Evaluation of the Assisted Places Scheme*. Basingstoke: Falmer Press.

Entwistle, N. (ed.) (1990) *Handbook of Educational Ideas and Practices*. London: Routledge.

Feinberg, W. (1983) *Understanding Education: Towards a Reconstruction of Educational Inquiry*. Cambridge: Cambridge University Press.

Floud, J., Halsey, A.H. and Martin, F.M. (1957) *Social Class and Educational Opportunity*. London: Heinemann.

Francis, M. and Morrow, J. (1994) *A History of English Political Thought in the Nineteenth Century*. London: Duckworth.

Gallie, W.B. (1955) 'Essentially Contested Concepts', *Proceedings of the Aristotelian Society*, LVI, pp. 167–98.

Gamble, A. (1986) 'The Political Economy of Freedom', in R. Levitas (ed.) *The Ideology of the New Right*. Cambridge: Polity Press, pp. 25–54.

Gamble, A. (1988) *The Free Economy and the Strong State*. Basingstoke: Macmillan.

Gardner, P. (1984) *The Lost Elementary Schools of Victorian England*. London: Croom Helm.

Gilmour, I. (1992) *Dancing with Dogma*. London: Simon and Schuster.

Goodson, I. (1985) *Social Histories of the Secondary Curriculum: Subjects for Study*. London: Falmer Press.

Goodwin, B. (1992) *Using Political Ideas*. Chichester: Wiley.

Gordon, P. and Lawton, D. (1978) *Curriculum Change in the Nineteenth and Twentieth Centuries*. London: Hodder & Stoughton.

Gordon, P. and White, J. (1979) *Philosophers as Educational Reformers: The Influence of Idealism on British Educational Thought and Practice*. London: Routledge & Kegan Paul.

Gordon, P., Aldrich, R. and Dean, D. (1991) *Education and Policy in England in the Twentieth Century*. London: Woburn Press.

Gosse, E. (1949) *Father and Son*. Harmondsworth: Penguin Books.

Grace, G. (1985) 'Judging teachers: the social and political contexts of teacher evaluation', *British Journal of Sociology of Education*, 6, 1, 3–16.

Grace, G. (1987) 'Teachers and the state in Britain: a changing relation', in M. Lawn and G. Grace (eds) *Teachers: The Culture and Politics of Work*. Lewes: Falmer Press, pp. 193–228.

Grace, G. (1993) 'On the study of school leadership: beyond educational management', *British Journal of Educational Studies*, XXXXI, 4, 353–65.

Green, A. (1990) *Education and State Formation: The Rise of Education Systems in England, France and the U.S.A.* Basingstoke: Macmillan Press.

Green, A. (1991a) 'The peculiarities of English education', in Education Group II *Education Limited: Schooling, Training and the New Right in England since 1979*. London: Unwin Hyman, pp. 6–30.

Green, A. (1991b) 'The structure of the system: proposals for change', in C. Chitty (ed.) *Changing the Future Redprint for Education*. London: Tufnell Press, pp. 59–82.

Green, D. (1987) *The New Right: The Counter-Revolution in Political, Economic and Social Thought*. Brighton: Wheatsheaf Books.

Green, T.H. (1888) 'Liberal Legislation and Freedom of Contract', in R.L. Nettleship (ed.) *Collected Works of Thomas Hill Green*. London: Longmans.

Gutmann, A. (1987) *Democratic Education*. Princeton, NJ: Princeton University Press.

Habermas, J. (1974) 'The public sphere', trans. S. Lennox and F. Lennox, *New German Critique*, 3, pp. 49–55.

Hall, S. (1988) *The Hard Road to Renewal*. London: Verso.

Halsey, A.H., Floud, J. and Anderson, C.A. (eds) (1961) *Education, Economy and Society*. Glencoe, IL: Free Press.

Hamilton, D. (1989) *Towards a Theory of Schooling*. Lewes: Falmer Press.

Hanham, H.J. (1971) *The Reformed Electoral System in Great Britain 1832–1914*. London: The Historical Association.

Hartnett, A. and Naish, M. (1986) 'Conceptions of education and social change in a democratic society', in A. Hartnett and M. Naish (eds) *Education and Society Today*. Falmer: Falmer Press, pp. 1–17.

Hartnett, A. and Naish, M. (1990) 'The sleep of reason breeds monsters: the birth of a statutory curriculum in England and Wales', *Journal of Curriculum Studies*, 22, 1, 1–16.

Harvey, D. (1990) *The Condition of Postmodernity*. Oxford: Basil Blackwell.

Haviland, J. (1988) *Take Care, Mr Baker*. London: Fourth Estate.

Hayden, G. (ed.) (1987) *Education and Values: The Richard Peters Lectures*. London: University of London Institute of Education.

Hayek, F.A. von (1976) *The Road to Serfdom*. London: Routledge & Kegan Paul.

Hearn, F. (1985) *Reason and Freedom in Sociological Thought*. London: Allen & Unwin.

Held, D. (1987) *Models of Democracy*. Cambridge: Polity Press.

Hillgate Group (1986) *Whose Schools? A Radical Manifesto*. London: Hillgate Group.

Hoggart, R. (1957) *The Uses of Literacy*. Harmondsworth: Penguin Books.

Hollis, M. (1971) 'The pen and the purse', *Proceedings of the Philosophy of Education Society of Great Britain*, 5, 2.

Honderich, T. (1990) *Conservatism*. London: Hamish Hamilton.

Hopkins, A. (1978) *The School Debate*. Harmondsworth: Penguin Books.

Horowitz, I. (ed.) (1963) *Power, Politics and People*. New York: Oxford University Press.

Horton, R.N. (1967) 'African traditional thought and western science part II', *Africa*, 37, pp. 155–87.

Hurt, J.S. (1971) *Education in Evolution: Church, State, Society and Popular Education 1800–1870*. London: Rupert Hart-Davis.

Hurt, J.S. (1979) *Elementary Schooling and the Working Classes 1860–1918*. London: Routledge & Kegan Paul.

Inglis, F. (1989) 'Managerialism and morality: the corporate and the republican school', in W. Carr (ed.) *Quality in Teaching: Arguments for a Reflective Profession*. Lewes: Falmer Press, pp. 35–54.

Inglis, F. (1993) *Cultural Studies*. Oxford: Blackwell.

Jackson, B. and Marsden, D. (1966) *Education and the Working Class*. Harmondsworth: Penguin Books.

Johnson, R. (1970) 'Educational policy and social control in early Victorian England', *Past and Present*, 49, 96–119.

Johnson, R. (1991a) 'A new road to serfdom? A critical history of the 1988 Act', in Education Group II *Education Limited: Schooling, Training and the New Right in England since 1979*. London: Unwin Hyman, pp. 31–86.

Johnson, R. (1991b) 'My New Right education', in Education Group II *Education Limited: Schooling, Training and the New Right in England since 1979*. London: Unwin Hyman, pp. 87–113.

Johnson, R. (1992) 'Radical education and the New Right', in A. Ruttansi and D. Reeder (eds) *Rethinking Radical Education: Essays in Honour of Brian Simon*. London: Lawrence and Wishart, pp. 267–98.

Johnson, R.W. (1985) *The Politics of Recession*. London: Macmillan.

Jonathan, R. (1986) 'Education and the needs of society', in A. Hartnett and M. Naish (eds) *Education and Society Today*. London: Falmer Press, pp. 135–45.

Jones, G. (1966) 'Further thoughts on the franchise 1885–1918', *Past and Present*, 34, 134–8.

Jones, K. (1989) *Right Turn: The Conservative Revolution in Education*. London: Hutchinson-Radius.

Jordan, G. and Ashford, M. (eds) (1993) *Public Policy and the Impact of the New Right*. London: Pinter.

Jowell, R., Witherspoon, S. and Brook, L. (1989) *British Social Attitudes: A Special Report.* Aldershot: Gower.

Kaestle, C.F. (1983) *Pillars of the Republic: Common Schools and American Society.* New York: Hill and Lang.

Kamenka, E. (ed.) (1983) *The Portable Karl Marx.* Harmondsworth: Penguin.

Kazamias, A.M. (1966) *Politics, Society and Secondary Education in England.* Philadelphia: University of Pennsylvania Press.

Kemmis, S. (1986) *Curriculum Theorising: Beyond Reproduction Theory.* Geelong, Victoria: Deakin University Press.

Kemmis, S. (1990) *Curriculum, Contestation and Change: Essays on Education.* Geelong, Victoria: Deakin University Press.

Kenway, J. (1990) 'Education and the Right's discursive politics: private versus state schooling', in S.J. Ball (ed.) *Foucault and Education: Disciplines and Knowledge.* London: Routledge, pp. 167–206.

King, A., Crewe, I., Denver, D., Newton, K., Norton, P., Sanders, D. and Seyd, P. (1993) *Britian at the Polls 1992.* Chatham, NJ: Chatham House.

King, D.S. (1987) *The New Right: Politics, Markets and Citizenship.* Basingstoke: Macmillan.

Knight, C. (1990) *The Making of Tory Education Policy in Post-War Britain 1950–1986.* London: Falmer Press.

Knights, B. (1978) *The Idea of the Clerisy in the Nineteenth Century.* Cambridge: Cambridge University Press.

Knowles, L.C.A. (1937) *The Industrial and Commercial Revolution of Great Britain during the Nineteenth Century.* London: Routledge.

Kogan, M. (1971) *The Politics of Education: Edward Boyle and Anthony Crosland in Conversation with Maurice Kogan.* Harmondsworth: Penguin.

Labour Research (1984) 'Pressure groups', February, 73, 2, 37–42.

Labour Research (1987) 'Getting to know what is right and wrong', October, 76, 10, 7–11.

Labour Research (1990) 'The right sort of education', June, 79, 6, 11–12.

Langford, G. and O'Connor, D.J. (eds) (1973) *New Essays in the Philosophy of Education.* London: Routledge & Kegan Paul.

Lawn, M. and Grace, G. (eds) (1987) *Teachers: the Culture and Politics of Work.* Lewes: Falmer Press.

Lawton, D. (1980) *The Politics of the School Curriculum.* London: Routledge & Kegan Paul.

Lawton, D. and Chitty, C. (eds) (1988) *The National Curriculum*, Bedford Way Papers 33. London: University of London Institute of Education.

Levitas, R. (1985) 'New Right utopias', *Radical Philosophy*, 39, spring, 2–9.

Levitas, R. (1986) (ed.) *The Ideology of the New Right.* Cambridge: Polity Press.

Leys, C. (1985) 'Thatcherism and British manufacturing: a question of hegemony', *New Left Review*, 151, 15–25.

Lindley, R. (1986) *Autonomy.* London: Macmillan.

Lindsay, K. (1926) *Social Progress and Educational Waste: Being a Study of the Free Place and Scholarship System.* London: Routledge.

Lipietz, A. (1992) *Towards A New Economic Order: Postfordism, Ecology and Democracy.* Cambridge: Polity Press.

Lippmann, W. (1922) *Public Opinion*, New York: Free Press.

Lippmann, W. (1925) *The Phantom Public.* New York: MacMillan.

Lowe, R. (1976) 'The divided curriculum: Sadler, Morant and the English secondary school', *Journal of Curriculum Studies*, 8, 2, 139–48.

Lowe, R. (1988) *Education in the Post-War Years: A Social History.* London: Routledge.

MacIntyre, A. (1981) *After Virtue: a Study in Moral Theory.* London: Duckworth.

MacIntyre, A. (1987) 'The idea of an educated public', in G. Hayden (ed.) *Education and Values: The Richard Peters Lectures*. London: University of London Institute of Education.
Maclure, J.S. (1986) *Educational Documents: England and Wales 1816 to the Present Day*. London: Methuen.
Maclure, S. (1988) *Education Re-formed*. Sevenoaks: Hodder & Stoughton.
Macpherson, C.B. (1966) *The Real World of Democracy*. Oxford: Oxford University Press.
Macpherson, C.B. (1973) *Democratic Theory: Essays in Retrieval*. Oxford: Clarendon Press.
Macpherson, C.B. (1977) *The Life and Times of Liberal Democracy*. Oxford: Oxford University Press.
Marquand, D. (1988) *The Unprincipled Society: New Demands and Old Politics*. London: Fontana.
Marx, K. (1983) 'The Eighteenth Brumaire of Louis Napoleon', in E. Kamenka (ed.) *The Portable Karl Marx*. Harmondsworth: Penguin, pp. 287–323.
Mathieson, M. and Bernbaum, G. (1988) 'The British disease: a British tradition?', *British Journal of Educational Studies*, XXVI, 2, 126–74.
McCulloch, G. (1988) 'The Norwood Report and the secondary school curriculum', *History of Education Review*, 17, 2, 30–45.
McCulloch, G. (1991) *Philosophers and Kings: Education for Leadership in Modern England*. Cambridge: Cambridge University Press.
McCulloch, G. (1993a) 'Spens v Norwood: contesting the educational state?', *History of Education*, 22, 2, 163–80.
McCulloch, G. (1993b) *Lessons from the Class of 1994? History as Education*, inaugural lecture. Lancaster: Lancaster University.
McDermott, J. (1981) *The Philosophy of John Dewey*. Chicago: University of Chicago Press.
McKenzie, J. (1993) *Education as a Political Issue*. Aldershot: Avebury.
McPherson, A. and Raab, C. (1988) *Governing Education: A Sociology of Policy since 1945*. Edinburgh: Edinburgh University Press.
Mill, J. (1937) *An Essay on Government*. Cambridge: Cambridge University Press.
Mill, J.S. (1895) *Principles of Political Economy*. New York: Appleton.
Mill, J.S. (1937) *An Essay on Government*. Cambridge: Cambridge University Press.
Mill, J.S. (1951) 'Considerations on representative government', in H.B. Acton (ed.) *Utilitarianism, Liberty and Representative Government*. London: Dent and Sons.
Mill, J.S. (1965) 'Principles of political economy', in J.M. Robson (ed.) *Collected Works of J.S. Mill Vol. 3*. Toronto: Toronto University Press.
Mills, C.W. (1963) 'Mass society and liberal education', in I. Horowitz (ed.) *Power, Politics and People*. New York: Oxford University Press.
Monroe, P. (ed.) (1914) *Enyclopaedia of Education*, 4. New York: MacMillan.
Morgan, G. (1986) *Images of Organisation*. London: Sage Publications.
Morris, N. (1973) *Four Periods of Public Education as Revisited in 1832, 1839, 1846, 1862: James Kay-Shuttleworth*. Brighton: Harvester Press.
Murphy, J. (1972) *The Education Act 1870: Text and Commentary*. Newton Abbot: David and Charles.
Nettleship, R.L. (ed.) (1888) *Collected Works of Thomas Hill Green*. London: Longmans.
Newsome, D. (1961) *Godliness and Good Learning*. London: John Murray.
Newson, K. (1993) 'Caring and competence: the long, long, campaign', in A. King, Crewe, I., Denver, D., Newton, K., Norton, P., Sanders, D. and Seyd, P. *Britian at the Polls 1992*. Chatham, NJ: Chatham House, pp. 129–70.
Nozick, R. (1974) *Anarchy, State and Utopia*. Oxford: Basil Blackwell.

O'Hear, A. (1988) *Who Teaches the Teachers?* London: Social Affairs Unit.

O'Connor, D.J. (1973) 'The nature and scope of educational theory', in G. Langford and D.J. O'Connor (eds) *New Essays in the Philosophy of Education.* London: Routledge & Kegan Paul.

OECD (1992) *Education at a Glance.* Paris Centre for Research and Innovation.

Oestereicher, E. (1982) 'The depoliticization of the liberal arts', *Social Research*, 49, 4, 1004–12.

Ozga, J. (1988) *Schoolwork: Approaches to the Labour Process of Teaching.* Milton Keynes: Open University Press.

Parekh, B. (1982) *Marx's Theory of Ideology.* London: Croom Helm.

Parkinson, M. (1970) *The Labour Party and the Organisation of Secondary Education.* London: Routledge & Kegan Paul.

Pateman, C. (1970) *Participation and Democratic Theory.* Cambridge: Cambridge University Press.

Perkinson, H.J. (1980) *Since Socrates: Studies in the History of Western Educational Thought.* London: Longman.

Peters, R.S. (1979) 'Democratic values and educational aims', *Teachers' College Record*, 8, 3, 463–81.

Pietrasik, R. (1987) 'The teachers' action 1984–1986', in M. Lawn and G. Grace (eds) *Teachers: The Culture and Politics of Work.* London: Falmer Press, pp. 168–89.

Plaskow, M. (ed.) (1985) *The Life and Death of the Schools Council.* London: Falmer Press.

Plato (1974) *The Republic.* Harmondsworth: Penguin.

Popper, K. (1947) 'Utopia and violence', in *Conjectures and Refutations* (3rd edition). London: Routledge & Kegan Paul.

Popper, K.R. (1962) *The Open Society and its Enemies, Volume Two* (4th edition). London: Routledge & Kegan Paul.

Popper, K.R. (1972) 'Two faces of common sense: an argument for common sense realism and against the common sense theory of knowledge', in *Objective Knowledge: An Evolutionary Approach.* Oxford: Clarendon Press.

Pring, R. (1977) 'Common sense and education', *Proceedings of the Philosophy of Education Society of Great Britain*, 11, 57–77.

Purvis, J. (1991) *A History of Women's Education in England.* Milton Keynes: Open University Press.

Purvis, J. (1992) 'The historiography of British education: a feminist critique', in A. Ruttansi and D. Reeder (eds) *Rethinking Radical Education: Essays in Honour of Brian Simon.* London: Lawrence and Wishart, pp. 249–66.

Raab, C.D. (1993) 'Education and the impact of the New Right', in G. Jordan and N. Ashford (eds) *Public Policy and the Impact of the New Right.* London: Pinter, pp. 230–50.

Ranson, S. (1988) 'From 1944 to 1988: education citizenship and democracy (Part 1: Transforming the government of education)', *Local Government Studies*, 14, 1, Jan/Feb 1988, 1–19.

Ranson, S. (1993) 'Markets or democracy for education', *British Journal of Educational Studies*, XXXXI, 4, 333–51.

Reid, W. (1985) 'Curriculum change and the evolution of educational constituencies: the English sixth form in the nineteenth century', in I. Goodson *Social Histories of the Secondary Curriculum: Subjects for Study.* London: Falmer Press, pp. 289–311.

Reid, W. and Filby, J. (1982) *The Sixth: An Essay in Education and Democracy.* London: Falmer Press.

Reid, W. and Holt, M. (1986) 'Structure and ideology in upper secondary education', in A. Hartnett and M. Naish (eds) *Education and Society Today.* London: Falmer Press, pp. 89–108.

Richards, D. and Hunt, J.W. (1950) *An Illustrated History of Modern Britain*. London: Longmans, Green and Co.

Rizvi, F. (1989) 'In defence of organisational democracy', in J. Smyth (ed.) *Critical Perspective on Educational Leadership*. Lewes: Falmer Press, pp. 205–34.

Rizvi, F. and Kemmis, S. (1987) *Dilemmas of Reform*. Geelong, Victoria: Deakin Institute for Studies in Education.

Robson, J.M. (ed.) (1965) *Collected Works of J.S. Mill Vol. 3*. Toronto: Toronto University Press.

Roderick, G. and Stephens, M. (eds) (1982) *The British Malaise: Industrial Performance, Education and Training in Britain Today*. London: Falmer Press.

Rothblatt, S. (1976) *Tradition and Change in English Liberal Education*. London: Faber & Faber.

Rousseau, J.J. (1968) *The Social Contract*. Harmondsworth: Penguin.

Rousseau, J.J. (1974) *Émile*. London: Dent.

Rowntree, D. (1989) 'The side effects of assessment', in B. Cosin, M. Flude and M. Hales (eds) *School Work and Equality*. London: Hodder & Stoughton, pp. 76–84.

Rubinstein, D. (1979) *Education and Equality*. Harmondsworth: Penguin.

Rubinstein, W.D. (1993) *Capitalism, Culture and Decline in Britain 1750–1990*. London: Routledge.

Rusk, R.R. (1979) *Doctrines of the Great Educators* (15th edition). London: Macmillan.

Ruttansi, A. and Reeder, D. (eds) (1992) *Rethinking Radical Education: Essays in Honour of Brian Simon*. London: Lawrence and Wishart.

Said, E. (1994) *Representations of the Intellectual: The 1993 Reith Lectures*. London: Vintage.

Salter, B. and Tapper, T. (1985) *Power and Policy in Education: The Case of Independent Schooling*. London: Falmer Press.

Sampson, A. (1962) *Anatomy of Britain*. London: Hodder & Stoughton.

Sandel, M. (ed.) (1984) *Liberalism and its Critics*. Oxford: Basil Blackwell.

Savage, G.L. (1983) 'Social class and social policy: the civil service and secondary education in England during the interwar period', *Journal of Contemporary History*, 18, 261–80.

Schlesinger, P. (1988) *Putting Reality Together: The BBC and Its News*. London: Sage.

School Curriculum and Assessment Authority (1993) *National Curriculum and Its Assessment: Final Report*. London: School Curriculum and Assessment Authority.

Schumpeter, J. (1942) *Capitalism, Socialism and Democracy*. New York: Harper and Row.

Scruton, R. (1984) *The Meaning of Conservatism*. London: Macmillan.

Selleck, R.J. (1968) *The New Education 1870–1914*. London: Issac Pitman.

Shannon, R. (1974) *The Crisis of Imperialism*. London: Hart-Davis MacGibbon.

Silver, H. (1980) *Education and the Social Condition*. London: Methuen.

Silver, H. and Brennan, J. (1988) A *Liberal Vocationalism*. London: Methuen.

Simon, B. (1965) *Education and the Labour Movement 1870–1920*. London: Lawrence and Wishart.

Simon, B. (1976) *The Two Nations and the Educational Structure 1780–1870*. London: Lawrence and Wishart.

Simon, B. (1985) *Does Education Matter?* London: Lawrence and Wishart.

Simon, B. and Chitty, C. (1993) *S.O.S.: Save Our Schools*. London: Lawrence and Wishart.

Simon, R. (1991) *Gramsci's Political Thought: An Introduction*. London: Lawrence and Wishart.

Smyth, J. (ed.) (1989) *Critical Perspective on Educational Leadership*. Lewes: Falmer Press.

Somerville, J. (1992) 'The New Right and family politics', *Economy and Society*, 21, 2, 93–128.

Statham, J., Mackinnon, D. and Cathcart, H. (1989) *The Education Fact File*. London: Hodder & Stoughton.

Stone, L. (1969) 'Literacy and education in England 1640–1900', *Past and Present*, 42, 69–139.

Tapper, T. and Salter, B. (1992) *Oxford, Cambridge and The Changing Idea of the University*. Buckingham: Open University Press and SRHE.

Tawney, R.H. (1922) *Secondary Education for All: A Policy for Labour*. London: George Allen & Unwin and the Labour Party.

Tawney, R.H. (1966) *The Radical Tradition*. Harmondsworth: Penguin.

Thompson, E.P. (1968) *The Making of the English Working Classes*. Harmondsworth: Penguin.

Tibble, J.W. (ed.) (1966) *The Study of Education*. London: Routledge & Kegan Paul.

Torrington, D. & Weightman, J. (1985) 'Teachers and the management trap', *Journal of Curriculum Studies*, 17, 2, 197–205.

Turner, R.H. (1961) 'Modes of social ascent through education: sponsored and contest mobility', in A.H. Halsey, J. Floud and C.A. Anderson (eds) *Education, Economy and Society*. Glencoe, IL: Free Press, pp. 121–39.

Vernon, P.E. (1964) *Intelligence and Cultural Environment*. London: Methuen.

Wardle, D. (1976) *English Popular Education 1780–1975*. Cambridge: Cambridge University Press.

Warnock, M. (ed.) (1962) *John Stuart Mill*. London: Fontana.

Welsh, D. (1993) 'The New Right as ideology', in G. Jordan and N. Ashford (eds) *Public Policy and the Impact of the New Right*. London: Pinter, pp. 46–58.

Westbrook, R.B. (1991) *John Dewey and American Democracy*. New York: Cornell University Press.

White, J. (1989) *The Aims of Education Re-stated*. London: Routledge & Kegan Paul.

Wiener, M. (1981) *English Culture and the Decline of the Industrial Spirit 1850–1980*. Cambridge: Cambridge University Press.

Wilkinson, R. (1964) *The Prefects*. London: Oxford University Press.

Williams, R. (1965) *The Long Revolution*. Harmondsworth: Penguin.

Williams, R. (1977) *Marxism and Literature*. Oxford: Oxford University Press.

NAME INDEX

Acton, H.B., 47, 51
Aldrich, R., 20
Arblaster, A., 27, 45
Arnold, M., 10, 50, 61, 67, 71, 75, 76, 86, 87, 94, 95, 110, 112, 115, 179, 184, 199
Arnold, T., 76, 111, 115
Auld, R., 146

Baker, K., 164
Ball, S., 160
Barnett, C., 124
Bell, A., 81
Bell, D., 6
Bennett, N., 146, 159
Bentham, J., 48–9, 58, 67, 75, 80, 179, 199
Berlin, I., 27, 28
Bernbaum, G., 75–6
Bernstein, B., 104
Beveridge, W., 125
Blatch, Baronness, 169
Bosanquet, N., 135
Bowe, R., 160
Boyle, E., 139, 156, 157
Boyson, R., 129, 143, 145–6, 147, 157, 161, 162, 181
Bucanan, J., 138

Burke, E., 27, 128, 132–3
Burt, C., 97
Bury, M., 124
Butler, R., 156

Cairncross, A., 124
Callaghan, J., 107
Carlisle, M., 162
Carlyle, T., 87, 132
Carr, E.H., 199
Chesterton, G., 132
Chitty, C., 168
Churchill, W., 153
Clarke, F., 67
Clarke, K., 170
Clegg, A., 142
Coe, J., 150
Coleridge, S., 76
Collard, D., 133
Collingwood, R., 70
Colquhoun, P., 79
Condorcet, M., 108
Cox, C., 145, 156, 158, 170, 181
Cox, C.B., 145, 156, 158
Crosland, A., 104–5, 142

Darwin, C., 59, 75
Dewey, J., 10, 15, 54–66 *passim*, 67, 120, 183, 184, 185, 186, 191, 197

SUBJECT INDEX

EDUCATION REFORM
A CRITICAL AND POST-STRUCTURAL APPROACH

Stephen J. Ball

This book builds upon Stephen J. Ball's previous work in the field of education policy analysis. It subjects the ongoing reforms in UK education to a rigorous critical interrogation. It takes as its main concerns the introduction of market forces, managerialism and the National Curriculum into the organization of schools and the work of teachers. The author argues that these reforms are combining to fundamentally reconstruct the work of teaching, to generate and ramify multiple inequalities and to destroy civic virtue in education. The effects of the market and management are not technical and neutral but are essentially political and moral. The reforms taking place in the UK are both a form of cultural and social engineering and an attempt to recreate a fantasy education based upon myths of national identity, consensus and glory. The analysis is founded within policy sociology and employs both ethnographic and poststructuralist methods.

Contents
Preface – Glossary – Post-structuralism, ethnography and the critical analysis of education reform – What is policy? Texts, trajectories and toolboxes – Education, Majorism and the curriculum of the dead – Education policy, power relations and teachers' work – Cost, culture and control: self-management and entrepreneurial schooling – 'New headship' and school leadership: new relationships and new tensions – Education markets, choice and social class: the market as a class strategy in the UK and USA – Competitive schooling: values, ethics and cultural engineering – References – Index.

176pp   0 335 19272 6 (Paperback)   0 335 19273 4 (Hardback)

FOR EDUCATION
TOWARDS CRITICAL EDUCATIONAL ENQUIRY

Wilfred Carr

A recent review of his work describes Wilfred Carr as 'one of the most brilliant philosophers now working in the rich British tradition of educational philosophy . . . His work is rigorous, refreshing and original . . . and examines a number of fundamental issues with clarity and penetration'.

In *For Education* Wilfred Carr provides a comprehensive justification for reconstructing educational theory and research as a form of critical enquiry. In doing this, he confronts a number of important philosophical questions. What is educational theory? What is an educational practice? How are theory and practice related? What is the role of values in educational research? Is a genuinely educational science possible? By appealing to developments in critical theory, the philosophy of science and the philosophy of the social sciences, Wilfred Carr provides answers to these questions which vindicate the idea of an educational science that is not 'on' or 'about' education but 'for education' – a science genuinely committed to promoting educational values and ideals.

Contents
Introduction: Becoming an educational philosopher – Part 1: Theorizing education – The gap between theory and practice – Theories of theory and practice – Adopting an educational philosophy – What is an educational practice? – Part 2: Towards a critical educational science – Can educational research be scientific? – Philosophy, values and an educational science – Whatever happened to action research? – The idea of an educational science – Epilogue: Confronting the postmodernist challenge – Notes – References – Bibliography – Index.

160pp   0 335 19186 X (paperback)   0 335 19187 8 (hardback)